"With the recent explosion of interest in s[...]
a curiosity—indeed, it is a tragedy— tha[...]
erature is conspicuous by its absence. With Curtis and Brugaletta[...]
ful book, thankfully, that has now changed. With an eye toward spiritual
formation and a sturdy focus on the Wisdom Literature, they weave together a rich, powerful, and weighty treatment of core biblical themes that
constitute the very essence of a life well lived. This book should be studied
by all who are interested in the spiritual life."

—J. P. MORELAND
Distinguished Professor of Philosophy
Talbot School of Theology

"The quest today for deep spirituality often leads people to explore practices that drive a deep wedge between the spiritual life and the daily rou-
tines of 'secular' living. Professor Curtis and Dr. Brugaletta . . . call us to the
practice of biblical wisdom as the means that the Spirit of God uses to guide
believers in every sphere of life. . . . Carefully connecting the wisdom of the
Old Testament with Jesus' summons to discipleship in the kingdom of God,
this book is based on years of study and teaching by top-level scholars, yet it
is also applicable and accessible for readers at all stages of spiritual growth.
Curtis and Brugaletta have provided the church with a vitally important . . .
understanding of the way that God designed His creation to be lived in by
His people. . . . I hope that it is read by many."

—MICHAEL WILKINS
Dean of the Faculty
Professor of New Testament Language and Literature
Talbot School of Theology, Biola University

"This is a remarkable book. For many Christians it will even be—dare I say
it?—something of a revelation. Many of us, after all, read the Old Testament
for its thrilling stories, its majestic poetry, its moving anticipation of the Word
made Flesh. But very few of us would ever look to it as a practical source of
spiritual discipline—that is, until *Discovering the Way of Wisdom*. Edward
Curtis and John Brugaletta have, without sacrificing scholarship or torturing

the biblical text beyond recognition, shown that the Wisdom Literature contains more wisdom than we—certainly more than I—had ever dreamed. I hope this book will become the spiritual classic it deserves to be."

—Ronald K. Tacelli, SJ
Associate Professor of Philosophy
Boston College

"This work provides a valuable and much needed complement to the emphasis in contemporary spirituality on developing a relationship with God through contemplation and spiritual disciplines. Through the teachings of the wisdom books of Scripture, Curtis and Brugaletta remind us that spiritual formation also takes place by following God's principles in the ordinary relationships and circumstances of our this-worldly life. In a marvelous blend of scholarship and practical application that makes for interesting reading, this work is vital for all who desire to truly grow in their relationship with God and 'work out' their salvation with Him in all of life."

—Robert Saucy
Distinguished Professor of Theology
Talbot School of Theology

"In *Discovering the Way of Wisdom,* Curtis and Brugaletta provide very helpful mile markers for those who are on that journey. Paul prays for the believers in Colossae to grow in 'wisdom and understanding' (Col. 1:9). . . . This work is a handbook for such a journey, by exploring the Scriptures that the early church had for guidance—the Old Testament Wisdom Literature. I look forward to recommending it to those who genuinely want to know the path that leads not only to the wise thing to do but the wise way to do it."

—Paul Sailhamer
Ministry Consultant, Southern California

DISCOVERING *the* WAY *of* WISDOM

DISCOVERING *the* WAY *of* WISDOM

SPIRITUALITY IN THE WISDOM LITERATURE

Edward M. Curtis
John J. Brugaletta

Kregel
Academic & Professional

Discovering the Way of Wisdom: Spirituality in the Wisdom Literature

Published by Kregel Publications, a division of Kregel, Inc., P.O. Box 2607, Grand Rapids, MI 49501.

Cover design: John M. Lucas

ISBN 0-8254-2404-6

Printed in the United States of America

04 05 06 07 08 / 5 4 3 2 1

CONTENTS

PREFACE

Throughout the life of the church, Christians have been interested in spiritual growth and the path by which maturity is reached, but the past few years have seen a great resurgence of interest in the subject. Many of the recent discussions about "spiritual formation" (the current term for this area of practical theology) view spiritual development through the lenses of philosophy, psychology, medieval mysticism, or any number of other disciplines both ancient and modern. Although many of the recent contributions are helpful and provide important and essential insights into spiritual growth, from the perspective of one whose specialty is the Old Testament, something seems to be missing. This impression is strengthened when one considers that the Old Testament is the soil from which the New Testament teachings about regeneration and sanctification emerge.

The importance of the Old Testament Wisdom Literature is evident in the number of times the Gospels show Jesus teaching from this part of the Old Testament. Even such uniquely New Testament teachings as the Beatitudes have their precursors in the "blessed are" statements found primarily in Psalms and Proverbs. Years of studying the Wisdom Literature have convinced me (Edward) of the vital nature of this material for bringing about progress in one's spiritual life. At the same time, as I have taught this material, I have often seen what some have called the "A-ha of discovery" as students recognize in the Wisdom Literature elements that have been missing in their Christian lives. They realize that these are elements that have the power to enable and energize them along the road to maturity in Christ.

A college senior recently said about a Proverbs elective that she took from me, "This class should be required for every student here. This is real spiritual formation! I am amazed at how much I have learned about what God wants me to be and how I can use wisdom to achieve it."

In the same class was a student who has been in ministry and Christian leadership for more than twenty years, much of that time teaching biblically related classes in various settings. He said that although he knew that his life "needed serious spiritual adjustment," he did not expect to find it through studying the Old Testament, and certainly not from a book such as Proverbs. He said, "Little did I know what was in store for me." What he discovered in the study were "fundamental principles for how life is to be lived under a God worthy of my fear, worthy to be glorified in truth." The student described the discovery that turned things around for him: "I had never really understood that wisdom is finding the patterns God put into the greater creation and into me, especially as a new creation in Christ, and that finding these patterns is wisdom. Spirituality was never quite so earthy in my orthodox circles." One result of "spiritual growth" for this student was the realization that he needed to give serious attention to his finances. He recognized that developing the discipline to appropriately manage his resources would contribute significantly to his spiritual development.

We would never claim that this book should replace all of the other works that consider spiritual formation from other perspectives; those works provide many essential insights. Nor would we argue that this book is a comprehensive treatment of the contributions of wisdom to spiritual growth. Wisdom's method is to stimulate thought and reflection rather than provide exhaustive answers; it encourages the kind of life application of the material that both allows the exploration of the broader dimensions of the principles and generates skills in living. The goal is to produce a craftsman who can respond to the circumstances of life in a fallen world in ways that reflect Yahweh's order and move a person toward godliness and spiritual maturity. The acquisition of wisdom, like spiritual growth, is a lifelong enterprise that, as Proverbs 2:5 makes clear, leads us to intimacy with God. This book is designed to introduce the reader to the potential of Old Testament Wisdom Literature for teaching us about God's order and encouraging us to practice God's truth so as to get those principles written onto the tablets of our hearts. The outcome of the process is godly character and the kind of maturity in which God takes delight.

I (Edward) am grateful to Talbot School of Theology and Biola University for granting me a sabbatical to work on this book, and to Tyndale Theological Seminary in the Netherlands for providing me a relatively stress-free environment for bringing the project to its conclusion. I am grateful to my "colleague in growth" and coauthor John Brugaletta for his work on the project. John contributed several chapters, provided insightful input on the chapters that I authored, and edited my work, considerably improving its style and clarity. Thanks are also due to Kregel Publications for their willingness to publish this work and to Jim Weaver for his helpful suggestions.

Finally, John and I want to thank our wives, Joy Curtis and Claudia Brugaletta, two truly excellent women. Their wisdom and patience have taught us much about how loving relationships can contribute to spiritual growth. As Proverbs 18:22 (NASB) says, "He who finds a wife finds a good thing and obtains favor from the LORD," and John and I see the truth of that every day. A project such as this takes a great deal of time, and we are grateful to our wives for their encouragement and patience as we worked on this book.

THE CRUCIBLE OF WISDOM

Sara was obviously perplexed as she sat in the chair in my (Edward's) office. She had asked if she could talk with me after class, and now she was telling me that her spiritual life was a great disappointment to her. She was not experiencing the "joy of the Lord" or the abundant life that she thought she would find in Christ. When she finished explaining the frustrations of her spiritual life, I asked her where she worked and how things were going there. She seemed somewhat surprised that I would ask her about such secular things in a conversation about her spiritual life. When she told me that she worked in an office in a nearby town, I suggested to her that she might be able to learn some things in interaction with her fellow employees that could help her with her spiritual growth. Sara was visibly irritated by my response and said, "I came here to talk about my spiritual life. The people I work with are pagans, and they certainly can't teach me anything about spiritual growth. I want to experience the Holy Spirit's power in my life, and I doubt that I can learn anything useful about that from my job."

Sara's view of spiritual formation is quite typical today, and many people in the church think that spiritual growth and sanctification are such "spiritual" activities that the ordinary activities of life can contribute little to them. Certainly spiritual growth does not take place apart from the work of God's Spirit, but I had observed several things about Sara over the course of the two semesters that she had been in my class. The class met at eight in the morning, but Sara rarely got to class on time and sometimes did not come at all. She often was late with her assignments, but she clearly was capable of doing excellent work. I also knew from the essays that she had written for me and from comments that she made both inside and outside of class that she had problems managing her finances and that those same traits created problems for her at work. In my estimation, Sara would have great difficulty making significant progress in developing discipline, self-control, diligence, etc. I would never suggest that the Holy Spirit plays no role in the development of those qualities, but I would argue that the normal activities of life also contribute significantly to their development. For example, a friend recently told me that his experience in the military helped him immensely in becoming a disciplined person and that discipline serves him well in his spiritual life. Another friend told me that a course on time management radically transformed his life, and again, what he learned in that seminar continues to help him significantly in his spiritual development.

If such settings seem unpromising environments for spiritual growth, the Old Testament Wisdom Literature strikes most people as being equally secular and unpromising. Those who hope to learn about God's ways do not often expect to find them reflected in books such as Proverbs and Ecclesiastes. But the purpose of this book is to show that these wisdom portions of the Bible are not as irrelevant to matters of faith as many people believe.

Several factors in the wisdom books contribute to the notion that they are, perhaps, too secular to be helpful to the believing Christian. First, the book of Proverbs, as an example of the Wisdom Literature generally, contains much that is not mentioned elsewhere in biblical revelation. Second, the wisdom books include many principles that are also found in the literature and traditions of different peoples throughout the world, not just those of the Israelites. Indeed, the ideas in certain biblical proverbs existed outside the Bible long before they became a part of the Bible.

But an even more significant factor is the fact that the biblical proverbs generally deal with rather ordinary and secular areas of life. Proverbs treats the importance of careful planning and diligence, the value of controlling one's temper, and the wise use of money; a lecturer could put together a very useful business or management seminar using only material from Proverbs. If the biblical source of the material were not revealed, the seminar would probably be welcome in almost any secular organization—even in the public schools. In fact, many successful programs such as Dale Carnegie's *How to Win Friends and Influence People* emphasize a number of the biblical principles found in the book of Proverbs. But the truth is that there are ways to see clear and real relationships between the Wisdom Literature and the more explicitly "theological" material elsewhere in Scripture (even though scholars continue to debate exactly how they relate).

What Is Wisdom?

To discuss this relationship between the wisdom books and the more theological material in the Bible, it will be useful to have a working definition of the relationship between the two concepts "wisdom" and "spirituality." First, wisdom is not merely the ability to think rationally. Reason alone might persuade us to go naked when the weather is pleasant—if we ignore the fact that more than rational thought is behind the wearing of clothing. Among the things that impel most of us to live with our bodies covered, to name only three, are custom, self-consciousness about our bodies, and the human desire to be associated with a group or movement.

But if wisdom is not pure reason, neither is it pure spirituality. Both the man who bombs an abortion clinic and the woman who rejects the neighborliness of the woman next door because the woman is not a Christian are acting unwisely, although both could sincerely say that they are acting spiritually.

Wisdom, then, is not isolated thinking, and it is not isolated worship. Could it be the two united? Perhaps, but even that seems to be an anemic picture of wisdom: rational worship. Something is still missing, but what? Only everything else that goes into making the essential human being: fear, awe, hunger for justice, thirst for mercy, the appreciation of others, and more—probably much more.

Why, then, does wisdom not include those "human" characteristics that are classified as foolishness: wanton violence, incontinent lust, disregard for the dignity of others, and so on? The reason is that wisdom generally describes the human being at the top of his form, at the best. It shows us the child of God who is acutely aware not only of God but also of earthly surroundings.

Think of an electric lamp. To function as it was designed to do, it must be both attached to a source of power at one end and placed strategically by a hand and mind at the other end. Only then does it shed light in areas where light may be useful. Similarly, the wise Christian is aware of God's immeasurable power, will, and affection while simultaneously working effectively and intelligently in the world.

Put differently, living wisely means receiving power from God to live and act as He designed us to live and act. He does not always tell us what choices to make. That is why He gave us the power to reason; He wants us to make some of the decisions. But He wants us to make them with Him at the center of our decision-making faculty, and thus according to His will and truth. That is what is meant by deciding wisely.

The Provisions for Human Wisdom in Scripture

All of Scripture affirms that God created the world, including human beings, and God designed man to function in certain ways within the world that He made. God gave man dominion over the world and assigned him the task of looking after the Garden. To succeed in this task, the man had to be able to think and understand something about the world around him. These human abilities are evident in the earliest chapters of Genesis, when Adam was able to name all of the animals that God brought to him.

Human abilities are also suggested in Genesis 2:5, which implies that certain plants could not grow on the earth until man was there to cultivate them.[1] The human knowledge and action required for cultivating these plants is like those described in Isaiah 28:23–29. Although Isaiah says that this knowledge comes from God, the conduit through which it comes from Him seems to be human discovery through experiment and reason. The results are then passed down from generation to generation, and the tradition continues to develop as each generation and individual receives and sometimes modifies it.

All of Scripture assumes that human beings have the ability to learn and discover as they study the world and human society, both of which have provided material for various fields of study and technological accomplishments. Although the biblical authors give no theological justification for these human discoveries, their existence seems to be rooted in the biblical doctrine of Creation: God created the world and designed into it the orderly principles by which it operates. Because it is a cosmos, an orderly system, and not a random universe of accidents, it can be studied and truths about it can be discovered.

---

1. According to Genesis 2:5, these plants needed sufficient water and cultivation for them to grow. The man was needed to cultivate the plants, and he could have addressed partially the need for water by irrigation.

Moreover, God designed human beings in His image, which includes the ability to think. The two fit together: the world is designed such that it can be understood, and human beings are designed to understand.

At the same time, we must recognize that there are limits to what man is able to discover and know. He is finite. He is a creature, not God. And Scripture regularly makes it clear that man, with all of his remarkable abilities, must understand who he is and function in submission to the sovereign Creator of the world. In addition to those limitations, man is fallen. Although that fact further limits the human creature, nothing in the Bible ever suggests that the impairments that came with the Fall completely destroyed the abilities that God designed into human beings.

Some scholars have described the material in the Wisdom Literature as "horizontal revelation" because much of it consists of observations made by human beings about their world, the world that is "horizontally" around them rather than what is "vertical" to them (i.e. God). As John Goldingay points out, "The challenge presented by life itself [is] to live in a way which works, which is in conformity with life as it is and with the world as it was created."[2] The Wisdom Literature generally presents the results of the human search for these useful principles. The inclusion in Scripture of such practical discoveries affirms the importance—and necessity—of such knowledge. It reflects the significance of man's ability to discover truth by studying his world and society.

Whereas most of Scripture focuses on the consequences of the Fall and the way to restore man's relationship with God, the Wisdom Literature deals primarily with man's life in the world. Proverbs contains a veritable landscape of principles that come out of human experience and reflect people's observations about what succeeds and what fails in life. Job, Ecclesiastes, and certain psalms reflect the struggles of individuals to square their experiences with the theological ideas they had come to believe. In particular, they struggle with such puzzles of life as why righteous people suffer, or with questions about the meaning of life itself. The focus of the Wisdom Literature on this life and the absence of stated theological themes, together with struggles such as that of Ecclesiastes to find agreement between orthodox theology and the realities of life in a fallen world, give it its somewhat secular flavor.

---

2. John Goldingay, "The 'Salvation History' Perspective and the 'Wisdom' Perspective Within the Context of Biblical Theology," *Evangelical Quarterly* 51 (1979): 203.

Although such issues are not mentioned often in the more theological parts of Scripture, they constitute an important part of living. Furthermore, God clearly is concerned that His redeemed people function well in these areas of practicality. Derek Kidner says,

> There are details of character small enough to escape the mesh of the law and the broadsides of the prophets, and yet decisive in personal dealings. Proverbs moves in this realm, asking what a person is like to live with or employ.[3]

And Roland Murphy notes,

> There were other areas of life not really touched by the Decalogue: Personal diligence, self-control, attitudes toward the poor, pride, trust in one's judgment, etc. In short, the development of responsible character, over and above the goals of the Decalogue, form the heart of wisdom teaching.[4]

The overall perspective of the Old Testament is wider and far more integrated than that shared by most believers today, primarily because the Old Testament blurs the distinction between secular and sacred. But this blurred distinction makes good sense when one thinks about it. C. S. Lewis argued that it would be neither feasible nor wise "to become exclusively and explicitly religious." He said,

> Before I became a Christian I do not think I fully realized that one's life, after conversion, would inevitably consist in doing most of the same things one had been doing before, one hopes in a new spirit, but still the same things. . . . Conversion [does not] obliterate our human life.[5]

---

3. Derek Kidner, *Proverbs,* vol. 15 of Tyndale Old Testament Commentaries (Downers Grove, Ill.: InterVarsity, 1964), 13.
4. Roland Murphy, "Wisdom and Yahwism," in *No Famine in the Land: Studies in Honor of John L. McKenzie* (Claremont, Calif.: Institute of Antiquity and Christianity, 1975), 119.
5. C. S. Lewis, "Learning in War-Time," in *The Weight of Glory and Other Addresses* (New York: Macmillan, 1962), 23.

Rather, he says,

> All our merely natural activities will be accepted, if they are offered to God, even the humblest, and all of them, even the noblest, will be sinful if they are not. Christianity does not simply replace our natural life and substitute a new one; it is rather a new organization which exploits, to its own supernatural ends, these natural materials.[6]

Becoming a believer then does not wall off the secular from the sacred; it does however require that all worldly activities be performed with God in mind and then offered up to God—done for His glory. Lewis even argued that when an activity can no longer be done humbly as unto the Lord—that is, when it becomes an end in itself or when it generates pride in us—the believer may well need to give up the activity. As Lewis puts it, "The time for plucking out the right eye has arrived."[7]

It seems obvious that God designed human beings to function in the world that He created and that a reciprocal relationship exists between people and the world. God placed the man in the Garden to cultivate it and keep it (Gen. 2:15), and God gave human beings dominion over the earth and its creatures (Gen. 1:28; Ps. 8:6–8). Anthony Hoekema suggests that the command God gives in these passages is "to serve and preserve the earth as well as to rule over it."[8] It seems clear that God equipped human beings for the work that He assigned them. Certainly the Fall has impaired man's function as steward over the earth, but it has not entirely destroyed his ability to perform his role.

Even before the Fall it seems that unimpaired man was incomplete, and the test to which he was subjected in the Garden was necessary for him to become "complete" or mature. In some sense the same was true even for Jesus, who, according to Hebrews 5:8–9, "learned obedience through what he suffered," and was "made perfect [complete]" through those experiences.[9]

---

6. Ibid., 25.

7. Ibid., 28.

8. Anthony A. Hoekema, *Created in God's Image* (Grand Rapids: Eerdmans, 1986), 80.

9. Note also the comment in Luke 2:52 about Jesus as He grew from a child into an adult: "Jesus kept increasing in wisdom and stature, and in favor with God and men" (NASB).

It seems, from all of this, that an individual's experience in the world is a necessary part of bringing him to maturity and making him a complete person. The world is where normal human development (physical, emotional, relational, etc.) takes place. In Kidner's words, wisdom's function in Scripture "is to put godliness into working clothes; to name business and society as spheres in which we are to acquit ourselves with credit to our Lord, and in which we are to look for his training."[10]

The world is also the realm in which sanctification takes place, and much of that process both presupposes and requires the context of the world. Again Kidner points out:

> If we could analyze the influences that build up a godly character to maturity, we might well find that the agencies we call natural vastly outweighed those that we call supernatural. The book of Proverbs assures us that this, if it is true, is no reflection on the efficiency of God's grace; for the hard facts of life, which knock some of the nonsense out of us, are God's facts and His appointed school of character; they are not alternatives to His grace, but means of it.[11]

Even such "spiritually" generated qualities as the fruit of the Spirit—love, joy, peace, patience, kindness, goodness, faithfulness, gentleness, and self-control—are not qualities that are infused into a believer who merely sits on a hillside praying. Rather, they are developed in a process that takes place with God's Spirit working in the believer *while that believer is functioning in the world.*

Thus, what seemed at first glance to have nothing to do with character formation may well play a highly important role in the process. Sanctification—or spiritual formation—is usually defined as a work of God that involves the believer's responsible participation. The Old Testament does not provide us with a comprehensive treatment of spiritual formation because it is the redemptive work of Christ that makes the Christian doctrine of sanctification possible, and it is the New Testament revelation that explains spiritual formation in its full Christian sense. The Old Testament Wisdom Literature has little to say about the work of God in the process of

---

10. Kidner, *Proverbs*, 35.
11. Ibid.

sanctification, but in its focus on the believer's participation in the process, it emphasizes many elements that are crucial in living wisely and in moving toward maturity in one's relationship with God.

As an example, for the Israelite the search for wisdom had to begin with a deep commitment to God and a genuine submission to God's authority and truth. The theme of the book of Proverbs is that the fear of the Lord is the beginning of wisdom/knowledge. The fear of the Lord is the essence of piety in the Old Testament, and it begins with a recognition of who God is—the all-powerful, sovereign Creator of the universe—and a contrasting recognition of who we are—creatures made by God. As a result of this awareness, those who fear the Lord live under the full acknowledgment that God's authority is over them.

Anyone's life, when it is suffused with such awareness, will necessarily be characterized by an appropriate humility and obedience. Without such an attitude, the search for wisdom will not succeed. Gerhard von Rad cautions,

> The search for knowledge can go wrong because of one single mistake at the beginning. One becomes competent and expert as far as the orders of life are concerned only if one begins from knowledge about God. . . . Israel was of the opinion that effective knowledge about God is the only thing that puts a man into a right relationship with the objects of his perception.[12]

That is, Israel realized that any attempt to understand reality and discover the principles by which the world operates must begin with a worshiping submission to God, who created that world and those principles. Spiritual formation cannot take place apart from such a commitment by the believer at the very beginning.

It is this acknowledgment of God and His authority over a person that makes the difference between what James calls "earthly wisdom" and the wisdom that comes from above. The fool says in his heart that there is no God, and his thinking and behavior proceed from that beginning point. The resulting human wisdom is often characterized by pride and an amoral pragmatism. In contrast, the person who fears God relates all of his thinking

---

12. Gerhard von Rad, *Wisdom in Israel,* trans. James Martin (Nashville: Abingdon, 1972), 67.

and doing to God's reality. Rather than trusting his own judgment and perception of things, he or she welcomes the revelation of God that comes through His Word and accepts that revelation as authoritative truth.

The Wisdom Literature also recognizes that qualities such as self-discipline are important if one is to have any sort of success, including success in growing spiritually. The importance of choices, together with the self-disciplined care that one must take in making them, is something that Proverbs affirms regularly, as do other wisdom books. The fear of the Lord is a choice that people must deliberately make; it is not a thing that comes about by default in the life of a believer. The search for wisdom, as Proverbs 2 makes clear, requires perseverance and determination of the sort that is required in a search for treasure.

Such qualities as diligence, wise commitment to the task, the sort of single-minded resolve that will not allow secondary goals to distract the searcher from the more important goal, and the ability to make careful choices are essential if one is to acquire wisdom. Proverbs 2:5 makes clear that the kind of wisdom in view here involves more than the acquiring of worldly knowledge or professional skills. It tells us that the search for wisdom leads the disciple to both "the fear of the LORD" and "the knowledge of God."

God's revelation to His people in Scripture plays a central role in both spiritual formation and the acquisition of wisdom. Psalm 1 identifies regular meditation on God's instruction as a key principle that leads to success and prosperity in everything the godly person does, and Psalms 19 and 119 expand on the role of God's Word in spiritual growth. According to Psalms 111 and 112, frequent reflection on God's works and character causes certain of God's attributes to be reproduced in the believer. Psalms 37 and 73, along with the book of Job, provide practical and profound instruction for people who are victims of injustice; they show that often one must simply trust God in circumstances that provide little visible evidence of His care and concern.

But the Wisdom Literature is not content with the believer merely adhering externally to religious values. When Proverbs 3 suggests writing its principles on the tablets of the heart, it is urging us to internalize these principles, to make them an integral part of us and our daily decisions. Proverbs is just as deeply aware of the importance of the heart as Jesus is in the New Testament.

Such material emphasizes the importance of a deep and intimate relationship with God, and it affirms the belief that maintaining and developing such a relationship with God is a central part of both wisdom and spiritual formation. Thus, the Old Testament Wisdom Literature gives its own unique perspective on principles that are recognized elsewhere in the Bible as vital to bringing a believer to maturity.

The Wisdom Literature also teaches the importance of morality and of ethical values, making clear that the pragmatic interest in what will succeed is presided over by a recognition of what is right. This fact sets Israel's Wisdom Literature apart from that of her neighbors. The godly person should value personal reputation above money or power. One should be discreet and avoid rash decisions and reactions. She should control her tongue and use money carefully and wisely. He should be a faithful friend, prepared to help a friend in need, even in desperate need. The mature disciple should be kind and compassionate and able to control his temper. He should avoid strife. In all of this, the Wisdom Literature serves largely the same function in the Old Testament as the book of James does in the New Testament: it makes clear that God's truth must be acted upon in practical and tangible ways, and it provides numerous examples of what that sort of practical obedience looks like.

In all of these ways, the Wisdom Literature complements the more patently redemptive and theological material upon which the Bible student usually focuses. Sinful human beings need to be redeemed and brought into a right relationship with God, and the redemptive message that dominates most of the Bible generally focuses on these issues. But at the same time that redeemed people work out their salvation in the world, they need to know how God expects His people to behave in a fallen world, and that is where Wisdom Literature provides vital help and insight.

I recently saw Sara again, and she reported that she has made much progress since our earlier conversation. Her spiritual life is back on track, and she seems to have matured significantly. She is still working in a largely secular environment, but she has found that the challenges of that secular setting afford her wonderful opportunities to practice and develop a more godly and mature Christian character. She is still studying Proverbs and regularly finds that book useful in dealing with the issues that she faces in her job. She also told me that she has developed new time-management skills and self-discipline in her job and finances and is amazed at how these new skills have improved her spiritual life. She has also come to appreciate the value of friends who encourage her and keep her accountable. Sara then told me that her experience the last few years has convinced her of the wisdom of what her pastor often says: "If you want to get things right, you have to practice doing things right." By gaining wisdom and putting it into practice in the ordinary routine of life, Sara is understanding the fear of the Lord and finding the knowledge of God, just as Proverbs 2:5 said that she would.

Chapter One

LOGOS AND OLD TESTAMENT WISDOM

In Shakespeare's play *Henry V,* King Henry is put in a difficult position when one of the companions of his youth is caught robbing a French church. Henry himself had commanded that all such offenders be put to death, and now he must decide between human affection and justice—whether to pardon his friend, thereby sending a message to his nation that he will use his royal power to gratify himself, or to be consistent and even-handed in administering the law to all of his subjects. His decision is not an easy one; his fondness for the man is genuine. But one measure of Henry's wisdom is that he places the larger good above the smaller: personal friendship is important to him, but his God-given task of serving England is more important. As Shakespeare paints Henry's portrait in scene after scene like this one, we recognize more and more clearly an admirable man, one who is pulled by his emotions as powerfully as any of us but who knows when his emotions are pulling him astray and who exerts himself to disobey those emotional prompts when they threaten to mislead his words and actions.

Similarly, the wise man, as depicted in the Old Testament Wisdom Literature, is able to disobey the fickle winds and currents of emotions' weather to stay on a true course toward some important destination. He is, we are told, teachable: "Whoever heeds instruction is on the path to life, but he who rejects reproof leads others astray" (Prov. 10:17). It is often humiliating to be corrected, but the person who hungers for wisdom will put aside this personal emotion when it hinders learning.

The Old Testament wise person is also discreet, thinking calmly before speaking or acting: "Good sense makes one slow to anger, and it is his glory to overlook an offense" (Prov. 19:11). Anger urges one strongly to rash words and even violent actions, but those who have wisdom have learned to control their anger, using it sparingly, and only when it leads to a higher good than mere self-expression.

The ideal wise man of the Old Testament knows that people do not normally hold fast to every word they speak; therefore, when he overhears someone slighting him, he can be forgiving. After all, he himself has not always been perfectly wise and has spoken disparagingly of others: "Do not take to heart all things that people say, lest you hear your servant cursing you. Your heart knows that many times you have yourself cursed others" (Eccl. 7:21–22). Once again, the instinctively human reaction—to focus on the emotional pain of being insulted by one whom we had thought to be loyal—is suppressed, and taking its place is a calm reflection that we ourselves once uttered similar words about others, and yet we did not mean them deeply.

People who are seeking wisdom are advised in the book of Proverbs to avoid illicit sexual relationships, as in 5:20–21 ("Why should you be intoxicated, my son, with a forbidden woman and embrace the bosom of an adulteress? For a man's ways are before the eyes of the LORD, and he ponders all his paths"), and to discipline their children so that self-discipline will become engrained in them, as in 22:6 ("Train up a child in the way he should go; even when he is old he will not depart from it"). Once again, the emotional commands of lust are to be set aside in favor of a wise self-discipline in the first instance, while in the second it is the natural tenderness that a parent feels for the young son or daughter that must be overcome for a more long-lasting and higher form of happiness than the mere avoidance of physical punishment. Again, several proverbs warn against laziness: "A little sleep, . . . a little folding of the hands to rest, and poverty will come upon you like a robber" (Prov. 6:10–11). The immediate pleasure of unnecessary rest, we are to understand, is trivial when contrasted with the loss of property that might result.

Said briefly, wisdom sets our priorities straight; God's truth is more important than any feelings we might have of personal humiliation, anger, or pain. And this principle is extended to include a healthy fear of the Lord, love among friends, and general integrity as more important than wealth, luxuries, and good looks, as exemplified in the following passages from Proverbs: "Whoever walks in uprightness fears the LORD, but he who is devious in his ways despises him" (14:2); "Whoever covers an offense seeks love, but he who repeats a matter separates close friends" (17:9); "Riches do not profit in the day of wrath, but righteousness delivers from death" (11:4); "Better is a little with righteousness than great revenues with injustice" (16:8); "Like a gold ring in a pig's snout is a beautiful woman without discretion" (11:22).

The elements of our lives hold differing values, but when we are forced to choose among these elements, our immediate and unthinking reaction is to choose the one that offers immediate pleasure, revenge, or power. Wisdom tells us what those relative values really are and cautions us to choose with an eye to the larger picture of life.

But so far, with one exception, these maxims sound very much like the products of a secular philosophy: learn from the wise; control your anger; do not take seriously what others say of you; never neglect your chores; avoid illicit sex. The one exception, of course, is that "the fear of the LORD is the beginning of wisdom" (Ps. 111:10; see also Prov. 1:7). The obvious question to be asked at this point is, "Why should such practical precepts require a fear of the Lord before they can be accepted?"

In any answer to this question, one must first admit that wisdom in the ancient world was international; it existed among the Egyptians, the Edomites, the Arabs, the Babylonians, and the Phoenicians, to name only those cultures in which the Old Testament recognizes it (1 Kings 4:30; Job 1:3; Isa. 19:11–12; 47:10; Jer. 49:7; Ezek. 28:3ff.; Dan. 1:4, 20; Obad. 8; Zech. 9:2; Acts 7:22). But as Derek Kidner points out, "While the Old Testament scorns the magic and superstition which debased much of this thought (Isa. 47:12–13), and the pride which inflated it (Job 5:13), it can speak of the gentile sages with a respect it never shows toward their priests and prophets. Solomon outstripped them, but we are expected to be impressed by the fact; and Daniel excelled the wise men of Babylon as one who stood at the head of their own profession (Dan. 5:11–12)."[1] If the ancient Hebrews surpassed their neighbors in wisdom, what enabled them to do so? The only major element of their lives that distinguished them from those neighbors was the God whom they worshiped—Yahweh. It was from Yahweh, they saw, that all wisdom comes, and Yahweh is the distinctively Israelite name used in the following passage in Proverbs when Wisdom says,

---

1. Derek Kidner, *Proverbs,* vol. 15 of Tyndale Old Testament Commentaries (Downers Grove, Ill.: InterVarsity, 1964), 17.

> The LORD possessed me at the beginning of his work, the first of his
> acts of old. Ages ago I was set up, at the first, before the beginning of
> the earth. . . . Before the mountains had been shaped. . . . When he es-
> tablished the heavens, I was there. . . . when he assigned to the sea its
> limit . . . , when he marked out the foundations of the earth, then I was
> beside him, like a master workman, and I was daily his delight. (Prov.
> 8:22–23, 25, 27, 29–30)

Set this beside Psalm 33:6, 8–9: "By the word of the LORD the heavens
were made. . . . Let all the earth fear the LORD . . . ; for he spoke, and it came
to be." It begins to be clear that God's Wisdom and God's Word (LXX[2] *logos*)
are synonymous in this context. And in the New Testament, the Logos, Jesus
Christ, is spoken of in much the same terms: "In the beginning was the
Word, and the Word was with God. . . . All things were made through him"
(John 1:1, 3). Or, as Paul puts it, "By him all things were created. . . . he is
before all things, and in him all things hold together" (Col. 1:16–17). The
author of the book of Hebrews speaks of God as having "created the world"
through Christ, by whom He "upholds the universe by the word of his power"
(1:3). Christ is "the power of God and the wisdom of God" (1 Cor. 1:24),
and He is "God's mystery . . . in whom are hidden all the treasures of wisdom and knowledge" (Col. 2:2–3).

It is clear, then, that many of the biblical authors describe Jesus in terms
of God's Wisdom. And even Jesus acknowledged this of Himself when He
said, "The queen of the South . . . came . . . to hear the wisdom of Solomon,
and behold, something greater than Solomon is here" (Matt. 12:42; Luke
11:31). What Jesus is referring to as having arrived in Him is not wisdom
alone; it is the entire kingdom of God. But included in the kingdom that
Christ has brought to earth, in addition to the function of the temple (Matt.
12:6) and God's call to repentance, as exemplified by Jonah (12:41), is God's
wisdom, whose greatest exemplar thus far had been Solomon. Darrell Bock
says of this passage, "Jesus is the bearer of God's wisdom,"[3] and we may add
confidently that He was that in a greater sense than the wisest of men had
been. Put differently, if the Old Testament Wisdom Literature instructs us

---

2. The Septuagint (LXX) was an early Greek translation of the Old Testament
   that the early church used regularly.
3. Darrell L. Bock, *Luke,* vol. 3 of IVP New Testament Commentary (Downers
   Grove, Ill.: InterVarsity, 1994), 214.

in that mode of life that is the way "we are meant to live," and if Jesus Christ demonstrates how redeemed man would act and react (John 13:15; Rom. 8:29; 2 Cor. 3:18; Eph. 4:13; Phil. 2:5; 1 Peter 2:21; 1 John 2:6), then the Wisdom Literature, in its description of order, lays the groundwork for our comprehension of Christ's teaching.

It has become a cliché among many Christians to ask, when they must make a difficult decision, "What would Jesus do?" The question is valid, but the answer is many times hard to find in the New Testament. Consider, for example, the topic of anger, which the New Testament never addresses directly. At least one example exists, however, of Jesus apparently experiencing anger when He cleanses the temple (John 2:14–16; see also, Matt. 21:12; Mark 11:15). All four of the Gospels mention this incident, but John's account includes a significant detail that the synoptics lack: "Making a whip of cords, he drove them all out of the temple" (John 2:15). The facts that the whip consisted of more than one cord and that He made the whip implies strongly that the task involved tying several knots. A space of time, then, elapsed between Jesus' decision to drive out the money changers and the eventual act of doing so. Moreover, He spent that time performing an act for which a man who was having a temper tantrum would have little patience. We may, if we like, try to circumvent the message in John's gospel by thinking of one or two people who meticulously prepared for their acts of violence, but we would be better advised to consider that John most likely included the detail for a reason: to convey the fact that Jesus was in full control of His anger when He used the whip.

The debate could go on forever, but the book of Proverbs clarifies the matter: "Whoever is slow to anger is better than the mighty, and he who rules his spirit than he who takes a city" (16:32). It would be hard to believe that the embodiment of God's wisdom had, in His humanity, violated this and the many similar injunctions in God's Word against being ruled by anger (see Ps. 37:8; Prov. 15:18; 19:11; 22:8; 29:11). Our culture generally is embarrassed by any display of anger, but the Wisdom Literature, as it always seems to do, takes the sane approach to this volatile emotion: keep it under the control of reason, and use it only when it applies properly to the situation at hand.

Another way in which the Old Testament Wisdom Literature can be an invaluable guide in everyday life is in giving practical suggestions for living life more wisely. For example, whereas the New Testament is as unequivocal as the Old Testament about the sinfulness of adultery (Mark 7:20–23), the New Testament offers few suggestions as to techniques to help avoid this sin. But in the book of Job, part of Job's claim to righteousness is this statement: "I have made a covenant with my eyes; how then could I gaze at a virgin?" (Job 31:1). This is not the same as Jesus' finding the sin of adultery in the mere "look[ing] at a woman with lustful intent" (Matt. 5:28); whereas Jesus teaches that sin is internal as well as external, the book of Job implies that a helpful technique is available to those (especially men) who wish to avoid this sin before it enters them: don't look! But an even more effective piece of advice for maintaining chastity is in the Wisdom Literature. It may be paraphrased, "Don't go there!" The advice, in essence, is to stay away from the place of temptation: "I have perceived among the youths, a young man lacking sense, passing along the street near [the harlot's] corner" (Prov. 7:7–8). Mere proximity (which, in this case, includes the opportunity for not only sight but also other sensory stimuli) to the occasion of sin encourages sinful behavior.

But no one should take any of this as saying that everything in the New Testament may be found in the Old Testament; the New Testament is not redundant. On the contrary, the New Testament takes us into the very nature of holiness and all of the unseen world in which we have faith, for which we have hope, and through which we love. Because Jesus speaks of a landscape that is for us an "undiscovered country," He must use metaphors such as "Father" and "kingdom" and the earth-based stories of the parables. But in reaching such heights of heavenly reality, He stands on and presumes our knowledge of the wisdom conveyed to humanity through the writers of the Old Testament. It is this presumed knowledge that the New Testament sees no need to reiterate but that our culture has come to ignore and that the church has neglected as an aid in spiritual growth.

Christ, then, does not deny Old Testament wisdom when He leaves it unmentioned. Yet, although He often transforms the practicality of Old Testament Wisdom Literature so as to concentrate on the eternal context to life, His discourse has an essentially rational and ultimately practical basis. It is as if one were to say to a blindfolded man, "Although this path along which I lead you is steep and rocky, if you stay on it, it will take you to a plateau at the top. All will be well there, and you will see that every other path would have taken you to a wasteland or a swamp." We are that blind man, for our perceptions are severely limited. We have no more direct knowledge of a wider world beyond our tangible surroundings than a newborn infant knows of anything beyond the room in which it has, thus far, spent its life. But an utterly reliable Source has told us of a city and a life that are more extensive than our poor eyes can see. Because the Source of this information is reliable, some of us believe it—we take it as fact. And because we accept it as fact, it would be irrational of us to ignore it. To ignore it would be sinful (and therefore irrational to the point of insanity). Christ can cure insanity if that is the cure that is needed, but, by all appearances, most of us need His cure for foolishness instead. And the cure for foolishness is wisdom. And wisdom resides in the Logos. And the Logos is Christ Jesus, who "dwelt among us . . . full of . . . truth" (John 1:14).

What Is *Logos?*

But before we go on to see how Christ's teachings are an extension of the Wisdom Literature, it will be worth our while to explore the concept of *logos* further, for in doing so we can better understand and appreciate the breadth of meaning carried by this Greek word in New Testament times, thereby understanding more of what John's gospel means in applying the term to Christ. Let's begin by looking again at the first three sentences of the fourth gospel: "In the beginning was the Word, and the Word was with God, and the Word was God. He was in the beginning with God. All things were made through him, and without him was not any thing made that was made." On this seemingly simple but actually meaning-packed passage is based much of the Christian doctrine of Jesus Christ's divinity. And so much is clearly evident. But when we study the word *logos* in the original Greek text, we see more than the simple English "word," or the mere concept of divinity. That is, we see that the word *logos* means more than the English term *word,* or any other single term in English, can convey.

One glossary to the Greek New Testament lists six meanings of *logos,*[4] but for our purposes, the most interesting segments of meaning are *Word* (of God) and *message. Word* is perhaps what we English speakers think of when we hear the word *logos,* recalling such phrases as the one Paul uses in Colossians 1:5 ("the word of truth, the gospel"). But *message* begins to open our eyes to a concept that we possibly had never considered. When applied to God's Word,

---

4. Warren C. Trenchard, *Complete Vocabulary Guide to the Greek New Testament,* rev. ed. (Grand Rapids: Zondervan, 1992), 65.

the term *logos* means not only the expression of God's thoughts but also God's expressible (but sometimes not yet expressed) thoughts. As Matthew Henry put it in his commentary on the fourth gospel, *"Word* is twofold: *word conceived* and *word uttered."*[5] It is easy enough to see that some thoughts remain unexpressed whereas others are expressed, but how is an expressible thought different from other, inexpressible thoughts? A moment's reflection will tell us that to express a thought (i.e., to convey it to the understanding of another being), we must put it in a form that is comprehensible to the recipient. In terms of a human recipient, the thought must be put in some sort of humanly understandable order. When we try to communicate with another human being, we must select words that are appropriate to our meanings and then arrange them in sentences that "make sense" to the human mind. There is no room for what we would call randomness in this ordering process; randomness in expressing a thought would produce what would seem like incomprehensible gibberish. In the same way, the thoughts themselves must become orderly. I believe it would not be going too far to say that Jesus Christ, at least in part and as we perceive Him, is that within God that is thinkable by the human being—that which can possibly make some sense to such limited beings as we are.

If that is so, then how pregnant with significance are the verses in John's gospel that follow. What they evidently are saying is that the world—all of creation—was made orderly and open to reasoning; it is conceivable by the human mind *because* God made it through Christ, who is the embodiment of intelligibility. Or, to put it another way, we are able to think about the world because it was designed to be thinkable. It has posed a philosophical problem for centuries that, although the human mind in the act of thinking seems to be such a different phenomenon from the material universe, it goes on performing what seems like an impossibility in interacting dependably with the other.[6] The fact is, however, that the mind does interact dependably with creation, a point that led the great physicist Albert Einstein to write, "The fact that [the physical universe] is comprehensible is a miracle."[7]

---

5. Matthew Henry, *Commentary on the Whole Bible,* ed. Leslie Church (Grand Rapids: Zondervan, 1960), 1506.
6. *Cambridge Dictionary of Philosophy,* ed. Robert Audi, s.v. "dualism" (Cambridge: Cambridge University Press, 1995), 210.
7. Albert Einstein, *Ideas and Opinions* (New York: Bonanza, 1954), 292.

Clearly, the phenomenon we are considering is an unexpected boon of cosmic dimensions. As early as 500 B.C., Greek philosophy, in searching for something that was stable in a universe of change, arrived at the concept of the *logos,* though only as a force, not as a living being. The Alexandrian Jewish scholar Philo, a contemporary of Christ, wrote in Greek of "the *Logos* of God," by which he meant an ideal (i.e., both flawless and more real) version of the universe. Philo was not a Christian but a Jew who venerated the Law of Moses; his concept of Wisdom and the *Logos* stopped short of seeing them as incarnate in the form of a man on earth. But as James Dunn has said, "What pre-Christian Judaism said of Wisdom and Philo also of the Logos, Paul and the others say of Jesus."[8]

Bruce Waltke, in writing about the biblical concept of wisdom, defines it as "the fixed order of reality."[9] This unchanging order of reality is the hallmark of the *Logos,* and it is the foundation upon which godly wisdom is based. Waltke also cites Proverbs 3:19–20: "The LORD by wisdom founded the earth; by understanding he established the heavens; by his knowledge the deeps broke open, and the clouds drop down the dew," remarking that "the point of this statement seems to be that wisdom is the principle that accounts for order and life found in creation."[10]

Having come thus far, we may now approach Psalm 19 and the apparent dichotomy of its parts. Of the fourteen verses of this psalm, the first six strike most casual readers today as a hymn to nature and to the ways in which nature displays the glory of God. Then the rest of the psalm praises God's written law, which "[makes] wise the simple." Whereas this apparent split nature of Psalm 19 has posed a problem for some commentators, we can see in the light of John's gospel that the split is only apparent, not real. The psalmist who joined these two concepts in one hymn knew perfectly well why he was joining them. He saw that when God created the world He did so as a silent expression of His own nature and inner order: the days are measurements of time; His "line" measures space; His sun's regular passage over the world is not only orderly but also like "a bridegroom coming out of his chamber (NASB)," part of a known ritual, a ritual being the prescribed order of a religious ceremony.

---

8. James D. G. Dunn, *Christology in the Making,* 2d ed. (Grand Rapids: Eerdmans, 1980), 167.

9. Bruce K. Waltke, "The Book of Proverbs and Ancient Wisdom Literature," *Bibliotheca Sacra* 136 (1979): 226.

10. Ibid., 223.

God's orderliness is designed into the universe, says the psalm, and it is therefore conceivable by those creatures made in His image, people, the rational and ensouled creatures, those who are capable of living according to His order—that is, those who are capable of wisdom.

Apparently, it is this concept of order in creation to which Jeremiah refers when he records God as having said,

> I placed the sand as the boundary for the sea,
>   a perpetual barrier that it cannot pass;
> though the waves toss, they cannot prevail;
>   though they roar, they cannot pass over it.
>   But this people has a stubborn and rebellious heart;
>   they have turned aside and gone away.
>   They do not say in their hearts,
>   "Let us fear the LORD our God,
> who gives the rain in its season,
>   the autumn rain and the spring rain,
> and keeps for us
>   the weeks appointed for the harvest."
>   —Jeremiah 5:22b–24[11]

In other words, God in His wisdom has created a world in which things are in their proper places (the sea, for example), and events come at their proper times (the autumn and spring rains, and the harvest). Space and time are ordered and regulated.

This relates to the account in Genesis of God's creation of the world, which is in great part a process of separating things that are different and gathering together things that are similar. In Genesis 1:4, "God separated the light from the darkness"; in verse 9, He separated the seas from the land; in verse 14, He "separate[d] the day from the night," which, in turn, allows for units (measurements) of time—"seasons . . . days and years"; and in verse 26, God made human beings as rulers (and hence in the image of the one perfect ruler, God Himself) over this ordered and arranged world.[12]

---

11. See also Psalm 104, as well as sections in Job 38ff.
12. Similarities of Genesis 1 to the Babylonian creation account once were thought to indicate borrowing. However, the existence of such parallel accounts demonstrates neither that the biblical creation account is borrowed or that it is

But our topic is still Psalm 19, and we see that once the psalmist has praised the order of the created world, he turns to his primary topic, God's *written* law and its necessity for anyone who hopes to have wisdom. But the point has been made: God's order, God's way of doing things, is not only spelled out in Scripture but also perceivable in creation. The world was designed to make sense to us because God, in His lovingkindness, chose to plant us human creatures in a world in which we could flourish and over which we could function as stewards. Clearly, we are meant to observe, think about, and interact with the world by using our reasoning abilities.

The latter half of Psalm 19 lists several results or rewards for the one who is obedient to God's law: a revived soul, wisdom (v. 7), joy, illumination (v. 8), and warning—presumably against sins (v. 11). And Psalm 119 repeats, develops, and adds to this list: adherence to the wisdom of God brings blessedness (vv. 1, 2, 56), freedom from unrighteousness (vv. 3, 101) and shame (v. 6), a purity in one's life (v. 9), delight (v. 24), wisdom (vv. 98, 104), insight (v. 99), light for one's path (v. 105), and great peace (v. 165). If we were to reorder the items in this list as they might occur in everyday life, we might end up with something like the following: learning and living by God's law imparts *wisdom* to the believer, which warns him about stumbling blocks ahead *(light for one's path),* giving *insight* and producing an ever greater *purity in one's life, a freedom from unrighteousness,* followed by the cognitive and emotional responses to this new life—*freedom from shame,* the feeling of *delight,* a sense of *blessedness,* and great *peace.* It is a process that, once begun and adhered to (through meditation on God's Word), leads step-by-step away from a life of sin and into blessedness and peace, a consummation devoutly to be wished. It is, of course, no coincidence that many of these qualities are in harmony with Jesus' list of the Beatitudes in Matthew 5:3–11. Among those listed there as blessed are those who love

---

nonhistorical. As one commentator remarks, "It is gratuitous to conclude from the mere existence of parallels to Genesis 1–11 in mythological form that the biblical account must also be nonhistorical. One can also judge that the events of Genesis 1–11 are historical. That being the case, it would not then be at all surprising if the story concerning them should come to be mythologized in pagan traditions, while being preserved in authentically historical form within the stream of tradition of which Gn 1–11 is the inspired deposit." Meredith G. Kline, *Eerdmans Bible Commentary,* ed. D. Guthrie et al. (Grand Rapids: Eerdmans, 1970), 79.

righteousness, are merciful, are pure in heart, and create peace between antagonists.

Jesus and *Logos*

But if we have seen that Jesus Christ is God's Word and God's Wisdom, where are we to find all of these things in Him? Leaving wisdom in general until the last, we may apply the preceding list from Psalm 119 to what we know about the incarnate Lord from the Gospels. Regarding His warning us about stumbling blocks or tests ahead, we might well think of Luke 14:28–32:

> For which of you, desiring to build a tower, does not first sit down and count the cost, whether he has enough to complete it? Otherwise, when he has laid a foundation and is not able to finish, all who see it begin to mock him, saying, "This man began to build and was not able to finish." Or what king, going out to encounter another king in war, will not sit down first and deliberate whether he is able with ten thousand to meet him who comes against him with twenty thousand? And if not, while the other is yet a great way off, he sends a delegation and asks for terms of peace.

The two vignettes, taken in themselves, urge us to have foresight, to plan carefully before committing ourselves to a task. This is wisdom in the Old Testament sense—good, practical advice on how to live one's life in this world. But when we read the New Testament passage in context, we see that Jesus applies Old Testament wisdom to another level of reality—God's kingdom. The advice, "Consider the cost and whether you can afford it before building a tower or going into battle," now becomes, "Consider the cost and whether you are willing to pay it [give up all earthly attachments] before following Me into the kingdom of God." It remains practical advice, but now practicality has taken a larger view of life; now the spiritual world is taken into account, and a reasonable sense of priorities says clearly, "Be prepared to give up those things that decay to attain the things that are eternal."

As to producing greater purity in one's life, Wisdom in the *Logos* has evidently affected the sinful woman in Luke 7:37–50 so profoundly that her repentance has brought her to weep at Jesus' feet. Adultery in the book of Proverbs is to be avoided because it results in "wounds and dishonor," "disgrace," and the offended husband's "revenge" (6:33–34). But none of this would apply if one were merely to look at someone while thinking lustful thoughts; yet, Jesus equates such a look with the act itself and as sinful (Matt. 5:27–28). Clearly sin in the New Testament is both internal and external, spiritual as well as physical. Where Job saw avoiding such stares as a useful technique in refraining from the act of adultery, Jesus sees it as something itself to be avoided for the very practical reason that it can end in one's destruction. It is as practical as advising someone not to walk on a rotted bridge over a deep gorge.

Freedom from shame is another benefit of Old Testament wisdom that is found in the teachings of Jesus, though again in a deeper sense. Proverbs 25:6–7 advises, "Do not put yourself forward in the king's presence . . . ; for it is better to be told, 'Come up here,' than to be put lower in the presence of a noble." This lesson clearly has the same source as Luke 14:8–10, where we find the situation in greater detail:

> When you are invited by someone to a wedding feast, do not sit down in a place of honor, lest someone more distinguished than you be invited by him, and he who invited you both will come and say to you, "Give your place to this person," and then you will begin with shame to take the lowest place. But when you are invited, go and sit in the lowest place, so that when your host comes he may say to you, "Friend, move up higher." Then you will be honored in the presence of all who sit at table with you.

Shame is always shame, but this is the same Jesus who suffered the ultimate earthly shame of His time—crucifixion—while ultimate honors awaited Him beyond His earthly life. So it seems highly unlikely that His meaning in this passage should be limited to earthly honor, as is that of the parallel passage in Proverbs. The interpretation that better suits all of the circumstances is that this is another of Jesus' many parables, nearly all of which use earthly matters to describe heavenly matters. The host, then, is God; the wedding feast is (as usual) the heavenly banquet; and the seating order represents relative degrees of sanctification. Again, the message is twofold: "Avoid spiritual arrogance by assuming always that your level of holiness is low, leaving to the Father the possibility of raising it," but also, "Practice humility in your earthly life in preparation for your heavenly life."

Once again, Old Testament wisdom provides the solid, physical stairway to the Upper Room of New Testament wisdom. In the Old Testament stairway, we could see only the stairs, with an occasional glimpse through a small window; less than the immense vista from the Upper Room. But the priorities of the two realms are the same: humility is better than pride. Note, however, that the New Testament view from the Upper Room apparently cannot be reached except by climbing the Old Testament stairs.

Jesus, God's *Logos,* is Wisdom itself, and as such He presents to us the graduate seminar in wisdom, the prerequisite of which is the undergraduate course in wisdom. But, as we noted earlier, wisdom reflects and interacts with the order intrinsic in the universe, the order embedded there at the creation. Clearly, Old Testament wisdom is an "owner's manual" that tells us how to work with this complicated device—the universe—revealing what its inherent patterns and design are. Jesus' teaching builds on this: "I have come not to abolish [the Old Testament] but to *complete* [it]" (Matt. 5:17 PHILLIPS). This is the statement of Him through whom both heaven and earth were created (see Prov. 3:19), and who, therefore, has firsthand knowledge of the "blueprints" of both.

There are many demonstrations of the fact that heaven is Christ's accustomed habitat, but the one that seems most interesting in its offhanded candor is recorded in Matthew 22:30, where He answers the Sadducees' trick question concerning the marital state in the afterlife by saying, "They neither marry nor are given in marriage, but are like angels in heaven." He then goes on to confront the real reason for their question, but only after giving us a glimpse of His being originally from that otherworld, explaining its patterns of behavior to someone who has never visited the place. Or, to use a different metaphor, He is the painter who is, for the time being, painted into a small but important part of the canvas—He through whom all things were made is now a part of the world He made.

Readers of Proverbs and other books of Old Testament Wisdom Literature often ask how the seemingly secular prescriptions of these parts of Scripture can be seen as the Word of God. But this division of "secular" biblical wisdom from more "spiritual" wisdom is based, as Bruce Waltke notes, "on a modern-day viewpoint of life," which is to say that the cause of our difficulty is our own secular view of everything that is practical and does not explicitly proclaim its religious nature. "From the sages' perspective," Waltke continues, "each proverb is an expression of 'wisdom,'" an order intrinsic to reality that was instituted by God. Waltke then quotes Henry Frankfort, writing on ancient Wisdom Literature in general, as saying, "When a predestined order is recognized . . . all rules of conduct become practical rules. There can be no contrast between *savoir-faire*—worldly wisdom— and ethical behavior."[13]

What form of civilization would be possible if people were unable to perceive some kind of order in the world around them? For example, for thousands of years wood has been perhaps the most useful of building materials. It is soft enough to be workable but also strong enough to support great loads. It has tremendous tensile strength, and it is remarkably durable. But if human beings were unable to understand that every tree— no matter how different its leaves—is a "tree," a member of a certain group of things, they would have had to cut down plant after plant (grapevines, oats, lilies, and occasionally a beech or a pine tree), experimenting again and again for all of mankind's existence. It would have been an endless process of trying to find wood and never learning from their occasional successes. We human beings would have had to "reinvent the wheel," not only every generation but also every day and every moment. The world would have been a complete puzzle. Only a rare tree, found by pure chance, would have provided enough lumber to build a house, a bridge, or a ship. We would have been unable to add to our "mental map" of categories, to discover patterns in nature. We would have been unable to obey God's command to "rule over" and "subdue," to be stewards of the world.

And what is true of patterns in physical objects is true also of the division of time into days, months, and years. Without such a natural regularity in segments of time, the human race would never have been able to know when to plant crops so that they might grow for harvest. If farmers could not perceive and count on the planting season of spring arriving once each solar year followed by the growing season of summer, agriculture, and therefore civilization, would be impossible.

Could Paul be referring to this God-created order in Romans? In 1:20 he writes, "His invisible attributes, namely, his eternal power and divine nature, have been clearly perceived, ever since the creation of the world, in the things that have been made. . . ." Paul evidently has something in mind about the created world that displays what he calls God's "eternal power and divine

---

13. Henri Frankfort, *Ancient Egyptian Religion,* 2d ed. (New York: Columbia University Press, 1948; New York: Harper Torchbooks, 1961), 65.

nature." In the original Greek, the word translated "eternal power" is *dynamis,* simply "power"; the word translated "divine nature" is *theiotes,* "divinity," or the qualities that distinguish God from His creatures. The question then is, What does Paul mean by God's "power" and "divinity" as they are experienced in nature?

We can tell something of what he means by what he says as he continues this topic. He next criticizes the idolatry of people who worship God's creatures—human beings and animals—instead of the Creator of those subordinate beings (1:23). From this, we can deduce what he means by "power" in this context—the ability to create the world as evidenced by the existing world itself, an ability that no man or animal has. Similarly, we can deduce something of what Paul means by "divinity" when he continues his criticism by attacking homosexuality among women (v. 26) and men (v. 27). If there is a visible prohibition of such same-sex lusts in nature, it is in the nearly universal heterosexuality of animals.[14] This fact not only would be obvious in the everyday behavior of sheep, goats, dogs, and wild animals but also would agree with the strong implication in the description we have of God's creation of the world. In Genesis 1:22, God commands the newly created sea creatures and birds to "be fruitful and multiply," and Genesis 1:27–28 specifies that mankind was created "male and female," followed immediately by a repetition of the command to "be fruitful and multiply." Put simply, then, God designed the world of animals so that a union of the two sexes would reproduce the species, and this design is within the human race as well.[15]

This is not to say that creation provides a Bible on its own, one on which a natural religion may be established; nevertheless, Paul does seem to be

---

14. In discussing sin as it relates to a natural theology, Alister C. McGrath raises the topic of chaos theory as a new avenue for the exploration of the phenomenon of sin, and asks "whether the disordering to be discerned within the natural world . . . can be regarded as reflecting or resting upon a concept of sin" (*Nature,* vol. 1 of *A Scientific Theology* [Grand Rapids: Eerdmans, 2001], 289).

15. The fact that occasional exceptions occur in certain species and in certain individual animals might be explained by the intermediate level of order referred to earlier as "chaos theory." See McGrath, *Nature;* also James Gleick, *Chaos: Making a New Science* (New York: Penguin, 1987); and M. Mitchell Waldrop, *Complexity: The Emerging Science at the Edge of Order and Chaos* (New York: Touchstone, 1992).

saying that some aspects of God's law, some lines of His divinely instituted order, do manifest themselves in creation.[16] And so, because human beings are made in the image of God, they are able to study the world and discover parts of that divine order as it is displayed in creation. We are, of course, limited in how much we can thus discover, both because we are finite creatures and because we are fallen. But even with such limitations, wisdom has a way of making itself known to the human heart through our careful observation of the world around us.

To summarize our thinking to this point, divinely ordained order, the fixed order of reality, is the result of God having created everything through the Logos, Christ; that is, the world has a generalized consistency that is roughly as regular as the grain in a pine board. Although the grain is almost never as straight as a laser beam, it nevertheless tends clearly to run in the same general direction, the direction of growth in the tree from which it came. Alister McGrath puts it thus: "The divine *logos* is embedded within the structures of the created order—including human rationality—thus allowing humanity to gain at least some access to a knowledge of God through creation, as an anticipation and preparation for the recognition of the *logos* incarnate in Christ."[17] We can see it in the board because we have been made in the image of God, and so we have the ability to reason and perceive such patterns and regularities. Therefore, when we use that board, we would be "wise" (translate here "practical") to take that grain into account, to respect it.

Let's assume that we are building a small shelf that is meant to hold a fifty-pound object. We select a piece of one-inch-thick wood that measures twenty-four inches on each side. The grain runs, let's say, from side A to side C, parallel to sides B and D.

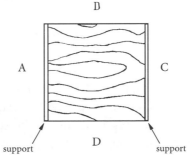

---

16. Charles M. Laymon, ed., *The Interpreter's One-Volume Commentary on the Bible* (Nashville: Abingdon, 1971), 772a.
17. McGrath, *Nature,* 253.

Because of the direction of the wood grain, if we support the shelf on sides A and C, the shelf will hold the weight placed on it. But if we place the supports on sides B and D, leaving A and C unsupported, the shelf will most likely split along the grain, dumping the object it was meant to hold. This carpenter's principle, like many proverbs, is a generalization; some woods, such as oak and ironwood, might hold heavy objects even under the worst methods of carpentry. But virtually no advantage is to be gained by ignoring the principle, and success while ignoring it is rare and depends upon unusual circumstances. In the vast majority of cases, there is both a wise procedure and a foolish procedure. True wisdom is not a set of rules handed down for the ego gratification of the Legislator; it is a collection of guidelines formulated for the benefit of a species that cannot yet understand the way the universe works. The follower of wisdom's ways is not a slave humiliated by means of laws passed to make human life more difficult than it might otherwise be; on the contrary, those who follow wisdom are like mechanics who are taught how an automobile works. Wisdom makes it easier, not harder, to live.

Let's think of the preceding illustration, that of building a shelf as an illustration of God's law or God's way with things. His way with things permeates everything—from the way an anthill operates; through human behavior and the design of the solar system; to the birth and death of animals, people, and stars. Everything seems to exist and behave according to certain principles or rules. There is both a right way and a wrong way to deal with people, animals, and inanimate objects, just as there is a right way and a wrong way to use a piece of wood. The grain of Christ's apprehensible character shows itself in innumerable dimensions of the world. A few of these are the wisdom inherent in generosity (Prov. 3:27–28); in avoiding adultery (6:20–35); in not availing oneself of prostitutes (7:4–27); in lovingkindness, truth, and fear of the Lord (16:6); in the quiet life (17:1); in restraint of one's speech (17:27); and in marriage (18:22).

Taking only some of these precepts, we may imagine what life would be like without them. Admittedly, not everyone exhibits generosity, but what sort of world would this be if no one ever gave to the needy or lent a neighbor a helping hand? As intolerable as life now is for some people, it would be intolerable for more people, even worse than intolerable for some people, if there were no generous acts at all. Likewise, although our lives are probably more troubled than we'd like for them to be, at least occasional oases of quiet occur in most lives—dinnertime perhaps, times set aside for prayer and bedtime. Life would be (and is for some) a continual torment without these periods set in an orderly fashion.

And what of truth? It is fashionable in some academic circles today to say that there is no truth, only differing opinions based on individual points of view. But for the airline pilot whose task is to land his passenger-laden airplane at O'Hare Field in Chicago, the location of that airport is not arbitrary; it is in one place and only one place on the face of the earth. Similarly, the physician who diagnoses a patient's illness is not free to be creative or to indulge his personal whims in his conclusions, for if the treatment that follows is based on an untrue diagnosis, the patient may die needlessly. And as a final example, imagine an innocent man on trial for murder. If he is convicted of a murder that he did not commit, how would justice be served merely because twelve people were of the opinion that he did commit the murder? It would not be served at all. And if, a year after his conviction, conclusive evidence of his innocence was found, causing a majority of the jurors to change their minds, did the truth change with their opinions? Not at all. Behind all of the opinions, feelings, prejudices, reasoning, and politics, the immutable fact remains: he did not commit the murder.

This is the sort of truth about the universe—the immutable facts of its tendencies, fiber, and texture—on which wisdom is based. In all matters that the human mind can comprehend, truth exists, and we are commanded to acquire it and never lose sight of it (Prov. 23:23). Jesus Himself attested to His identification with this ultimate truth when He answered Thomas's question by saying, "I am the way, and the truth, and the life" (John 14:6). This is the truth of which Jesus said He had come to bear witness, and at the same time the truth about which He said those who are in harmony with it hear His voice (18:37). It is also the truth of which Pilate spoke when he asked, "What is truth?" Pilate's perception of the truth in Christ's case (His innocence) was in conflict with the procurator's political position, and the latter was more important to Pilate than the truth.

If we fear the Lord more than we fear the disapproval of our peers, we will seek the Lord's truths, the Lord's ways, and the Lord's wisdom and take them to heart. In some cases, it will be of practical use to us, whereas in other cases it will be vital to our earthly survival, and in still others it will bring us closer to understanding and knowing God. It is this growing nearness to understanding and knowing God that is both the goal and the motivation in our quest for spiritual maturity.

Questions for Thought and Reflection

1. Consider the times in your life when you have made decisions that you later regretted. List as many such instances as you can remember. Now look at each item and ask yourself if you made that decision on emotional grounds. How would you make those same decisions today? (Note: Rather than saying *what* your decision would be, tell *how* you would come to that decision.) Although you might never have to make that same exact decision again, you will make thousands of others, so outline a basic plan for making future decisions of any kind.

2. Pick a craft that uses one of the following materials: metal, textiles, leather, clay, glass, or paper. Jot down the things that you think you would need to know about the nature of that material to make a useful object (not a piece of art for its own sake) of it. When you have made your list as complete as you can, go to a library, builders' supply, or crafts store and glance through a book about using this material. How many traits can you detect in the raw material that make it useful to the human race?

3. When a friend telephones you one day, you sense that she is upset, but you have no idea why. Then she tells you of a trip that she took recently to her hometown, a place she had not seen for thirty years. She says that the place was entirely different; she could hardly find her way around town, no one knew her, and it didn't feel like home anymore. You have heard such accounts before, and you begin to console her on the sadness brought about by change in the things we love. But then she interrupts you to say that she knows all of that, and that's why she often looked at old photographs of her hometown and reminisced about its people, streets, houses, and shops. She wanted it to stay the same. And she really did believe that it would be the same. So why wasn't it? Explain where the fault lies in her logic.

4. Although many of the patterns that are a part of God's order are evident in the physical world, where do similar patterns exist in other areas, such as the social, moral, or ethical realms? Are there patterns that generally lead to success in life or in relationships? If so, do you think that those principles are a part of God's design?

Chapter Two

PROVERBS' PORTRAIT OF A WISE PERSON

Israel's wisdom had many things in common with that of both other peoples around them and many other cultures around the world, both ancient and modern. This fact should surprise no one because the Old Testament recognizes that all people are made in God's image and that, even after the Fall, they are able to identify many of the patterns of nature and human behavior that God built into the fabric of the universe at Creation. Therefore, we should expect many common insights among the peoples of the world. The thing that sets Israel's wisdom apart from that of all others is that they recognized the reality of God's special relationship with them: God had chosen them, made a covenant with them, and revealed Himself to them in a variety of ways. He had done so through His prophets, through Scripture, and in history (Heb. 1:1).

The wisdom gained from general revelation often deals with such practical matters as how to build a house, certain aspects of raising children, or behaviors that contribute to success in life (e.g., the advantages of rising early, often phrased, "The early bird catches the worm")—matters that are not addressed in special revelation. Sometimes, wisdom struggles with complex issues that have significant theological implications but that are not dealt with comprehensively in special revelation (e.g., questions about why the righteous suffer or why, as Ecclesiastes puts it, wicked people are treated like the righteous ought to be and vice versa). Such attempts to understand the nature of things, as long as they did not conflict with Yahwistic theology, were appreciated as important and legitimate. At the same time, Israel viewed wisdom secured apart from the knowledge of God as incomplete and sometimes even deceptive. Wisdom discovered from general revelation needed, where possible, to be integrated with that received through God's special revelation of Himself to understand Yahweh's order in the most complete way possible.

The book of Proverbs devotes considerable attention to developing its picture of the wise person and contrasting that image with its portrait of the foolish one. Although the fundamental difference between these individuals lies in the fact that the wise person fears the Lord but the foolish person does not (a concept that will be discussed at length in a subsequent chapter), the picture in Proverbs often includes a number of characteristics of the wise person that seem to have little to do with anything spiritual. The church often neglects these elements of character and behavior in its teaching about sanctification and spiritual development. One suspects that a connection exists between the church's failure to teach Christians about the importance of such things as good manners, common sense, basic decency, and appropriate speech and the fact that Christians often do not have a very good reputation when it comes to such virtues. At the same time, our failures in these areas often undermine our credibility in the eyes of the world. The woman who is zealous about doing good works but who has an unsanctified mouth that cuts like a sword; the deacon who knows every detail of orthodox theology but who finds fault with everything anyone does either in the church or in his own home; the young man who is passionate about Bible study, prayer, and ministry but who does not pay his bills on time and is deeply in debt; or the wonderfully gifted pastor or teacher who regularly loses his temper and yells at his staff or the people with whom he does business—these are people whom the apostles James or John would say are not complete or mature believers.

Although the New Testament recognizes the inconsistency of such individuals, it provides few details about wise behavior or the process by which such behavior and character are developed. It is clear that sanctification plays a major role in producing such results, but experience does not support the idea that God's Spirit mysteriously infuses people with good time-management skills or with financial discipline. The Old Testament has much to say about many of these matters. Behind the New Testament's echoes of the Old Testament, the New Testament seems simply to presuppose these teachings as it focuses on the role of God's Spirit in bringing the believer to maturity. If this perception is correct, neglect of what the Old Testament Wisdom Literature has to say about these matters is likely to produce a skewed teaching that results in many Christians' "shooting themselves in the foot" when it comes to living life as it was meant to be, that is, according to Yahweh's order.

Wisdom's Perspective on Life

The texts we will be considering come largely from the book of Proverbs, which is part of the Old Testament Wisdom Literature; thus, they share the basic perspective that characterizes wisdom. Wisdom thinking is anchored in the doctrine of creation. God created all things, and the universe exhibits order because God created it that way. What is more, the Wisdom Literature does not see the order that God designed into the world as limited to the physical realm. Cause-and-effect relationships exist in the moral, ethical, social, and spiritual realms as well, and they exist because that is the way God designed His world and His creatures to function. An important part of human responsibility is to search for that order and thus learn to live in harmony with the cosmos. In contrast to the Law and the Prophets, in which God's truth is often revealed directly from heaven to its recipient, the wisdom material seems largely to have resulted from careful human observation of the world and society. This was then selected, under the direction of God's Spirit, for inclusion in inspired Scripture. Theophanies are rare in Wisdom Literature, and at least one function of the one in the book of Job seems to be to show the limits of the wisdom that man can discover apart from that special revelation.

Note, however, that these cause-and-effect relationships between action and outcome were seen by the Wisdom Literature in general terms rather than as invariable and absolute. The book of Proverbs consists largely of statements that are, by their very nature, generalizations on truth rather than invariable promises or exhaustive descriptions of reality. An extrabiblical proverb such as "A stitch in time saves nine" affirms the importance of taking care of a problem while it is small and can be repaired with only minimal effort, in contrast to neglecting the problem until it is more serious and thus more difficult to repair. In reality, some problems cannot be fixed by any amount of effort no matter how early they are discovered, and some minor problems need no attention because they will never develop into major problems. It has been said that a single proverb captures a tiny cross section of truth, and so a more comprehensive understanding of a subject must be developed by putting together a number of related proverbs to create a broader mosaic. Many different proverbs describe a wise person; a single one in isolation rarely provides a full portrait of such a character.

What Is a Proverb?

An important skill that wisdom seeks to inculcate in its students is the ability to identify the variables that are presupposed in each proverb and to discern which proverb or set of proverbs appropriately applies in a given situation. Failure to develop skill in application is vividly described in Proverbs 26:7, 9 where a proverb in the mouth of a fool is compared first to legs that hang down from a lame man and then to a drunk man carrying a thornbush as he staggers through a crowd of people. Like the lame man's legs, a proverb known but not applied appropriately will not accomplish that for which it was designed. Even worse, the proverb, like the thornbush carelessly carried by the drunken man, can do damage and cause pain to others if it is not applied appropriately.

The form of a proverb seems designed not only to cause truth to register with those who hear it but also to stimulate thought about how the proverb applies to life. Proverbs such as 26:4–5 illustrate the ambiguity and tension inherent in wisdom's approach. The first proverb says, "Answer not a fool according to his folly, lest you be like him yourself." The second proverb says, "Answer a fool according to his folly, lest he be wise in his own eyes." Thus, the wise person must become a craftsman who is able to know how to respond wisely and effectively to any situation that might confront him. Proverbs such as those we've just quoted alert us to the challenges that lie hidden in the real world. As Kidner says, "The secondary purpose of Proverbs is to introduce the reader to a style of teaching that provokes his thought, getting under his skin by thrusts of wit, paradox, common sense and teasing symbolism, in preference to the preacher's tactic of frontal assault."[1]

At first glance, the proverbs might seem to leave no room for exceptions, but, as Garrett notes, this conclusion results from

---

1. Derek Kidner, *Proverbs*, vol. 15 of Tyndale Old Testament Commentaries (Downers Grove, Ill.: InterVarsity, 1964), 58–59.

our failure to grasp the hermeneutics of wisdom literature. By its very nature and purpose, wisdom emphasizes the general truth over some specific cases and, being a work of instruction, frames its teachings in short pithy statements without excessive qualification. It is not that the wisdom writers did not know that life was complex and full of exceptions, but dwelling on those cases would have distracted attention from their didactic purposes. . . . general truths are the stock in trade of Proverbs.[2]

In fact, wisdom books such as Job and Ecclesiastes make clear that the sages recognized that exceptions to the general principles occur, and these books reflect some of the tensions that result when experience seems to be at variance with traditional understandings of how things work in life—tensions that will be considered in later chapters and that make their own unique contribution to spiritual growth.

The wisdom authors also clearly recognized that wisdom is limited by God's sovereignty, and it is God's purpose that ultimately determines outcomes. Proverbs 16:9 says, "The heart [or mind] of a man plans his way, but the LORD establishes his steps." Proverbs 21:30–31 says, "No wisdom, no understanding, no counsel can avail against the LORD. The horse is made ready for the day of battle, but the victory belongs to the LORD." The purpose of such statements was not to discourage people from acquiring and using wisdom in every area of life. As von Rad says, "Its aim is, rather, to put a stop to the erroneous concept that a guarantee of success was to be found in practicing human wisdom and in making preparations. Man must always keep himself open to the activity of God, an activity which completely escapes all calculation, for between the putting into practice of the most reliable wisdom and that which then takes place, there always lies a great unknown."[3]

Nevertheless, and in spite of the ambiguities and generalizations that dominate the wisdom approach to understanding life and the world, the Wisdom Literature identifies many important principles that reflect Yahweh's order, and it is possible to put the individual proverbs together in a way that

---

2. Duane Garrett, *Proverbs, Ecclesiastes, Song of Solomon,* vol. 14 of The New American Commentary (Nashville: Broadman & Holman, 1993), 57.

3. Gerhard von Rad, *Wisdom in Israel,* trans. James Martin (Nashville: Abingdon, 1972), 101.

allows the pictures of the wise person and the foolish person to develop before our eyes. The pictures might not be comprehensive, and we will from time to time identify components that come from other sources, both within Scripture and from general revelation. In the pages that follow, we will put together a general outline of what Proverbs says about the wise person and the fool, and, in so doing, recognize several important characteristics of the person who lives according to God's truth and receives His commendation and blessing.

Proverbs' Picture of Wise and Foolish Men

Proverbs uses a variety of terms for the semantic domains "wisdom/wise"[4] and "folly/fool."[5] In the following discussion, we normally will not differentiate among these terms, unless it seems important to do so. Von Rad[6] has suggested that the author of Proverbs 1:1–5 (where most of the terms for wisdom are used) is seeking to communicate a rather comprehensive idea for which no adequate term exists, so he conveys the idea by clustering together a number of different, but closely related, terms. We would argue that what is true for the introductory verses of Proverbs generally holds true for the entire book and that the same basic idea is valid for the terms indicating folly as well. We will deal with both the wise person and the fool, each as a single composite character.

Although many of the attitudes and behaviors that characterize the wise person in Proverbs fall into categories that strike the casual reader as "secular" and "nonspiritual," it is important to affirm that the material in Proverbs is set in a broader theological context, one that clearly sees the knowledge of God as the beginning point for wisdom. "The fear of the LORD is the beginning of knowledge/wisdom" (Prov. 1:7; 9:10), and true wisdom is not acquired apart from diligently seeking God (Prov. 2:1–10) within a life of faith and obedience (Prov. 3:5–7). Although wisdom consists in skill, the ability to succeed, and the ability to formulate a plan that allows a person to

---

4. Some examples are terms such as *wisdom, discipline, insight, knowledge, prudence,* and *good sense.*
5. The words used cover a continuum that ranges from the person who is naive and uninformed, to the scoffer who knows exactly what he or she is doing and who violates God's order with great determination and delight.
6. Von Rad, *Wisdom in Israel,* 13.

accomplish successfully a desired objective, what Proverbs offers is not an amoral pragmatism. The results of the wisdom with which Proverbs is concerned include such things as righteousness, justice, equity, prudence, and discretion (Prov. 1:3–4), while it also promises to deliver one from evil ways and evil people (Prov. 2:12–19). This wisdom enables a person to find favor and good success in the sight of God and man (Prov. 3:4). Clearly, this wisdom is not the worldly wisdom that both the Old and New Testaments regularly warn against and condemn, precisely because worldly wisdom results from human autonomy and independence from God. At the same time, what Proverbs shows us is that these seemingly secular aspects of wisdom are vitally important; they are necessary for one to be "complete" and mature. They are qualities that must be cultivated, not apart from a life of faith but as an essential component of it.

Teachability: An Essential Virtue

A wise person is teachable, and this as much as any other single characteristic distinguishes the wise person from the fool. The wise person is open to instruction in all of its forms (teaching, correction, rebuke, and discipline), and he learns from it, whereas the fool rejects it and continues to pursue his own self-destructive course. The importance of receiving teaching and instruction is affirmed throughout the book of Proverbs, with the sections in the early chapters of the book framed as a parent's teaching to a son regularly beginning with words such as, "Hear, my son, your father's instruction, and forsake not your mother's teaching" (1:8); "My son, do not forget my teaching, but let your heart keep my commandments" (3:1); "Hear, O sons, a father's instruction, and be attentive, that you may gain insight" (4:1). The results of embracing the teaching and instruction are stated in Proverbs 19:20—"Listen to advice and accept instruction, that you may gain wisdom in the future"—and Proverbs 10:17—"Whoever heeds instruction is on the path to life, but he who rejects reproof leads others astray."

A number of proverbs contrast the ways in which the wise person and the fool respond to instruction and correction. Proverbs 13:1 says, "A wise son hears his father's instruction, but a scoffer does not listen to rebuke." Proverbs 15:5 says, "A fool despises his father's instruction, but whoever heeds reproof is prudent." The fool may sometimes quietly reject advice and ignore correction, but often his response is much more negative and intense. The fool's antagonism toward instruction and correction is often directed against the person who offers the rebuke, whereas the wise person welcomes the correction and appreciates the person who offers it. As Proverbs 9:7–9 says, "Whoever corrects a scoffer gets himself abuse, and he who reproves a wicked man incurs injury. Do not reprove a scoffer, or he will hate you; reprove a wise man, and he will love you. Give instruction to a wise man, and he will be still wiser; teach a righteous man, and he will increase in learning." Proverbs 23:9 says, "Do not speak in the hearing of a fool, for he will despise the good sense of your words."

This basic difference between the wise person and the fool has little to do with intellectual ability; rather, it has to do with attitude, and the fool's resistance to correction ensures that he or she will never become wise. The extent of the foolish person's refusal to listen and be deterred from his unwise course is expressed in Proverbs 17:10—"A rebuke goes deeper into a man of understanding than a hundred blows into a fool"—and Proverbs 27:22—"Crush a fool in a mortar with a pestle along with crushed grain, yet his folly will not depart from him." Whereas the wise person is corrected by words, the fool does not get the message even after experiencing the pain of corporal punishment.

The attitude that separates the wise person from the fool is pride. The fool sees no reason to take advice from anyone because he thinks so highly of himself and his opinions that he is certain he has no need to listen to anyone else. Proverbs 12:15 says, "The way of a fool is right in his own eyes, but a wise man listens to advice." The nature of this pride, at least in extreme cases, is described in Proverbs 13:10: "By insolence [*zadon*] comes nothing but strife, but with those who take advice is wisdom." The word *zadon,* translated "insolence" here, is used of "the arrogance of those who must have everything their own way and will not be kicked around."[7] McKane says about the verse, "Insolence or arrogance is contrasted with a willingness to confer and be guided by a consensus of informed opinion. The contrast suggests that *zadon* indicates particularly a contempt for all other opinions, such as is characteristic of the person who takes his own omniscience for granted and will not be deterred from unwise and contentious courses by advice from any quarter."[8] The wise person has the humil-

---

7. Kidner, *Proverbs,* 90.
8. William McKane, *Proverbs,* Old Testament Library (Philadelphia: Westminster, 1970), 453–54.

ity to recognize that his opinions and behavior are not without error and is open to correction and instruction—from both God and others.

Proverbs 12:1 also affirms the importance of openness to instruction in acquiring wisdom, but it states the idea in a way that suggests that we may, in fact, be dealing with a fundamental principle of God's order. The proverb says, "Whoever loves discipline loves knowledge, but he who hates reproof is stupid." The word translated "discipline" is the Hebrew word *musar,* a word that is used frequently in the Wisdom Literature. The purpose of *musar* is normally educative, to change attitudes, thinking, or behavior. The methods that are encompassed in *musar* cover a broad range, from the provisions that God bestowed upon His people in the wilderness to instruction, correction, and even the harsh discipline of corporal punishment. The method of *musar* seems to have been essentially whatever it took to accomplish the task of education. Thus, the disciple is embracing a wide range of methods to guide him to the goal of being wise. He or she recognizes that the blessings of wisdom are well worth any difficulties that might be encountered in the process of reaching that goal. The person who hates reproof is described with an unusual adjective that is related to a word for animal or beast. Therefore, the statement suggests that the person who rejects the path that leads to wisdom will be relegated to functioning not like a human being, as God designed him, but rather like an animal. McKane says that the word "denotes the absence of the rationality which differentiates men from animals."[9] Clifford says, "To reject correction is to choose an animal level of consciousness."[10] The pattern seen in these verses from Proverbs very likely reflects something about how human beings are designed to function both in their relationship with God and in their relationships with other human beings.

The early chapters of Genesis make clear that God is the Creator and we, as part of His creation, are His creatures. This fact defines our relationship with Him and establishes His legitimate authority over us. The fact that God is infinite and we are finite provides another basis for submitting to God's authority over us. God is omniscient, all-wise, powerful to a degree that we are not, and again these attributes establish a reason why we should listen to God and do what He says rather than depending on our own wisdom

---

9. Ibid., 441.
10. Richard J. Clifford, *Proverbs,* Old Testament Library (Louisville: Westminster/ John Knox, 1999), 129.

and understanding. Being fully human and functioning according to God's design requires that we live in dependence on and in harmony with God. Rejecting His authority and the order that He has established results in a life that operates below the level that God intended, and the person living thus cannot experience the fullness of life as it was meant to be.

Pride, Humility, and God

The Fall illustrates these points clearly. God gave the man and the woman whom He had created and placed in the Garden a single prohibition: "You shall not eat of the fruit of the tree that is in the midst of the garden." He also told them that if they did eat from that tree, they would die. The tempter presented to the woman an alternative and suggested that God was trying to withhold something good from them through the prohibition. He suggested that if they ate from the fruit of the tree, they would become like God. When confronted with these alternatives, rather than responding as a creature and depending on the Creator's instruction, the woman acted independently and autonomously, a reaction that is the essence of sin. As Kidner says, "As [the fruit] stood, prohibited, it presented the alternative to discipleship: to be self-made, wresting one's knowledge, satisfactions and values from the created world in defiance of the Creator."[11] Gerhard von Rad has said that what the serpent is claiming is "the possibility of an extension of human existence beyond the limits set for it at creation."[12] He describes the result of their disobedience as follows: "Man has stepped outside the state of dependence, he has refused obedience and willed to make himself independent. The guiding principle of his life is no longer obedience but his autonomous knowing and willing, and thus he has ceased to understand himself as creature."[13]

The Fall, with its picture of the paradigmatic sin, clearly shows us that sin is unbelief. The man and woman simply did not believe what God told them, and they both concluded that their own picture of reality and truth was more accurate than what God proclaimed. In addition to being unbe-

---

11. Derek Kidner, *Genesis*, vol. 1 of Tyndale Old Testament Commentaries (London: Tyndale, 1967), 63.
12. Gerhard von Rad, *Genesis*, Old Testament Library (Philadelphia: Westminster, 1972), 89.
13. Ibid., 97.

lief, sin is also rebellion. The man and woman were not willing to live within the freedom and dominion that they had as the creatures that God designed. They wanted more, and so they rebelled against God and disobeyed His instruction. It was pride and hubris that made the woman think that she could decide for herself what was good in her situation and that the result would be better than God's will for them. It was pride and hubris that prompted the man to reject the authority of the Creator and in independence seek to become like God. The consequences of these creatures' rebellion were devastating. They no longer understood themselves as creatures; as a result, they ceased to function as God had designed them, and they ceased to experience life as God intended it to be.

Scripture regularly calls the people of God to live in the humility that acknowledges God as Creator and themselves as His creatures. Just as pride keeps a person from depending on God and encourages him to assert his own independence and put his trust in things other than God, so it is that those who are humble are the ones who fear the Lord and seek Him. The words translated "humble" also mean oppressed, afflicted, and poor, and a person's physical circumstances often seem to force him or her to depend on others for survival and well-being. This attitude of dependence seems to account for these words being used to describe a person's relationship with God. Several passages (e.g., Deut. 8 or the prayer in Prov. 30:8–9) make clear that abundant resources can easily cause a person to forget God and the need to depend on Him. The author of Psalm 119 says in verse 67, "Before I was afflicted I went astray, but now I keep your word," and again in verse 71, "It is good for me that I was afflicted, that I might learn your statutes."

Apart from the passages that use the words in a socioeconomic meaning, dependence on God is the basic characteristic of humility. Dumbrell says that in the Wisdom Literature the humble "display . . . reverence for Yahweh by recognizing their place in the basic cosmic order, so that humility means the acquiring of a proper self-estimate."[14] In terms of man's relationship with God, humility means acknowledging, both theoretically and practically, that God is the Creator and sustainer of all things and that people are creatures. "Humility . . . is part of the cosmic ordering of the created universe, one of the essential factors by which life in God's creation proceeds. . . . Humility is the personal quality that makes integration into the world order

---

14. W. J. Dumbrell, *New International Dictionary of Old Testament Theology and Exegesis,* ed. Willem A. VanGemeren (Grand Rapids: Zondervan, 1997), 3:462.

possible and enables the possessor to know his place in the total system."[15] It is only as people recognize their place as creatures—while also recognizing themselves as persons made in God's image—that people can live in the dependence on God for which they were designed. This dependence on God makes a person teachable and prompts him or her to respond to God's instruction in the obedience of faith.

The prophet Isaiah makes clear what God approves of in people. As important as the temple was, both before and after the Exile, it was not building a house for God that attracted His attention—after all, He created the heavens and the earth, and all things belong to Him. In the last half of Isaiah 66:2, the Lord says, "This is the one to whom I will look: he who is humble and contrite in spirit and trembles at my word."

Pride, Humility, and Other People

Although Proverbs does recognize the necessity for humility in one's relationship with God and the negative consequences of pride in that relationship (e.g., Prov. 16:5 says, "Everyone who is arrogant in heart is an abomination to the LORD; be assured, he will not go unpunished"), most of the teaching about pride and humility in Proverbs is focused on interpersonal relationships. Humility in a person's relationship with God and openness to His instruction clearly is part of the order that God built into creation, but can the same be said with respect to our relationships with other people?

In Genesis 2, after God had created Adam and placed him in the Garden that He had planted, He said in verse 18, "It is not good that the man should be alone; I will make him a helper fit for him." Although considerable discussion exists about the exact meaning of the Hebrew expression used here, certain things are clear. The word translated "helper" is in no sense a demeaning term, nor does it indicate anything about status in the relationship. The word is often used of God, and it describes someone who has sufficient strength and resources to assist another at a point of weakness. What is implied by the use of the term is that the man, even before the Fall, was designed by God with both strengths and weaknesses. In the context of Genesis 2, this need was met by God's providing him a "complementary helper" whom God designed. In this author's (Edward) opinion, the helper

---

15. Ibid.

"corresponding to him" or "opposite him"—the literal meaning of the Hebrew term *ezer kenegdo*—is another human being made in God's image but
one designed to bring strengths to his points of weakness and vice versa.
God's design was to have the man and the woman fit together in every area
of life—physical, emotional, and spiritual—such that the man was com-
pleted through his wife. As Westermann says, "The man is created by God
in such a way that he needs the help of a partner; hence mutual help is an
essential part of human existence."[16]

Although Genesis 2:18–25 relates specifically to marriage and the way it
is designed to function, the human need for others, a need that is innate in
God's design, seems not to be limited to the help that comes from one's
spouse. Ecclesiastes 4 describes some of the benefits that relationships are
intended to provide. After describing the tragedy of valuing money and
things over relationships and family, Qoheleth says, "Two are better than
one, because they have a good reward for their toil. For if they fall, one will
lift up his fellow. But woe to him who is alone when he falls and has not
another to lift him up! Again, if two lie together, they keep warm, but how
can one keep warm alone? And though a man might prevail against one
who is alone, two will withstand him—a threefold cord is not quickly broken" (Eccl. 4:9–12).

The human need for instruction and correction that is affirmed in the
passages we have noted in Proverbs likely reflects this same component of
God's design: people in their finitude have weaknesses that are to be sup-
plied by others. Man's need for the help of others was magnified after the
Fall because his finitude is now compounded by his fallenness, and that
inherent human sinfulness both clouds his judgment as to what his weaknesses are and greatly increases his reluctance to acknowledge his dependence on either God or others. The New Testament passages that describe
the church as the body of Christ suggest the same idea: the people who
make up the body are designed—by nature, training, and experience—to
function in a wide variety of ways in the church. The entire body functions
as it was designed to function only when the various members use their
individual strengths to complement the weaknesses of others. We all have
strengths, so others need us; we all have weaknesses, so we need others. This
mutual dependence on one another seems to be a part of God's order.

---

16. Claus Westermann, *Genesis 1–11*, trans. John J. Scullion (Minneapolis:
Augsburg, 1984), 227.

As we noted earlier, humility enables the person who has it to know his or her place in the total system. It produces a proper self-understanding that includes a recognition of both one's strengths and one's inadequacies compared with other people in the community. Paul describes this fact in the introduction to one of the passages describing the interdependence of the members of the body of Christ. He says, "I say to everyone among you not to think of himself more highly than he ought to think, but to think with sober judgment, each according to the measure of faith that God has assigned" (Rom. 12:3). Humility involves not only the recognition of strengths and weaknesses but also a willingness to learn from others and to benefit from their strengths. Paul suggests that our attitude toward others in this regard is not unrelated to our humility toward God. He tells the Corinthian church that there is no place in the church for pride and arrogance based on the gifts that people possess and exercise because those strengths and abilities are gracious gifts from God and therefore do not constitute a legitimate reason for boasting (e.g., 1 Cor. 4:7). Humility is an important key to functioning in society as well as in one's relationship to God. And perhaps even more significantly, humility appears to be one of the fundamental elements of the order by which God's world functions.

In his *The Screwtape Letters,* C. S. Lewis recognized the importance of humility in Christian living and the dangers of failing to understand what humility involves. The senior devil gives the following advice to his junior colleague:

> You must conceal from the patient the true end of Humility. Let him think of it . . . as a certain kind of opinion (namely, a low opinion) of his own talents and character . . . fix in his mind the idea that humility consists in trying to believe those talents to be less valuable than he believes them to be . . . by this method thousands of humans have been brought to think that humility means pretty women trying to believe they are ugly and clever men trying to believe they are fools. And since what they are trying to believe may, in some cases, be manifest nonsense, they cannot succeed in believing it and we have the chance of keeping their minds endlessly revolving on themselves in an effort to achieve the impossible. . . . The Enemy [that is, God] wants to bring the man to a state of mind in which he could design the best cathedral in the world, and know that it was the best, and rejoice in the fact,

without being any more (or less) or otherwise glad at having done it
than he would be if it had been done by another.[17]

Humility is a necessary attitude for functioning according to God's design, but pride regularly keeps the sort of humility that Lewis describes from
becoming a reality. Pride prevents a husband or wife from acknowledging
his or her weaknesses and from benefiting from the strengths that a spouse
brings to their relationship. As a result, that individual will not make progress
toward becoming wise. Arrogance can destroy family relationships when
people are unwilling to submit to legitimate correction and modify their
behavior toward others. We can all think of people who had great potential
for accomplishing significant things but who failed to realize that potential
because they refused to listen to advice or receive correction from others.
Examples abound: the excellent athlete who will not listen to his coach; the
student who will not do what her teacher tells her is necessary to succeed;
the gifted employee who is terminated because he or she will not receive
correction and follow instruction relating to how things are done in that
particular organization; the pastor who will not listen to the counsel of his
congregation, staff, or leaders; the congregation that will not listen to the
biblical teaching of their pastor.

We regularly hear examples in the news of people who literally lose their
lives or end up in prison because they were so determined that nobody
could tell them what to do. We hear of Christian leaders who have fallen
into sin, and often we discover that long before the scandal occurred, they
refused to heed the warnings of friends and colleagues and their advice to
terminate the involvement that finally led to the disaster. We can think of
politicians who were too arrogant to listen to advice from those around
them and whose careers were destroyed as a result. We hear of government
agencies that were so committed to protecting turf that they refused to listen
to others in situations in which heeding the advice possibly could have
averted national disasters. We hear of CEOs or CFOs of major corporations
who are so blinded by pride and greed that they rejected warnings from
employees that could have prevented the collapse of the company. Failure
and disgrace often result because proud people are unwilling to listen to
advice and the correction that comes from others around them. The tragedy

---

17. C. S. Lewis, *The Screwtape Letters,* letter 14 (New York: Macmillan, 1959), 72–73.

is that, in many cases, openness to advice and correction and a teachable spirit could have produced a very different outcome. The wise (and godly) person welcomes counsel and discipline even when the correction is difficult to hear and painful to acknowledge (Prov. 27:6; Eccl. 7:5). Such people know that counsel and discipline have the potential to make them even wiser.

Proverbs affirms what many other parts of Scripture teach: that a welcoming attitude toward discipline and correction is a significant virtue that contributes to success throughout life. The person whose theme song in life is "I Did It My Way" will not acquire wisdom or become spiritually mature. There is a close connection between being open to advice and correction in the social realm and being open to the instruction and correction of God's Word.

Obtaining advice from others clearly brings benefits. We seek advice from lawyers, medical doctors, financial advisors, building contractors, and auto mechanics because we recognize that their education and experience give them specialized knowledge that we do not possess. We recognize the truth of Will Rogers's statement, "We are all ignorant, only in different subjects," and we are rarely threatened by seeking advice from others in our areas of ignorance. We often seek advice from people we respect or from those we believe can shed special insight on issues about which we are confused or struggling. Normally, people are open to the advice they solicit and for which they have to pay—although according to one interpretation of Proverbs 17:16 ("Why should a fool have money in his hand to buy wisdom when he has no sense?"), the fool may sometimes ignore the advice for which he pays.

We generally have more difficulty when the advice is unsolicited, or when it involves matters about which we consider ourselves informed or expert, or when it comes from competing disciplines or rival theological traditions. Most parents bristle when they are given advice about how to rear their children. Most teachers become defensive when their teaching methods are questioned. Many Christian leaders react with a vehement negativity when someone questions their godliness, integrity, or wisdom or when someone tells them that their sermons are too long. It becomes more difficult still when the person leveling the criticism is less qualified than we, or when they deliver the rebuke sarcastically or demeaningly. As we noted in the introduction, sanctification takes place in the context of the world, and God uses our experiences in the world as a means of grace by which He refines us and develops godly character in us. God's Spirit develops the qualities that He desires in us while we are functioning in the world. We have already cited several verses suggesting that humility is often developed through experiences of suffering and difficulty—a topic that we will explore in more detail in a later chapter—but it also seems certain that godly character (i.e., character that is consistent with God's order) is developed regularly as we respond to the teaching and correction of those around us.

Proverbs does not suggest that we must always agree with the instruction or rebuke. One of the interesting ironies is that the wiser a person becomes, the less often the criticisms will be legitimate, but the wiser a person becomes, the more open he or she becomes to instruction. In C. S. Lewis's terms, the person who is genuinely wise seems to be able to receive instruction and rebuke and evaluate it in the same nondefensive way that he would if he had thought of the idea himself. One wonders if a person who has trouble receiving correction from others can be genuinely open to the instruction of God's Word. Certainly such people will be receptive as long as they agree with the instruction and it is consistent with their agenda, but even King Saul was able to do that. Unless we recognize our weaknesses and our limits and unless we understand our need for others to point out what we cannot see or what we refuse to see in ourselves, we likely will never develop the humility that allows us genuinely to welcome God's instruction and say with the psalmist, "Search me, O God, and know my heart! Try me . . . and see if there be any grievous way in me, and lead me in the way everlasting!" (Ps. 139:23–24).

And the wise person not only is welcoming to counsel but also will actively seek it out. Proverbs 11:14b says, "In an abundance of counselors there is safety."[18] Obviously, a person cannot, and should not, follow all of the opinions that are given, but neither do we exercise wisdom when we select as our advisors only those who agree with us. Of course, there is no point in seeking the advice of a fool because, as Proverbs 13:20 says, "Whoever walks with the wise becomes wise, but the companion of fools will suffer harm." Proverbs 14:7 adds, "Leave the presence of a fool, for there you do not meet words of knowledge."

The pride that keeps the foolish person from accepting advice affects

---

18. Proverbs 15:22; 20:18; and 24:6 affirm the same point.

him in a number of negative ways. He will not listen to corrective counsel and so continues on a path that will lead to destruction. But because he is unwilling to listen to others, he also rarely understands the issues that are under discussion. And because he is foolish, even his lack of understanding does not prompt him to remain quiet and at least conceal the fact that he is not wise (see Prov. 17:28). According to Proverbs 18:2, "A fool takes no pleasure in understanding, but only in expressing his opinion," and Proverbs 18:13 describes the embarrassing consequences: "If one gives an answer before he hears, it is his folly and shame."

Job's friends illustrate the point as they and Job consider his tragic situation. Their thinking focuses on the reasons for Job's catastrophes and how Job should respond to them. But, because questions about suffering involve many issues concerning the nature of God and His activity in the world, together with other issues about whether the sufferer has done things that have contributed to the suffering, the questions are complex and rarely can be answered with total confidence. As the men discuss Job's situation, the friends are certain that Job must have done something to cause the suffering. Job, however, knows of nothing that he had done that could explain the severity of his suffering on the basis of the doctrine of retribution (the idea that people reap what they sow). As Job continues to affirm his innocence, the friends refuse to accept his claim and are unwilling to consider that there might be more to God's ways of working in the world than the doctrine of retribution—something that becomes quite important if Job is in fact innocent. Job's friends' refusal to listen to the facts or to consider that he might know some things that they do not is clear in Job 15:7–10, where Eliphaz says to Job, "Are you the first man who was born? Or were you brought forth before the hills? Have you listened in the council of God? And do you limit wisdom to yourself? What do you know that we do not know? What do you understand that is not clear to us? Both the gray-haired and the aged are among us, older than your father."

Because these men do not even entertain the possibility that Job might know something that they do not, they fail to understand the situation they are trying to explain. As a result of their dogmatic accusations, they cause Job significant misery. At least in the end of the book, God Himself corrects Job's friends, as Job 42:7 makes clear: "After the Lord had spoken these words to Job, the Lord said to Eliphaz the Temanite: 'My anger burns against you and against your two friends, for you have not spoken of me what is right, as my servant Job has.'"[19] Often in life, the self-sufficient fool walks away from his battered victims and goes smugly on his way, convinced that he has delivered the final word on the matter, when in reality he has little understanding of the situation about which he has pronounced judgment. Without the sort of humility that the Wisdom Literature recommends, one cannot develop the insight and sensitive compassion needed to minister effectively to those who are hurting. Jesus taught this same humility as a core value of God's kingdom (e.g., Matt. 5:3–5; 23:12; Mark 10:35–45), as did Paul (Rom. 12:3–8; Phil. 2:1–11) and others (James 4:6–10; 1 Peter 5:4–7). They all saw it as fundamentally necessary for God's people to function effectively according to God's order.

Questions for Thought and Reflection

1. People who are in love often act on the secular proverb that says, "Absence makes the heart grow fonder," only to find that the opposing maxim, "Out of sight, out of mind," was more appropriate to their situation. How is it that many of the same people repeat both of these contradictory sayings as if both were correct? Is it possible that both can be correct? Explain.

2. We say that we have certain obligations and duties toward God because He created us, and Christ Jesus encourages us to consider the Creator as our "Father." Make two lists, one of the various ways in which our normal obligations and duties toward our earthly parents are similar to those toward our heavenly Father, and another of ways in which they are different. Is one list appreciably longer than the other? If so, has this possibly had an effect upon your relationship with the heavenly Father?

3. Imagine yourself a medical doctor. You have not only earned an M.D. degree from a prestigious school of medicine but also have interned

---

19. To be fair, we should point out that Job made similar statements in Job 12:2–3 and 13:1–2. It seems that there is a difference in that Job has, in fact, considered what the friends had suggested but realized that their explanation was too simplistic and could not account for all of the facts in his particular situation. Note that at the end of the book Job seems to make the same mistake in that he fails to realize that his knowledge of the way God works is not exhaustive, and he is brought to his knees in confession.

in your specialty and have had your own successful practice for twenty years. You are an authority in your field. A female patient comes to your office with a list of symptoms that, when you check her records, you find she reported last year at this same time of year. You tell her that her ills are psychosomatic. Then the attending nurse, who is twenty-five years younger and far less experienced than you, suggests that evidence indicates that the patient could be pregnant. Describe your immediate, unconsidered reaction. Then describe the way you wish you would react if you had attained wisdom as well as knowledge.

4. In which areas of your life do you receive correction well? In which other areas are you uncomfortable with correction? Are there people from whom you receive correction more easily or less easily than from others (for example, a boss, a coworker, a teacher, a spouse, a friend, or a rival)? Why do you think these differences exist?

5. Can you think of a time when you (or someone you know) ignored advice from others and as a result suffered unpleasant consequences? Can you think of a time when you acted on the basis of your own intuition and against the advice of others and later saw that you had made the right decision? Can a person be open to advice/correction and at the same time reject the counsel of others?

Chapter Three

DISCRETION, BALANCE, AND PRIORITIES

In Luke 14:28–32, Jesus uses two stories to illustrate an important principle of wisdom. The first story emphasizes the importance of having sufficient resources before beginning a building project; otherwise, one might be left with an unfinished structure as a testimony to his or her lack of wisdom. The second story makes a similar point: a king who is of a mind to wage war against someone would be wise to assess carefully his chances of victory before beginning the war, and if it appears unlikely that he can defeat the opposing army, negotiations might be a better approach than war. In both instances, Jesus is emphasizing the wisdom of counting the cost before committing oneself to a major undertaking. In so doing, Jesus is affirming a principle found regularly in the Old Testament Wisdom Literature: the wise person is characterized by discretion in all of his affairs, whereas rash involvements are typical of the foolish person.

Just as humility and openness to instruction are defining characteristics of the wise person, so discretion separates the wise person from the fool. What we are calling discretion involves two slightly different but clearly related characteristics. First, discretion involves a calm and deliberate response to any situation or opportunity. The wise person does not respond in the heat of emotion but rather evaluates each situation and responds to it carefully and appropriately. The wise person does not rush to judgment but waits until he or she has sufficient information to make a good decision. In contrast, the foolish person proceeds recklessly, only to discover that he faces unanticipated difficulties for which he has insufficient resources or circumstances about which he was unaware.

Amaziah was a king of Judah who, according to 2 Kings 14:3, did what was right in the eyes of the Lord, but he also did one thing that has made him a classic example of rash and foolish behavior. When he defeated an Edomite army and captured the town of Sela, the victory evidently went to his head, and he became arrogant. He challenged Jehoash, the king of Israel, to battle and was determined to wage that war despite being warned that he was not strong enough to defeat Israel. Judah was defeated, Amaziah was taken prisoner, and Jehoash then came to Jerusalem and plundered the city, including the temple treasures.

The wise person clearly is both humble and open to instruction, as we discussed earlier. The wise man knows that "the one who states his case first seems right, until the other comes and examines him" (Prov. 18:17), and so he withholds judgment until he has sufficient information. He will also seek out others for counsel and guidance in his efforts to gain that knowledge. In contrast, the fool, quite unaware of his limited understanding, is quick to pronounce judgment and express his opinion as to what should be done. His rash response often leads to embarrassment, as Proverbs 18:13 says: "If one gives an answer before he hears, it is his folly and shame." Proverbs 18:2 adds, "A fool takes no pleasure in understanding, but only in expressing his opinion."

The wise man's humility also makes him aware of his own limitations. He understands that some endeavors are risky and that he might not have the ability or assets that would make it prudent to become involved. He considers carefully his own resources, the benefits that will result from success in the endeavor, or the loss that would result from failure, and he makes careful decisions in the light of such considerations. The foolish person, however, never stops to think that he might have limited skills or that the task may be too difficult for him to handle. He is supremely confident regardless of his limitations or the difficulty of the task, and so he takes unwise risks and often suffers the consequences.

This difference is seen in the contrast in Proverbs between the wise person and the naive or simple person. The Hebrew word translated "simple" means "to be open," and, in this instance, it describes a person who is open to everything and lacks the discrimination to determine which ideas are good and which ones are bad and to be avoided. This person is gullible and can be convinced of almost anything.[1] Proverbs 14:15–16 contrasts the two individuals: "The simple believes everything, but the prudent gives thought to his steps. One who is wise is cautious and turns away from evil [or trouble], but a fool is reckless and careless." The wise person is cautious and careful, and such deliberation enables him to avoid many of the problems that overwhelm the foolish person. Proverbs 27:12 says, "The prudent sees danger and hides himself, but the simple go on and suffer for it," and Proverbs 21:5 describes the contrasting outcomes: "The plans of the diligent lead surely to abundance, but everyone who is hasty comes only to poverty." Careful planning, combined with diligence, leads to success; rash commitments lead to trouble and poverty.

Proverbs presents several specific examples of how this general principle might work itself out. Although differences of opinion exist about the basic meaning of the section, Proverbs 25:7c–8 likely describes the danger of initiating a lawsuit on the basis of insufficient information.[2] The proverb says, "What your eyes have seen do not hastily bring into court, for what will you do in the end, when your neighbor puts you to shame?" The point seems to posit a person seeing what seems to be clear evidence that his neighbor has wronged him, and on that basis he enters into a lawsuit against him. When the case is heard, however, the person who initiated the complaint discovers that the evidence that he thought was irrefutable was only part of the truth, and he loses the case and suffers material loss and humiliation. Had he been more careful in determining all of the facts, he would not have pursued the matter.

A few years ago, someone filed a lawsuit against another party against much advice from friends and associates. The man was certain that he had been seriously wronged and was convinced that he had a great deal of evidence that supported his claim. He went ahead with the lawsuit, and after

---

1. Proverbs makes clear that there is hope for this person. Unlike the scoffer or another kind of fool, this person has not flatly rejected wisdom but remains open to it. If this person responds to wisdom, it has the power to give him the knowledge, resolve, and discernment that will allow him to make progress in becoming wise.

2. Some commentators argue that the warning is directed to those who may be called to testify in a case rather than to someone who rashly pursues a case against another party. In this case, it would be a warning against inappropriately disclosing information that was privileged or perhaps against testimony that was based on a very limited awareness of the facts.

several years in the courts (and who knows how much in legal costs), the court, on every single count, ruled against the person who filed the lawsuit. Obviously, this person did not know about some facts; otherwise, he surely would not have pursued the matter. His haste in bringing the case into court and his refusal to listen to the advice of many counselors proved to be very costly. In this particular instance, the person who initiated the lawsuit was a Christian, and his unwise response to what he saw as a grievous wrong against him did serious damage to the cause of Christ.

In a contrasting case, I (Edward) spoke with a friend who has experienced a great deal of trouble from a neighbor. After some years of this, the neighbor did something that caused several thousand dollars in damage to my friend's property. This was the last straw for my friend, and she was determined to seek damages against the man in small claims court. She sought the opinion of a lawyer friend of hers, and as he looked at the facts, he pointed out something that, if it were brought up in the proceedings, could have been devastating for my friend. She was spared potential embarrassment and trouble because she sought advice and followed it rather than pursuing the matter hastily.

Proverbs 25:14 says, "Like clouds and wind without rain is a man who boasts of a gift he does not give." Israel has limited rainfall, which typically comes only in the winter and early spring, and farmers are dependent on that rainfall for their crops. Think of a farmer whose crops must have rain to produce anything at all. Clouds begin to form in the west, and the wind begins to blow—clear signs that rain is on the way—and then the rain never materializes. The farmer would certainly be disappointed and frustrated and would possibly face the disaster of failed crops. The person who promises things that he or she never delivers causes this same sort of frustration and disappointment.

Certainly the proverb has in mind the boastful person who is always trying to impress others with claims and promises. Equally common, I suspect, are people who make promises that they will never keep because they responded to requests casually and hastily, without ever thinking about whether they were willing or able to do what they promised. I (Edward) recall a person who wanted my son to participate in a research project and in return offered to take him out for a treat at a special ice-cream place. My son did the survey, but the person never did what he promised. He did mention several times that he had not forgotten and would do it, but he never got around to it. We say things like, "I will be glad to help you move, and you are welcome to use my van," but then our schedule does not allow us to do what we promised. We glibly say, "If you ever come to California, you are welcome to stay with us," or "Let's go out to dinner. I will call you this week." Certainly there are times when promises are made in good faith and then circumstances beyond our control make it impossible to follow through. Some things are said in social contexts where everyone understands that these are not legitimate promises that people expect will be kept, but sometimes other people take our promises seriously, and our failure to do what we have said we will do not only disappoints others but also undermines our credibility and our reputation as people of integrity.

Simply following the advice of Proverbs and being deliberate and careful about what we say could help us immensely in terms of building a reputation that is blameless. Such careful responses are also far more consistent with Jesus' insistence that we should not need to take an oath to establish the truth of our words, but simply saying yes or no should be sufficient (Matt. 5:34–37; see also James 5:12). Such truthful words reflect God's order and honor Him.

Ecclesiastes 5:1–7 makes the point that rash vows should be avoided, especially in a person's religious life and relationship with God. The warning seems to be against making impressive promises to God (perhaps when we are caught up in the emotion of the moment), and then discovering on further reflection that we cannot possibly follow through on the vow. Proverbs 20:25 makes a similar point: "It is a snare to say rashly, 'It is holy,' and to reflect only after making vows." When a possession was declared to be holy, its owner lost the use of it for ordinary purposes; the item was then to be used exclusively for God's service. Such declarations, as well as other promises to God, should be made carefully and cautiously only after considering the implications of the vow. Rash, spur-of-the-moment promises are to be avoided in all areas of life, including a person's religious life and relationship with God. It is better not to make a vow at all than to make one and then be unable to fulfill it.

Although in many areas of life wisdom requires care and deliberation rather than haste, one final example from Proverbs will suffice. In the book of Proverbs, the wise person is one who has his tongue under control, and one important aspect of that tongue control involves patience and care in responding to others. Unlike the fool, the wise person listens carefully to what others are saying (Prov. 18:13) and, as a result, does not respond impulsively. The contrast is clearly seen in Proverbs 15:28: "The heart [or mind] of the righteous ponders how to answer, but the mouth of the wicked pours out evil things." The wise man restrains his lips (Prov. 10:19) and guards his mouth and tongue (Prov. 13:3; 21:23). This often will mean that the wise person will not be the first to speak on a matter. Such a person takes time to get sufficient information and to think carefully through the issues, knowing that it is usually better to say too little than to say too much too soon.[3]

By taking time to respond, and by carefully weighing his answers, the wise person is able to speak words that are insightful and appropriate for the circumstances. Several proverbs indicate that the care and thought that lie behind the words of the wise person enable him or her to speak the truth in a way that seems good to others. For example, Proverbs 16:23 says, "The heart [or mind] of the wise makes his speech judicious and adds persuasiveness to his lips." In contrast, according to Proverbs 15:2, "The mouths of fools pour out folly," the image being that of folly bubbling up and overflowing from the fool like water from a spring.

Although Proverbs identifies many other aspects of effective speech besides patience and careful deliberation in answering a person, it is doubtful that one can ever become an effective speaker without learning this kind of discretion. James emphasizes the importance of controlling the tongue when he says, "If anyone thinks he is religious and does not bridle his tongue but deceives his heart, this person's religion is worthless" (James 1:26). In James 3:1–12, he describes vividly the damage it can do both inside the church and beyond its boundaries. Again, the Wisdom Literature contains an abundance of teaching about the power of the tongue, for either good or evil, and about how the child of God can make progress toward speaking words that heal rather than those that cut like the thrusts of a sword (Prov. 12:18).

---

3. These statements, like the proverbs, are generalizations, and one can easily imagine circumstances in which they could be applied in ways that fly in the face of the intent of the biblical proverbs. For example, people can say too little and thereby deceive others, and the Bible makes clear that using words in that way is wrong. For example, Abraham's telling Pharaoh only that Sarah was his sister, while in one sense true (she was his half sister), was done intentionally to deceive the Egyptians. It is also sometimes the case that people say too little, or delay making decisions, because of indecisiveness, and clearly that is not a result of wisdom.

Discretion and the Power of Emotion

In addition to the general cautiousness and conservatism that character-ize the words and decisions of the wise person, Proverbs sees an even tem-per as a fundamental characteristic of the discretion that it commends. The wise person does not speak or act rashly out of anger or any other strong emotion such as frustration or intense desire. Such passion clouds the judg-ment and often results in words and actions that a person will later regret.

In Proverbs, drunkenness is folly precisely because it impairs a person's ability to behave wisely; instead, it produces words and actions that are the antithesis of wisdom. Proverbs 20:1 says, "Wine is a mocker [or scoffer], strong drink a brawler, and whoever is led astray by it is not wise." In Prov-erbs 31:4–5, King Lemuel's mother warns him to avoid wine because he cannot, under its influence, fulfill his responsibility to his people by making wise decisions that will ensure justice. The wine can cause him to forget what has been decreed and thus pervert justice. Proverbs insists that a vari-ety of strong emotions can, in a similar way, impair one's judgment and undermine wisdom.

Discretion and Anger

At times, anger is appropriate, as Jesus' response to the money changers in the temple makes clear, but Proverbs focuses primarily on expressions of hu-man anger that are not consistent with God's order and points out the prob-lems that anger can create for people. Proverbs recognizes that anger can impair judgment and bring about devastating consequences. Proverbs also recog-nizes that habitual anger can destroy both the angry individuals and those around them, a habit that can become so deeply ingrained that it is virtually impossible to bring it under control.[4] Proverbs sees this kind of anger as a clear symptom of folly and contends that a basic virtue of the wise man is his

---

4. Proverbs 19:19, although a difficult proverb in Hebrew, says, "A hot-tempered man must pay the penalty; if you rescue him, you will have to do it again" (NIV). Allen P. Ross says of this proverb, "A hot-tempered person will be con-stantly in trouble. . . . if you save this person from his legal troubles, you will have to do it again and again. Unless he changes, he will always need bailing out" (*Proverbs*, The Expositors Bible Commentary, ed. Frank E. Gaebelein [Grand Rapids: Zondervan, 1991], 5:1035).

ability to control his anger. Proverbs 29:11 states clearly the contrast between the wise person and the fool: "A fool gives full vent to his spirit, but a wise man quietly holds it back." As McKane says, "The fool is the slave of impulse and is at the mercy of every moment when [he feels] irritation. . . . [The wise man] is never driven by passion into foolish responses."[5]

The fool reacts instantly and aggressively to any affront, deliberate or otherwise, and his anger often gets him involved in strife and violence. Proverbs 12:16 says, "The vexation of a fool is known at once"; in contrast, "the prudent ignores an insult." The hot-tempered person stirs up strife (15:10 and 29:22), and often that strife gets out of control, and disaster results. Proverbs 17:14 says, "The beginning of strife is like letting out water," the picture being a person who wants to get a little water and pokes a tiny hole in a dam to get it. He will get the small amount of water that he wants, but unless the hole in the dam is repaired quickly, a major disaster may result. Likewise, a small outburst of anger can explode quickly into more anger than anyone present can accommodate.

People sometimes respond angrily to being cut off on a freeway or inconvenienced by another driver. They pursue the strife, and things quickly escalate out of control, with someone being killed or seriously injured as a result. Students become angry because of a classmate's remark or because of a bad grade on a paper, responding in ways that cause harm to someone or that get them expelled. Employees are often angered by something that has happened to them at work, and they kill or injure their fellow workers.

Several years ago, a man in Southern California got angry because some teenagers vandalized his Halloween display. He pursued the teenagers, taking a gun with him in his vehicle, but he was unable to find them. As he returned home, he found the boys in front of his house, and he approached them with the gun, "only intending to scare them." In the ensuing confrontation, however, he shot and killed one of the teenagers, and now the man is facing time in prison, and a family has lost their son. Such tragedies illustrate why Proverbs insists that an essential part of wisdom is the kind of self-control that does not pursue strife but rather responds in ways that cause anger to subside. In the inspired value system of Proverbs, "It is an honor for a man to keep aloof from strife" (Prov. 20:3), and "Good sense makes one slow to anger, and it is his glory to overlook an offense" (19:11). "Whoever is slow

---

5. William McKane, *Proverbs,* Old Testament Library (Philadelphia: Westminster, 1970), 635.

to anger is better than the mighty, and he who rules his spirit than he who takes a city" (16:32). Proverbs 25:28 says, "A man without self-control is like a city broken into and left without walls." The image of the damaged and unprotected city makes apparent that a person without self-control will be vulnerable to destruction because of spiritual immaturity.

The damage caused by an angry response is certainly not limited to death, serious injury, or prison time. Many times, it is the angry and ill-considered word that cuts like a sword (Prov. 12:18) and causes irreparable damage. Angry words to a child often leave significant scars. A seminary student once told me that he has his college diploma on a wall near the mirror where he dresses. He sometimes looks at the diploma in disbelief. A significant part of his understanding of himself was determined years ago by a father who used to angrily say to the student, "Boy, you're thick!" as he helped him with his homework. The scars left by those remarks made it difficult for the student ever to imagine that he could actually earn a college degree and then go on to graduate from seminary.

Angry words can do much to undermine or even destroy relationships, and I am sure that those words of the father to his son, my student, did little to deepen the relationship between the two of them. Although Proverbs 18:19 ("A brother offended is more unyielding than a strong city, and quarreling is like the bars of a castle") is very difficult in Hebrew, many commentators agree that the proverb describes the walls and barriers that are sometimes erected in relationships, barriers that are, as Kidner says, "so easy to erect, so hard to demolish."[6]

Words spoken in anger can do much to create those barriers. A promising career can be ruined by angry words to a supervisor or by rash comments about a boss. A reputation can be tarnished by angry words, as can a Christian witness. Few things on the path to spiritual maturity are more important than developing the self-control that enables a person to restrain an angry response, and then to respond with appropriate, well-chosen words that, according to Proverbs 25:11, are "like apples of gold in a setting of silver."

The New Testament also makes abundantly clear that inappropriate anger—including most human anger—is something characteristic of fallen humanity and should not characterize the people of God. Jesus, in the

---

6. Derek Kidner, *Proverbs,* vol. 15 of Tyndale Old Testament Commentaries (Downers Grove, Ill.: InterVarsity, 1964), 130.

Sermon on the Mount (Matt. 5:21–26), warns against being angry with one's brother. Anger, persisted in, can lead to hatred and finally even to murder, and such attitudes are not consistent with God's order and kingdom values.

Galatians 5:19–23 contrasts the deeds of the flesh with the fruit of the Spirit. Included among the deeds of the flesh are enmities, strife, jealousy, outbursts of anger, disputes, and dissensions; included among the fruit of the Spirit are patience, peace, and self-control. In Ephesians 4:17–32, Paul exhorts Christians to eliminate attitudes and practices characteristic of unbelievers and to develop qualities consistent with the likeness of God. Within this passage (in v. 26), he instructs believers to control their anger so as not to provide the Devil an opportunity to work his will. In verse 31 he tells them, "Let all bitterness and wrath and anger . . . be put away from you, along with all malice." He makes a similar point in Colossians 3:1–17. James says in 1:19–20, "Let every person be quick to hear, slow to speak, slow to anger; for the anger of man does not produce the righteousness that God requires."

Again the general exhortations of the New Testament seem to need to be complemented by the more specific and practical teaching of the Old Testament Wisdom Literature if the process of sanctification is to proceed as it should. The New Testament teaching likely presupposes the practical warnings and instruction of the Wisdom Literature, and if that teaching is neglected, growth toward spiritual maturity will be seriously impeded.

Finally, both research and observation affirm that anger, when persisted in, undermines the development of Christian character in that the anger feeds bitterness and an inability to forgive others. A former student once shared with me the struggle that she had in forgiving her ex-husband for the way he had hurt her in both their marriage and the divorce that ended it. She realized that she had to learn to forgive him because of what the anger was doing to her and because, as she put it, she did not want her daughter to grow up being reared by a bitter woman. Susan's experience is by no means unique. Anger, bitterness, and an unforgiving spirit can so poison a person that growth in godliness cannot occur.

Discretion and Finances

Proverbs has many things to say about money and wisdom. According to Proverbs 10:22a: "The blessing of the LORD makes rich," and generally the book of Proverbs sees wealth in positive terms. Although Proverbs recognizes that money can take a person's focus off God and undermine one's trust in the Lord, it also recognizes the benefit of money. It provides protection against many of life's difficulties—difficulties that can bring disaster on a poor person, as Proverbs 10:15 makes clear: "A rich man's wealth is his strong city; the poverty of the poor is their ruin." Proverbs also advises that money should never become the all-consuming quest of a person's life; it is far too uncertain for that. Proverbs 23:4–5 says, "Do not toil to acquire wealth; be discerning enough to desist. When your eyes light on it, it is gone, for suddenly it sprouts wings, flying like an eagle toward heaven."

Proverbs recognizes that normally there is a direct relationship between hard work and wealth. Proverbs 14:23 says, "In all toil there is profit, but mere talk tends only to poverty." Proverbs 10:4 agrees: "A slack hand causes poverty, but the hand of the diligent makes rich." Ecclesiastes 10:11 makes clear that even a highly skilled person (e.g., a person with the skill to charm a snake) will come to ruin if he does not use the skill in a timely manner. The proverb says, "If the serpent bites before it is charmed, there is no advantage to the charmer." The sluggard is the poster boy of Proverbs for the almost inevitable connection between his laziness and his poverty. Proverbs 20:4 says, "The sluggard does not plow in the autumn; he will seek at harvest and have nothing," and the song in 6:10–11 and 24:33–34 describes his almost certain fate: "A little sleep, a little slumber, a little folding of the hands to rest, and poverty will come upon you like a robber, and want like an armed man."

Proverbs also sees discretion as an essential part of wisdom in financial matters—first, in the careful deliberation and planning necessary for good financial management. Wisdom recognizes that one cannot spend money and still have it available for future needs and opportunities. Proverbs 21:20 says, "Precious treasure and oil are in a wise man's dwelling, but a foolish man devours it," and Proverbs 21:17 adds, "Whoever loves pleasure will be a poor man; he who loves wine and oil will not be rich." The wise person determines carefully how much to spend and how much to save on the basis of available resources and long-term financial goals, recognizing that considerable saving and sacrifice may sometimes be necessary to accomplish those goals. People with wisdom know that constant spending on pleasure will leave them poor. They also understand that "the plans of the diligent lead surely to abundance, but everyone who is hasty comes only to poverty" (Prov. 21:5).

It is not only hard work or vigorous activity but also careful planning, combined with diligence, that lead to the desired financial outcomes. The plan must be coherent, and things must be done in the right sequence to have sufficient resources to maintain a family and a household. Proverbs 24:27 says, "Prepare your work outside; get everything ready for yourself in the field; and after that build your house." In 27:23–27, we find the exhortation to anticipate future needs and arrange one's resources so those future needs can be met as they arise: "Know well the condition of your flocks, and give attention to your herds, for riches do not last forever; . . . When the grass is gone and the new growth appears and the vegetation of the mountains is gathered, the lambs will provide your clothing, and the goats the price of a field. There will be enough goats' milk for your food, for the food of your household and maintenance for your girls."

Proverbs recognizes the importance of diversifying one's resources so that when one source of income dries up, others will be available to meet the needs. Preferably, this will include some forms of wealth that are "stable and self-perpetuating,"[7] as McKane puts it. Clearly, the approach to financial management advocated by Proverbs involves careful and deliberate planning, in contrast to impulsive financial decisions made with little thought about future goals and consequences. According to Proverbs, wisely handled finances do not result from just letting things happen.

Both the need for careful and deliberate decisions, and the need to avoid being pressured into unwise commitments by strong emotional pressure, are illustrated by warnings in Proverbs against becoming responsible for someone else's debts through something like cosigning a loan.[8] On the one hand, Proverbs makes clear that generosity toward someone in need is a significant virtue that a wise or righteous person will cultivate. Like honoring God with one's wealth (Prov. 3:9), generosity is not only the right thing to do but also will contribute to one's own success and prosperity. Proverbs 14:31 says, "Whoever oppresses a poor man insults his Maker, but he who is generous to the needy honors him." Most of the loans in the Old Testament were not made to expand a business or to buy a bigger house; rather, they were loans that would help a truly poor individual survive economically; thus, there was little chance that even the principal would be repaid, and no interest could be charged on such loans. Despite the fact that a loan to a

---

7. McKane, *Proverbs*, 618.
8. This is called "going or becoming surety" in many of the older translations.

needy person would probably not be repaid, the loan was to be made with the awareness that this kind of generosity pleases God. Responsibility for repayment of the loan was to be left with God, who would repay both at the time and in the manner that He deemed appropriate. Proverbs 19:17 says, "Whoever is generous to the poor lends to the LORD, and he will repay him for his deed." Under the right circumstances, becoming surety for someone else's debt would seem to be a very generous thing to do.

On the other hand, it is the wise person's discretion that keeps him from such involvements. One mark of the wise person is that he or she carefully considers the risks and advantages of any proposal, and when involvement in a particular undertaking seems to be dangerous, or not to the lender's advantage, the wise person avoids it. There is, however, a dimension to becoming responsible for another person's debt that often makes it both more tempting and more difficult to refuse, and it is here that the wise person's refusal to allow his thoughts to become clouded by passion becomes especially important. It seems probable that the major purpose of these warnings is to guard against rash involvements rather than absolutely to prohibit ever becoming surety for someone else. This view is suggested by several of the warnings in Proverbs (e.g., Prov. 6:1; 11:15; 20:16; 27:13), which mention becoming surety for strangers and foreigners, people whom the cosigner probably would not know well. It is likely that the verses warn against rash involvements.

In typical Proverbs caricature, the picture that these verses paint is that of someone walking down the street. A man he does not know comes up to him and begins relating the sad story of how he has suffered some unfortunate reversals and how he and his family are about to go under financially (perhaps his wife and children are standing nearby, sobbing softly). The man goes on to explain that the ironic thing is that he has the potential not only to overcome these temporary setbacks but also actually to make a lot of money through a business venture in which he is involved. It cannot miss; he will become financially independent and perhaps quite wealthy through this undertaking.

Unfortunately, he must survive the next few months until his new scheme begins to take off; he needs money now to get him through the current difficulty. He has tried to borrow the money he needs, but he cannot get it because he has had some bad luck in the past that has affected his credit, or he has not yet established a credit rating, or he does not have any collateral, or whatever. If only he could find someone who would cosign for a loan, everything would be fine. It would not cost the cosigner a penny because the future looks so bright with the "cannot miss" business opportunity in which he is now involved. If only someone would help them—about this time the children begin crying louder, and the wife tries to console them by saying, "Don't cry children; everything will be okay. If some kind person would just help us get some money, we can get you poor children food."

The man who needs the loan asks in a plaintive voice, "Could you please help us out? We will repay the loan, and it will not cost you anything to help us."

The person who has been listening to this sad tale says that he would like to help, but he does not have enough money to do so—but he could sign a note for the man as long as he is sure that the man would be able to repay the loan. The man who needs the money, of course, laughs and assures him that repaying the loan would be no problem at all—he could easily repay ten times that amount given the future he has. The man cosigns the note and then forgets about it—until the loan agent comes to collect from the poor, gullible soul who believed the stranger's tale.

Agreeing to cosign for a stranger or a foreigner often involves being pressured into an unwise business arrangement because of sympathy for the person and failure to consider carefully the consequences of a default by the borrower. The warnings against becoming responsible for someone's debts also mention neighbors or friends, for the pressure to agree to such commitments usually comes not only from an awareness of the person's financial need but also from concern that a rebuffed relative will be angered by the refusal and the relationship strained or broken. Thus, a person, through emotional and social pressure, is dragged into an injudicious agreement whose full consequences he does not appreciate. Succumbing to the pressure is made easier by the supposition that becoming responsible for the person's debt will not actually cost anything because he does not expect the neighbor to default on the loan. Becoming surety is almost like signing a blank check because the person does not know exactly for what he or she is obligated. He does not know the full extent of what his involvement will cost him, nor can he be certain of the ability and resolve of the borrower to repay the loan.

As Kidner points out, this warning against surety "does not banish generosity—it comes closer to banishing gambling. A man's giving should be determined by him, and not wrung from him by events outside his control."[9] The wise person carefully determines the extent of her giving rather than having that determined by factors beyond her control. The wise man first realistically assesses the extent of his resources and then structures his generosity such that he is not faced with unanticipated giving that he cannot afford.

Proverbs recognizes that there are poor people whose circumstances leave them no choice but to borrow money, and it does not condemn borrowing. At the same time, however, Proverbs does recognize the unfortunate consequences that sometimes result from debt. "The rich rules over the poor, and the borrower is the slave of the lender," says Proverbs 22:7. In antiquity, slavery because of debt was often a literal reality. Today, that kind of slavery has been outlawed, but the loss of freedom that debt causes constitutes a tragic kind of bondage. The clear implication of Proverbs is that debt should be avoided whenever possible, and discretion should keep debt to a manageable minimum.

Discretion precludes impulse buying, especially when the purchase is charged because there is no cash available to pay for the item. A rabbinic proverb says, "When a fool goes to market, all the merchants rejoice." A wise person is not gullible or readily susceptible to smooth sales pitches and deferred payments. Neither is the wise person so enslaved to his desires that he cannot resist buying things that he neither needs nor can afford, ending up saddled with a heavy burden of debt. He is careful and deliberate about what he buys, and he always makes his decisions in the light of both genuine needs and available resources.

Although the relationship between wisdom in finances and spiritual maturity might not be immediately apparent, the New Testament makes very clear that one's attitude toward money is critical for spiritual growth. In Colossians 3:5, Paul says that greed or covetousness (which, according to F. F. Bruce, is a strong desire to possess more than one has, and particularly that which belongs to someone else)[10] amounts to idolatry because "it puts some other object of desire in the central place which Christ ought to occupy in our hearts."[11] Jesus made clear that "No one can serve two

---

9. Kidner, *Proverbs,* 71.

10. F. F. Bruce in Simpson and Bruce, *The Epistle to the Ephesians and Colossians,* New International Commentary on the New Testament (Grand Rapids: Eerdmans, 1957), 270.

11. F. F. Bruce, *Epistle to the Ephesians and Colossians,* 270.

masters, for either he will hate the one and love the other, or he will be devoted to the one and despise the other. You cannot serve God and money" (Matt. 6:24). He also said, "Where your treasure is, there your heart will be also" (v. 21). It would seem that spiritual maturity is not possible apart from a right attitude toward money, and the practical teaching of the Old Testament Wisdom Literature can do much to free us from the patently wrong attitude.

Ecclesiastes affirms that the meaning of life is not found in money or things, nor will they ever provide a person with ultimate satisfaction and fulfillment. Ecclesiastes also makes clear that things such as the fear of the Lord and relationships with family and friends are far more valuable than wealth. Proverbs 23:4–5 tells us to hold money loosely and warns us not to become obsessed with it because it can leave as quickly as it came. Developing such an attitude toward money allows us to focus more readily on God as our ultimate treasure and so make progress toward maturity without being distracted by material things.

The way of wisdom brought at least one Old Testament believer to recognize wealth's power to undermine a person's dependence on God and to pray that his financial circumstances not create an obstacle to a life that honors God. He says in Proverbs 30:8–9, "Give me neither poverty nor riches; feed me with the food that is needful for me, lest I be full and deny you and say, 'Who is the LORD?' or lest I be poor and steal and profane the name of my God." Such an attitude would free many people in the church from their bondage to the material, a bondage that Jesus says will severely retard growth toward spiritual maturity.

In addition, Proverbs makes clear that the same sort of discipline and careful deliberation that is required for responsibility in financial affairs is also necessary in acquiring wisdom. The early chapters of Proverbs emphasize the importance of diligence and planning in the quest for wisdom—wisdom that, according to Proverbs 2:5, brings a person to "understand the fear of the LORD and find the knowledge of God." Although it is possible for a person to be extremely focused and disciplined in one area while being careless in other parts of his life (e.g., an athlete who is extremely diligent about his sport but who is equally unconcerned when it comes to academics), Proverbs suggests that once the issue of priorities is resolved, discipline must affect virtually all of life. As one intentionally develops discipline and learns to avoid rash behavior in one area, other parts of life will be affected as well.[12]

Certainly, great wisdom and responsibility in finances do not amount to complete spiritual maturity, but Scripture indicates that those who do not correctly value wealth have little chance of becoming truly mature. Lack of wisdom in financial matters can hinder a person's progress toward maturity in a variety of ways. When individuals or organizations fail to meet financial obligations, their failure can undermine their reputation because the failure indicates to others a lack of integrity and maturity. Besides, debt and the way it restricts freedom can make it impossible to take advantage of opportunities that could contribute to personal development and Christian growth. I have had many students and friends who could not pursue certain ministry and educational opportunities because they had large credit card debts or student loan balances that kept them in bondage. It is a tragedy when unwise financial decisions restrict a person's freedom to do things that have great potential for moving that individual toward maturity. I also know people whose financial obligations force them to work so many hours that they have no devotional life, and they can no longer be involved significantly in the life and ministry of the church. Thus, even our financial attitudes and practices seem to be relevant to our spiritual development, and unless we diligently apply wisdom to such matters, we will be unable to live fully according to Yahweh's order and be the people God desires us to be.

Wisdom and Priorities

It has been said that the greatest tragedy in life does not lie in having attempted to do worthwhile things and failed but rather in succeeding at things that do not really matter.[13] Wisdom recognizes the importance of

---

12. Several years ago, I read an editorial describing a rabbi's suggestion that keeping kosher was a helpful antidote to sexual promiscuity for teenagers. His idea was that learning to say no to a ham sandwich or a cheeseburger will make it easier for a young person to say no to premarital sex or drugs.

13. One thinks of people who devote their lives to playing video games or become so obsessed with some sport or hobby that they neglect their family, career, or church. I remember seeing a cartoon that depicted a job interview. The interviewer was saying to the young man, "This is a very impressive résumé. Unfortunately, we do not have any openings for a highly skilled hacky sack player."

priorities, and, although it does not provide anything approaching a comprehensive treatment of priorities, it nevertheless identifies a number of important ones. An important part of wisdom lies in identifying priorities appropriately and then living life in ways that reflect those priorities.

The Wisdom Literature puts forth the relative importance of certain pairs of values, often in the "better than" proverbs that deal in various ways with relative values. The importance of being open to correction is recognized in Ecclesiastes 7:5–6: "It is better for a man to hear the rebuke of the wise than to hear the song of fools. For as the crackling of thorns under a pot, so is the laughter of the fools." Although the laughter of fools is more enjoyable to hear than correction, the rebuke of a wise man has the potential to reorient a person and move him or her along the path of wisdom. Thornbushes make a spectacular and loud fire for a short time, but they produce little heat and are of almost no value as fuel. In the same way, the laughter of fools is nothing but entertainment with no real substance.

Similarly, Ecclesiastes 7:2–4 says that it is better to go to a funeral than to a party, and the reason is given in verse 2: "for this is the end of all mankind, and the living will lay it to heart [or pay attention to it]." A similar point is made in Psalm 90, which is dominated by the idea of death and the shortness of human life in contrast to God's eternality. As the psalmist reflects on these realities, he says in verse 12, "So teach us to number our days that we may get a heart of wisdom." As Davidson comments, "To recognize our transitoriness and mortality is to recognize that many of the values which are placed on life—for example, wealth, status, and power—have no ultimate significance. What is needed is that wisdom . . . which will enable us to live responsibly in the light of a true, God-given understanding of what our human life really means."[14]

Priority in life must be given to those things that enable us to advance in wisdom, the high priority of which is reflected in other proverbs as well. For example, Proverbs 3:13–15 compares wisdom with wealth: "Blessed is the one who finds wisdom, and the one who gets understanding, for the gain from her is better than gain from silver, and her profit better than gold. She is more precious than jewels, and nothing you desire can compare with her." Proverbs 15:16 says, "Better is a little with the fear of the LORD than great treasure and trouble with it."

---

14. Robert Davidson, *The Vitality of Worship* (Grand Rapids: Eerdmans, 1998), 302.

Proverbs also makes clear that good family relationships are more important than money. Proverbs 15:17 says, "Better is a dinner of herbs where love is than a fattened ox and hatred with it." Proverbs 17:1 says, "Better is a dry morsel with quiet than a house full of feasting with strife." Ecclesiastes 4 talks about the tragedy of a person spending all of his time and energy working and accumulating wealth to the neglect of family. The passage describes "one person who has no other, either son or brother, yet there is no end to all his toil, and his eyes are never satisfied with riches, so that he never asks, 'For whom am I toiling and depriving myself of pleasure?' This also is vanity and an unhappy business" (Eccl. 4:8). Clearly, good family relationships are meant to have a higher priority than riches, and wisdom requires that we expend time and effort to ensure that those relationships develop positively.

Proverbs also makes clear that personal reputation, honesty, and integrity are more important than money. Proverbs 19:22 says, "What is desired in a man is steadfast love, and a poor man is better than a liar." Proverbs 22:1 says, "A good name is to be chosen rather than great riches, and favor is better than silver or gold," and 28:6 says, "Better is a poor man who walks in his integrity than a rich man who is crooked in his ways." Obviously, wisdom requires that we give priority to developing those virtues that are of greater importance within God's order.

Proverbs also recognizes the priority of certain human qualities above some other qualities that our culture values highly. Proverbs 11:22 says, "Like a gold ring in a pig's snout is a beautiful woman without discretion," and Proverbs 31:30 adds, "Charm is deceitful, and beauty is vain, but a woman who fears the LORD is to be praised." When such proverbs are considered in the light of our culture's adulation of charm, beauty, shape, size, and fashion, it is obvious how different is wisdom's value system from that which prevails in our world. As Kidner says about Proverbs 11:22, "The proverb puts it more forcibly than we might. Where we (to whom the outward is the impressive part) would have spoken of the lady [the one with beauty but no discretion] as a little disappointing, Scripture sees her as a monstrosity."[15]

Ordering life around wisdom's priorities would mean learning to value people, including those we choose in Christian leadership positions, for the qualities that wisdom values, without placing a premium on superficial

---

15. Kidner, *Proverbs*, 93.

qualities such as fame, beauty, and appearance. At the same time, the focus should be on developing those virtues that wisdom promotes—values such as the fear of the Lord, loyal love, integrity, and the like. Qoheleth, the author of Ecclesiastes, in considering the ultimate meaning of life, surveyed many different human activities (such as gaining wealth and power, gaining knowledge/wisdom as an end in itself, pleasure, building projects, and the like), trying to discover something that would produce an appreciable profit or advantage in life. His conclusion, after careful examination, was that although some of the things that he considered offered an advantage over other things (e.g., wisdom offers a significant advantage over folly), none of them gave ultimate meaning to life or resulted in an advantage that death did not finally obliterate. He concluded that all of these things ultimately lead only to vanity. His final conclusion is, "The end of the matter; all has been heard. Fear God and keep his commandments, for this is the whole duty of man" (Eccl. 12:13). Certainly, this statement reflects wisdom's highest priority, the priority that is prerequisite for becoming spiritually mature.

Questions for Thought and Reflection

1. Have you ever known anyone who was encouraged to think that "you can do anything at all if you really want to do it"? Did they seem to take this to mean that, if their desires were intense enough, they would not need to plan ahead, study, or work hard? Has this ever applied to you? In either case, if the person so advised ever acted on the belief, was he or she successful? Briefly describe the experience.

2. You are in a Bible study group of about ten people that has been meeting regularly for years. Two months ago, your boss wrongly accused you of unethical behavior on the job and fired you. Today, this boss joins your Bible study group. As the group discussion progresses, you say something about one of the passages in Scripture, at which point your former boss contradicts you in a way that makes you feel once more unjustly attacked. Do you respond at all? If so, describe your response. Is it limited to the question under discussion in your study group, or do you mention your conflict with this man at your former job? What tone will your response take? If you do not respond, explain in detail why not.

3. Have you ever witnessed rash responses that resulted in unpleasant or damaging outcomes? What steps would you say the responder needed to take to avoid such incidents?

4. Keep a journal in which you record the focus of your daily activities. How many hours or minutes did you spend on activities or worries relating to (1) money, (2) shopping, (3) eating, (4) helping others, (5) socializing, (6) reading the Bible, (7) reading other spiritually related materials, (8) watching television, (9) praying? After recording the objects of your attention daily for a week, calculate the time spent on each category. Are you satisfied with the amount of time that you spent on categories 4, 6, 7, and 9? If these four categories received little of your time, draw up a schedule for your day in which you devote greater priority to these. (Caution: be realistic. Eight hours per day of Bible reading, for example, might not be practical.)

5. A friend who is highly successful in a very competitive field describes a constant struggle that he faces. When he concentrates on the qualities that enable him to succeed in his job, those qualities often seem to spill over into the rest of his life, adversely affecting such areas as relationships. But when he concentrates on developing Christian virtues such as the fruit of the Spirit, he finds that he sometimes loses the competitive edge needed to succeed in his work. What would you advise my friend to do? In the struggle to maintain a proper balance among family, career, church, ministry, personal growth, community involvement, and the like, do you think a Christian is relegated to a life of "well-balanced mediocrity"? Might it be that sometimes a balanced Christian life requires us to redefine what *excellence* involves?

Chapter Four

DILIGENCE AND RESOLVE ON THE PATH TO MATURITY

In teaching at the same university for thirty years, I (John) watched wave after wave of awkward freshmen work through their studies for four years and more, finally graduating with poise and greater self-confidence. They dressed differently, spoke differently, and walked differently than they had four years earlier. They had entered as adolescents; they graduated well on their way toward becoming adults. I was watching one kind of growth. It was not always spiritual growth, but it was growth of a kind, and it can illustrate the transforming nature of spiritual growth.

Diligence

Even the apostle Paul—model of spiritual strength that he is for us—did not develop suddenly into the planter of churches and writer of canonical letters in the week or month after his Damascus road experience. When he writes to the Philippians, about twenty years after this conversion, he says, "I want to know Christ and the power of his resurrection . . . and . . . to attain to the resurrection from the dead. Not that I have already obtained all this, or have already been made perfect, but I press on to take hold of that for which Christ Jesus took hold of me. Brothers, I do not consider myself yet to have taken hold of it" (Phil. 3:10–13 NIV).

Although Paul wrote this letter from prison in Rome probably no more than two years before his death, he was still developing spiritually. Some people might argue that Paul's degree of diligence is beyond our abilities, but we are always ignorant of what we can do (a) when we are emulating a great model of behavior and (b) when we are doing it with God's help.

We can never overstate the value of diligence in the process of maturing spiritually. Eugene Peterson titles his book on the psalms of ascent *A Long Obedience in the Same Direction,* using the phrase as a guide in spiritual growth.[1] Although the phrase could be improved for Christians (he is quoting Nietzsche) by amending it to read "a long obedience in the *right* direction," it is nevertheless extremely helpful in that it encapsulates the invaluable concept of obedience extended over a long period of time but always to the same principle.

A single isolated act of obedience is like the first step in a walk of a hundred miles—necessary but, in itself, wholly insufficient. We might take that one step, or five steps, or twenty-five steps in the same direction, but we might then lose all that we had gained if we retrace our steps or veer off in another direction. Whether we call it persistence, endurance, resolve, or diligence, that consistency in our walk of sanctification, that staying on the same path, is vital to both the process and the end result. Abraham's faith did not become strong enough to agree to the sacrifice of his son to God in Genesis 22 merely by obeying God's command to leave his home in Genesis 12 and then doing nothing more. Only through a lifelong process of obedience did Abraham's remarkable faith deepen and solidify.

Developing Patience

Another thing that can keep us from growing in wisdom and sanctity is our tendency to desire only the quick fix. Most of us living in an era of electric lighting and internal combustion engines have been conditioned by instant light and almost-instant arrival times to think that everything should be instantaneous. When we are ill, we want the doctor to prescribe something that will take the illness away, and the faster it works the better. When we are hungry, we want food, and we want it now. When our children are unhappy, our friends neglect us, or our pay raise does not arrive on schedule, we seek the instant remedy, something that will rid us of inconveniences and let us get back to living our lives as we did before we had troubles. Peterson quotes Gore Vidal as calling this aspect of our world "today's passion for the immediate

---

1. Eugene H. Peterson, *A Long Obedience in the Same Direction* (Downers Grove, Ill.: InterVarsity, 1980).

and the casual" and then follows it by saying, "The Christian life cannot mature under such conditions and in such ways."[2]

Ecclesiastes 7:8 reads, "Better is the end [or 'outcome'] of a thing than its beginning, and the patient in spirit is better than the proud in spirit," reminding us that the early stages ("beginning") of a long process are much less satisfactory than its culmination, so we must learn to be patient in spirit. In Luke 21:19, Jesus is speaking of the last days when He says, "By your endurance [KJV reads 'patience'] you will gain your lives." I am a terrible gardener because I plant seeds one day and go out the next morning to see if they've sprouted yet. If true farmers expected such instant results and then gave up when there were no signs of them, we would all starve.

Moreover, God seems to have no intention of letting us "get back to living our lives as we did before we had troubles." He has something better in mind for us, if only we will be patient and continue cooperating with Him for our entire lives. We were not saved to remain the same people we used to be. If we say that we have been "born again," we must be prepared to grow as we did following our first birth. That physical growth from infancy to adulthood took approximately twenty years, but this spiritual development, the kind that flows out of regeneration, we must pray will continue throughout our lives. It takes patience, but not the sort of patience called for in waiting for a pot of water to boil, with all of the work being done aside from our attention. It is more the kind of patience needed to raise a child well—the daily attention to new and unexpected circumstances but always with the same goal in mind: the mature and sanctified adult. "Let patience have her perfect work," writes James (1:4 KJV).

Having the Right Goal

Notice, however, that if we want to walk to the corner grocery store, walking persistently in the wrong direction will not get us there. That is to say, believing anything at all, or modeling our lives on anyone at all—Alexander the Great, Genghis Khan, Doc Holliday—is like looking for a certain city by wandering aimlessly in a vast continent. As Proverbs 14:12 puts it, "There is a way that seems right to a man, but its end is the way to death." We must find the *right* direction to our goal before devoting our lives to the long journey there. But, like the man in the parable who found the treasure in a field, once

---

2. Ibid., 12–13.

we have found the right direction, we must put all other destinations behind us and adhere to the right destination. Once we have found the treasure of God's kingdom, we would be wise to "sell" (or devalue) everything else that we have or love in favor of that treasure (Matt. 13:44). We must develop ways to resist distractions that tempt us from our journey, those siren calls that beckon us aside to hinder our progress and stunt our growth.

One of the world's oldest and most interesting stories is of a man who goes away to war, fights for ten years, then meets with so many obstacles on his way home that it takes him another ten years to get there. His ship is blown off course, his crewmen are all killed in various perils, and he is trapped on an island for years, to relate only a few causes of his delay. But always, as soon as the current hindrance relents, he once again moves homeward toward his waiting wife and son. Few people have been so resolute in their quests as Odysseus, and his massive determination makes him admirable. And even when he reaches his homeland, he finds his task is incomplete because his palace is besieged by a horde of suitors for the hand of his wife, and he must fight his way through them. And then, even after he has accomplished that dangerous and distasteful task, he has one final frustration: his wife, who has not seen him for twenty years, looks at him in his beggar's disguise and refuses for a time to believe that he is her husband. He must persuade her that he is the man he actually is. But at every hindrance, every frustration, and every temporary defeat, Odysseus once again gathers his determination, remembers his paramount destination, and sets off again toward home.

Consider, however, that all Odysseus had waiting for him at home was his mortal wife, his mortal son, and his petty kingdom on a rocky island, all of it lasting for him another forty years at most, and probably less. By contrast, the culmination of our spiritual development will be with us beyond all boundaries of time and beyond all of our current comprehension of joy. Homer, who first wrote the story of Odysseus, gives us a glimpse of what he believes about the afterlife when the hero Achilles speaks from the world of the dead, saying, "I would rather follow the plow as [slave] to another man, one with no land allotted to him and not much to live on, than be king over all the perished dead," indicating perhaps the world's bleakest view of life after the grave.[3] As a result, Odysseus, who shares this view of the afterlife

---

3. Homer, *Odyssey,* trans. Richmond Lattimore (New York: HarperCollins, 1965), 11.489–91.

awaiting him, expends all of this energy, determination, and wakefulness on a goal that is shabby in contrast to ours. Because we have the right goal, the right home, in prospect would it not be shameful of us to be any less energetic, determined, and wakeful than Odysseus?

Lengthening Our Attention Span

Perhaps the greatest hindrance to our spiritual progress is our limited attention span. The word *watch* is often on Jesus' lips, and nowhere in the Gospels more urgently than in Gethsemane just before His betrayal, when His few select disciples do not stay awake to watch and pray with Him (Mark 14:34–41). Do we imagine that we would have performed better than they did in the presence of the Lord? If so, we must think more realistically. It had been an eventful day, the hour was late, and Jesus left them alone (for how long?) to go off some distance and pray. These circumstances induce one not only to physical sleep but also and more importantly to spiritual sleep, making it hard to keep alert. Perhaps it is significant that immediately after the disciples' repeated failure to "watch," Jesus was arrested and ultimately crucified. His words to Peter, James, and John might also be addressed to us: "Are you still sleeping and resting? Behold, the hour is at hand and the Son of Man is being betrayed into the hands of sinners" (Matt. 26:45 NASB). It seems almost as if we were to understand that all of us, since the Fall, have been suffering from an attention deficit disorder; perhaps it was, in part, our lax and sleepy watchfulness that finally made necessary Jesus' great torment and sacrifice.

Not only the mind wanders at such times but also the heart with it. The soldier on guard duty might be the best illustration of this principle. He has received and accepted his orders, and he fully intends to obey them. But his watch lasts four hours, and if there is no immediate reason to fear an attack, he has nothing tangible on which to focus his all-too-human attention. All he has to alert him is a vague memory of his commander's orders, and as time goes by in the silence, he relaxes and either forgets or ignores them. He no longer "watches"; he merely exists. He is, in effect, deaf and blind, leaving himself and his fellow soldiers open to surprise and death.

For our current purposes, the preceding illustration says much about those of us who make little or no spiritual progress. It is not that we are intentionally wicked; it is more that we are fallen human beings, creatures who live more according to the promptings of our five senses than we do by the Word of God. This fact, with a weak sense of urgency and the constant desire to relax our attention, arrests our spiritual growth and maintains in us a child*ishness* that is devoid of the child*likeness* that Jesus held up as our model. It is spiritual youth without the innocence that we mistakenly attribute to children. Only by repeatedly and persistently bringing our wandering attention back to our search for wisdom, to modeling ever more closely our thinking on that of God, can we grow spiritually. That is why we are urged to meditate daily on the Word of God.

Detecting Our Own Spiritual Immaturity

How do we detect spiritual immaturity in ourselves? First, we may always safely assume it. No mortal is on record as having attained complete sanctification in this life—not Moses, or King David, or any of the disciples. Second, we may be sure that we are spiritually immature until we can sincerely say with the inspired psalmist, "I find my delight in your commandments, which I love" (119:47). That is, many of us receive the Lord's commandments the way our younger children receive some of our rules for them—obedient, perhaps, but not delighted to have them imposed. As parents, we look forward eagerly to the day when they internalize our rules and obey them even when we no longer supervise everything they do. Until God's rules become our own and we obey them, not grudgingly or even dutifully but with the delight that we formerly reserved for eating delicious food or falling in love, we are immature in the spirit.

But we should use one more way to measure our spiritual growth since we usually measure with a prejudice in our own favor. Another such measurement that might not be quite so easy to cheat on is mentioned in Deuteronomy 8:2: "The LORD your God has led you these forty years in the wilderness, that he might humble you, testing you to know what was in your heart, whether you would keep his commandments or not." This was how God tested the Israelites so that they would know their own hearts (the Lord, of course, already knew them): four decades of wandering without a place to call their home, hunger and thirst, and afflictions of various sorts.

And what should be the gauge by which our spiritual maturity is measured when we are tested by adversity? It would seem to be twofold. First, it would be Job's test—whether one continues in faith and obedience when confronted with catastrophe—a test that Job passed but that some people fail. Second, it would be whether, once the period of affliction has ended, one responds to returned pleasures with gratitude to God: "And you shall eat and be full, and you shall bless the LORD your God for the good land he has given you" (Deut. 8:10). While this second gauge sounds easy, in reality it is as difficult for human beings as the first gauge; when the backache is gone, we often forget that we ever had a backache, and even more often we neglect to thank God for the relief, just as nine of the ten lepers in Luke 17:17 who had received Jesus' healing failed to return to praise God and thank Jesus.

There is a tendency among many people of our day to try to manufacture in themselves an extreme degree of compassion, so much so that they sometimes feel that even God Himself, the Creator and Source of all real compassion, is not as compassionate as they are. But in truth, Proverbs 17:24 tells us, "The discerning sets his face toward wisdom, but the eyes of a fool are on the ends of the earth," which may be interpreted to mean that the wise person uses the wisdom within reach of ordinary, daily progress, whereas the foolish person ignores the gradual acquisition of wisdom as he seeks to stretch his understanding beyond human capacity. Ecclesiastes advises, "Be not overly righteous" (7:16).

Other people mistakenly take maturity to mean skepticism, the attitude that a stubborn refusal to believe anything unfamiliar is the mark of a stable personality. Some of these people will end by disbelieving, *a priori*, in any miracles. Others, going too far in the opposite direction, feel that *love* (in its spiritual sense) means accepting every individual's belief system as equally true, no matter how flatly they contradict one another—which, of course, would mean that none is really true. Such people often will mouth their acceptance of all faith systems merely to be polite. Here, too, genuine belief dies.

Avoiding "Good Enough"

Evidence indicates that many of us need such a test to continue our spiritual development because many of us think that we are "good enough" already. More than a few pairs of characters in the Bible consist of one party being blessed while the other is not, the unblessed member feeling slighted and unjustly treated. The pattern is probably clearest in the clash between

Jesus and the Jewish leaders of His time. If the leaders had applied to themselves the standards that they imposed on others for adherence to the Law, they might have realized that they themselves had fallen short of satisfying the demands of holiness. But because they maintained a purposive blindness to their own inadequacies, they refused to agree that anyone capable of performing the miracles that Jesus wrought was clearly sent from God and was, therefore, not only holier than they but also holier than any person they had ever seen or heard described.

Saul and David form another such pair. Saul's version of a successful life seems to consist of political and military pragmatism. He thinks that certain actions ensure success. The only hindrance that he recognizes is how difficult it can be to perceive which actions are the correct ones. Should he wait for Samuel to arrive before attacking the enemy? He thinks he should because Samuel's cooperation seems to be an advantage in warfare. But when Samuel is inexplicably late in arriving, success seems more likely to lie in attacking promptly, even without Samuel. David, on the other hand, recognizes (most of the time) God as One who delivers what He promises, even when delivery seems highly unlikely. Saul saw this principle in action many times, initially in the duel between David and Goliath, but he never seems to have learned anything from it. His having been appointed king by the Lord seems to have meant to him that he was "good enough" and needed no deepening of his concept of and relationship with God. Thus, when David is more successful in battle than Saul and is anointed king in his stead, Saul is angry, apparently to the point of suffering fits of insanity.

To consider just one more example of such a pair, Cain and Abel seem to fit the pattern. Although our first question about these brothers often is why God rejected Cain's offering whereas He accepted Abel's, the answer stands palpably in Cain's reaction. First, it was anger, possibly directed at God. Second, it was murder. Clearly, Cain was jealous of God's looking favorably on Abel's sacrifice. Might he have killed Abel if God had regarded favorably *both* offerings? Probably not. And certainly Cain would not have committed murder, or even felt anger, if his had been the only offering to be favored. Therefore we may safely assume, I believe, that Cain considered his offering (and himself by extension) worthy of God's approval; he considered himself "good enough."

But the obvious evidence—his anger and his actions—points to Cain's not being nearly good enough. If Cain had been more mature spiritually, he would not have assumed, taken for granted, or even demanded God's approval of his offering. Hebrews 11:1 tells us that, in effect, Cain was deficient in faith—lacking, that is, in "the assurance of things hoped for, the conviction of things not seen" (NASB)—so it should not surprise us that he was angry and desperate when God's approval was not immediate and visible. It might well be that one of God's reasons for withholding approval of Cain's offering was to make visible in Cain's reactions his spiritual immaturity. And to what purpose would God have done so? Just as clearly, to give Cain (and us) an indication of his inadequacy and the possibility of amending it: "If you do well, will you not be accepted?" (Gen. 4:7).

Are we ever angry when our finances look grim, when we lose someone close to us, or when our prayers go unanswered for years? If so, we are in the company of Cain, one of the juvenile delinquents of the Bible.

Beyond Playing the Role

Does the reader have enough patience to hear of another hindrance to our spiritual maturation? We are role players. Like children who put on adults' clothing in an amusing attempt instantly to become adults, we sometimes take upon us the superficialities of life as it was lived by Jesus and His contemporaries.

That we know so little of the physical appearance and personal mannerisms of Jesus is an unappreciated blessing. Had the Bible told us His height, weight, eye color, hair color, whether He ever laughed, how He walked, His manner of speaking to a crowd, how long He paused before answering a question, or even His table manners, some of us would demand strict and Procrustean adherence to these nonessentials before accepting professing Christians. Thankfully, God has kept that information from us. The danger of knowing and possibly revering such external trappings is twofold: it not only excludes many excellent people from the saving fold but also persuades those who have gained entrance with such feigned credentials that they are "good enough" for anything and anyone, including God's approval. It should be enough to give such role players serious pause to remember that Jesus used a certain word for such a lifestyle—*hypocrite,* the Greek word meaning "actor"—what we have been calling a role player.

Some people will ask, "How, then, are we to imitate Jesus in our lives, knowing so little about Him as we do?" And the answer is by steeping ourselves in His wisdom, in His reactions to varying circumstances, in His way of assigning to different things different priorities, and in His way of approaching the Father. What we know of Him is what is useful for us to know of Him, an essential holiness that can be incorporated into the differing personalities of the human race and the changing ages of its existence. We human beings learn best by imitating, and we have been given the perfect model to imitate, but we must avoid caricature, even well-meaning caricature. Our spiritual life is not a costume competition.

I (John) remember my surprise at meeting an Israeli Christian pastor, a man who was clearly dedicated to working hard for the Lord among his people but whose personality and attitude in other matters was completely unlike American Christians of any denomination. To the eye and ear he was a Jew, but to the hearing heart, he was a true Christian. It taught me (a) to stop trying to "look like" a Christian in the mistaken notion that a changed appearance would soak into my soul and magically become genuine Christianity and (b) never to assess other Christians by externals alone.

Ignoring Faddism

Yet another stumbling block in the way of our maturing is our habit of snapping up the latest model, the newest fad, or the most recent topic of conversation. There is something about a mass movement that, though it repels some people, attracts others and attracts them with their unquestioning agreement. Most of us feel compelled to "jump on the bandwagon" without asking where the bandwagon is going. Western society has made so many sharp turns in the past four hundred years that we have been conditioned to accept change as soon as it seems to be the potential "wave of the future." Some of us even go further and try to predict the next wave before it takes hold of the world, thus putting us (to use a cliché) "on the cutting edge."

Although it might not be fair to label such people occultists, they are clearly gamblers at heart; when they win, historians look back on them as pioneers, or they make it big on the stock market. But when they lose, they look ridiculous to later generations. Consider, for example, the self-proclaimed pundits of the early twentieth century who predicted dinner tables in our homes that would be an extension of the dishwasher; after dinner we would tip the table over and all of the dishes, glasses, and flatware would go into the adjacent washer, to reemerge clean (and unbroken) for our next meal. Defenders of such dreamy predictions will say their time has not yet arrived, but they have been a long time coming, and there is still no sense that they are on their way to us. For the false prophet, the happiest eventuality is to be forgotten.

And why is such faddism a hindrance to spiritual growth? Because spiritual growth is primarily internal, whereas most fads are external; because spiritual growth is hard work, whereas most fads require little or no effort on our part; because spiritual growth is a long process that requires our daily attention, whereas most fads distract us with their promise of instant gratification. And once we have been distracted by such promises and then enjoyed a brief period of gratification, the quick pleasure dies with familiarity, and we have wasted precious years when we could have been cultivating our souls in preparation for the great heavenly reception.

Alexander Pope gave a rule of thumb in the eighteenth century for those wondering when to adopt a new fashion or trend: "Be not the first by whom the new is tried, Nor yet the last to lay the old aside." Although this advice does not recognize the possibility that the old might be superior to the new (sometimes it is), it is good, practical advice for those who fear embarrassment at being seen as either (a) immature in hastily embracing the ephemeral as if it were going to last or (b) stodgy in their tardy acceptance of inevitable change. Notice, however, that Pope's advice appeals most to those whose criterion for timely acceptance is the avoiding of embarrassment. This, too, is a hindrance to spiritual development. Although spiritual growth might seem as if it is occupied solely with the self, in reality it focuses on God, His wisdom, and our need to lose ourselves to gain self. But a preoccupation with our possible embarrassment differs from this in that it does center wholly on the self, revealing a type of narcissism in our fallen humanity.

Putting Trends Aside

Trends come in two types in our day: those that occur spontaneously, without a concerted effort to create them, and those that are created artificially by someone with a political or commercial agenda. The first type could be called natural, whereas the second is artificial. The Protestant Reformation is an example of a "natural" trend. Although some of its leaders (including Luther, Melancthon, and Calvin) campaigned for it, signs of its essential principles arose centuries before those leaders were born, probable evidence that the movement was inevitable; crushing it only delayed it. The second type of trend, the artificial, uses the fuel of money in the engine of the mass media to create artificial needs in the mind of the public. It is advertising. (By the way, whereas this is the major form that artificial trends take in a free-market economy, in a totalitarian regime they take the form of government propaganda—political advertising—as it did in the former Soviet Union.)

But it is impossible to create an artificial need—whether for a whole new wardrobe or the latest SUV—while telling the truth accurately and entirely. If it has to be created or manufactured, the need itself does not exist, so persuading someone that it does exist requires lying. And although lying can take many forms, it always has at its core a semantic corruption—a distortion of language. The automobile manufacturer whose poorly designed vehicles rolled over when making sharp turns made a public statement to the effect that none had rolled over in its testing. Although that statement might have been true technically, its implication—that its vehicles never, ever rolled over—was false; they did roll over.

Business ethics aside, we are deluged with such misleading information nearly every day of our lives. And although it has its influence on our buying behavior (no thriving corporation would continue to spend large amounts of money on something that did not increase their sales), we nevertheless sense that we are being lied to. The effect over time is to create in us the feeling that every statement is dishonest, every "truth" is relative to its teller's private desires, and ultimately, everything is self-serving on the part of someone. Although this assumption might be true much of the time for fallen mortals, we either forget or refuse to acknowledge that it does not apply to God. Therefore, some people disbelieve parts of the gospel record, arguing that the original reports were adulterated with propaganda on behalf of the young church. But this is not the worst effect of semantic corruption. The most insidious effect is at work when we read the Bible's statements of fact as advertising for our own "company," Christianity, approving of it heartily but believing it ourselves no more deeply than the CEO of a major corporation believes his own advertising.

How many Christians, if they could walk into God's throne room today, would walk up to the Father, pat Him patronizingly on the head, and say,

"Nice work, that Bible. Now, let's talk about what You and I believe"? None, I hope. Yet, if anyone did, how mature would he or she be in spirit? Not very. Their growth has been stunted, something that we must avoid whenever we can. Paul told the Corinthians that they were "infants in Christ" (1 Cor. 3:1), and we must ensure that we are not the same. The author of Hebrews says that spiritual babies drink milk, "But solid food is for the mature, for those who have their powers of discernment trained by constant practice to distinguish good from evil" (5:14).

Prioritizing

We have been placed in this world to live our mortal lives, and we must make our way through this world's periodic shifts and reshufflings, but living *in* this world does not automatically include living *for* this world. Distractions from our quest for spiritual wholeness are inevitable, no matter what we do, but if we forget that they are distractions from our goal and begin to treat them as the goal itself, we will be sidetracked by temporalities and live with undernourished souls.

Dante's *Divine Comedy* has a helpful image for it. Just as an upright flame is blown aslant by a gust of wind, then stands upright again when the wind has stilled, so should we always resume our attention to wisdom and its heavenly source as soon as our necessary but menial activities can be put aside.[4] Supper was called for in the gospel account of Mary and Martha, but Martha dwelled too assiduously on the distracting necessity and thereby missed out on an inestimable opportunity to hear what Jesus told her sister (Luke 10:40–42).

This is not to say that the concerns of this world are unimportant. Anyone who has gone without food, shelter, adequate clothing, or freedom of movement for any length of time is painfully aware of how important these things are. But they are less important than concerns of the spirit. The book of Proverbs often prescribes priorities using the rhetorical pattern "better *x* than *y*" (8:11; 12:9; 15:17; 16:16; 21:19; and 28:6 are some examples), and Jesus frequently adds to and expands upon them ("It is better for you to enter the kingdom of God with one eye than with two eyes to be thrown into hell," Mark 9:47, and, "Sell what you possess and give to the poor . . . ;

---

4. *The Divine Comedy,* vol. 3, *Paradise,* trans. Mark Musa (New York: Penguin, 1984), canto 4, lines 73–78.

and come, follow me," Matt. 19:21). Even when we consider that Jesus is not suggesting that we literally remove one of our eyeballs, we must note that He does not say, "It is better for you to enter the kingdom of God with no eyes at all." Nor does He say, "Sell your possessions and give to the poor . . . ; and touch no more food." That is to say, Jesus recognizes our need to live in this world for a time. If complete rejection of the material world were what God desired of us, Jesus would not have told Martha that "only one thing is necessary" for supper; He would have told her that food was not necessary at all. If material needs were entirely irrelevant for the Christian, Jesus would not have told His apostles to take only one change of clothes when they traveled; He would have told them nothing at all about clothes. But notice that Jesus definitely reduces to the minimum the attention that His followers should pay to their bodily needs. Vastly more important, He teaches, is the attention that we must pay to our souls.

Christianity is not a religion that considers matter to be intrinsically evil, but neither is Christianity a religion that worships matter. Our God not only created all matter and initially called it good but also blessed the world of matter by taking it upon Himself in the form of a human body, one that occasionally tired, one that slept, one that He cushioned with a pillow while on a fishing boat, one that ate bread, and one that ate fish even after the resurrection. Clearly, we are not to be dead to the world, but neither are we to make the world our first priority; our spiritual health depends upon our keeping our priorities straight.

Keeping a Sense of Urgency

But perhaps the best advice one could give a growing Christian is to maintain a sense of urgency. The five wise virgins and the five foolish virgins had to wait only a number of hours for the bridegroom to arrive; we have now waited more than two thousand years for our Bridegroom. Evidently, it was a task that was beyond half of them, but our task is far more demanding because it is much more extended. It is to live always as in preparation for the real possibility that tonight will be the last night of both our lives and the world. It is never to say, as we sometimes do at our jobs, "That's good enough" when we know that it is not the best we can do. It is never to say, "I'm saved, so I need nothing more" because it probably is not all that the Father would like to see in us. It is never to rest on our laurels, thinking that we have paid our spiritual dues (whatever those are) and can coast safely and effortlessly along for the rest of our lives.

Our task is not to do any of those things. It most definitely is, on the other hand, our job to keep alert constantly to how much we are in need of wisdom, to immerse ourselves regularly and often in God's Word, to remember always that "time must have a stop," the master of the house will return, the Bridegroom will arrive, and that the oil of the parable is not oil at all but sanctification. We will never be good enough to look God in the face, but, with God's help, we can always become better than we are. And once we have stretched every fiber of our being to do that over a long period of time, He will declare His approval, saying, "Well done, good and faithful servant."

But we must not think that what Jesus is advocating when He commands us to "watch" is what psychologists call obsessive-compulsive behavior. To distinguish between the two, we must think of the man who checks his computer for new e-mail messages every ten minutes, although he has no reason to expect one, or the woman who cleans her bathroom washbasin twelve times each day even when no one has used it.

Let's imagine two very different people driving from Seattle to Miami. One person (the obsessive-compulsive one) stops only for gasoline, candy bars, and bottled water. If he survives the ordeal at all, he arrives in Miami with both his body and his mind in danger of breakdown. (A life-and-death emergency might call for such a heroic effort, but we are not talking about such rare emergencies here.) The diligent driver, on the other hand, would leave Seattle at an appropriate hour, stop for lunch, drive until supper time, and then get a good night's rest before driving on toward Miami the next morning. He might stop now and then to spend thirty minutes or so at a historical site or some other interesting place or to visit a friend, but he would always keep in mind his overall destination—Miami—and he would be more and more uncomfortable the longer each delay lasted. He would never allow his progress to be sidetracked indefinitely, and he certainly would never let minor hindrances such as rain or detours become excuses for putting his goal aside. He is determined to reach Miami with all due dispatch, but no one could accuse him of being mentally ill on the subject of his itinerary. Nor is he compromising his dedication to reaching his goal by stopping when necessary. He can, like Dante's flame, be blown aside from it for a time, but he always returns to it when circumstances allow. He is not a monomaniac, but neither does he ever give up on what he had set out to do. That is diligence rightly understood: urgency under control, the prime quality called for in the process of spiritual growth. If we can imitate such diligence in our acquisition of wisdom, we will "seek it like silver and search for it as for hidden treasures" (Prov. 2:4); we will follow the proverb's advice and "not forget [wisdom's] teaching" (3:1); and we will not let her words "escape from [our] sight" but will "keep them within [our] sight" (4:21).

Of course, it is not always an urgent matter to reach Miami, or any other place, so let's look at diligence through the lens of another anecdote. Imagine that you and your family are staying at a cabin in the mountains. One morning, you find that one of your children is missing. The family is instantly alert and agrees to spread out in their search, each member looking in a different area. You begin searching your area with an image of the lost child in your mind, hoping, almost expecting, that the real child will replace that image as you walk around the next tree. But as the search goes on, a branch whips your face, and you spend a few moments consoling yourself for your stinging cheek. Then you see a patch of color that looks out of place in the woods, but it turns out to be only a wild mushroom. That mushroom makes you think of this child's refusal to eat mushrooms, and spinach as well, which in turn reminds you of Popeye cartoons that you watched in your own childhood. Soon, you are so lost in memories that you pay no attention to the distant cries of the lost child, although you would have heard them easily if you had kept in mind the original purpose for your being out walking in the forest that day. If we take the lost child as representing our incomplete self, we begin to understand Proverbs 4:23: "Watch over your heart with all diligence, For from it flow the springs of life" (NASB).

Wisdom, Both Moral and Practical, As a Prerequisite

The universal church has been divided for centuries on the question of salvation by works or by faith. But when the question moves from salvation to sanctification, everyone seemingly agrees that works—our everyday actions—are a necessary means to the desired end. The Christian who considers every word of the Bible to be true (including Proverbs 11:1 and 26:18–19) but who continually cheats clients, tells lies in self-protection or for gain, commits adultery, or otherwise lives contrary to the Word of God even while agreeing that the Bible speaks truth, nevertheless keeps that truth at arm's length. Such people look into the Bible the way a bathysphere enters the ocean, without absorbing any of it; this is right in the ocean but wrong in the Bible.

Spiritual growth requires that we steep ourselves in God's wisdom in the way a fish poaches in broth, absorbing its surroundings and becoming better by it. A patient must do more than believe that his doctor's prescription will cure him; he must also follow that prescription and take the medicine before he can benefit from it. "The sacrifice [read *worship*] of the wicked is an abomination to the LORD, but the prayer of the upright is acceptable to him" (Prov. 15:8). Even the devils know that the prescriptions of Scripture are valid, but they refuse to follow orders. Should we, forgiven and adopted as we are, follow their perverse lead? May God forbid it.

If we are to grow into spiritual adults, as my students grew into social adults, it will take us more than the four years of study that a bachelor's degree normally requires. It will take a lifelong attention to God's Word, an attention that includes both obedience and a judicious receptivity to the lessons of wisdom.

Questions for Thought and Reflection

1. Bob, a member of your church, came to the Lord six months ago. In chatting with you after worship one Sunday, he confides that he is disappointed in his progress. He says that he still has unwholesome urges, improper thoughts, and difficulty in forgiving certain people in his life. What general response would you give to all of his complaints?
2. Are there limits to the value of diligence alone? Have you ever been determined to accomplish something, worked hard at it, stuck with it, given it your all, and still failed in the end? If so, why do you think your efforts proved fruitless? What was missing?
3. Search the four Gospels for clues to Jesus' physical appearance. What clues do we get from Matthew, Mark, Luke, and John as to what our Savior looked like? List His physical characteristics and personal habits. If your reading produces less than satisfies you, search the rest of the New Testament and all of the Old Testament for further clues. Have you found enough to recognize Jesus by sight on a city sidewalk? What have your findings taught you about the way Christians ought to look?

4. People who say that advertising does not influence their buying habits either ignore the fact that no successful corporation would spend the large sums they do on advertising if it did not increase sales, or they consider themselves rarities in the human race. Putting aside the entertainment value of commercial ads, what buying trends do you see in our time that apparently are stimulated by advertising? What trends in general seem to be brought about by movies, television, or the daily news? How vulnerable are you to artificial trends?

5. What are some of the things in your life that shorten your attention span and distract you from the sort of focus on spiritual realities that will allow you to grow in your faith? What can you do to resist the power of these distractions?

Chapter Five

INTERPERSONAL RELATIONSHIPS

M ary enrolled in my (Edward's) class on Ecclesiastes and Song of Songs and participated regularly in discussions about marriage and healthy relationships between men and women. In both her comments in class and her papers, Mary seemed very skeptical about the positive potential for marriage, and she expressed some very negative opinions about men. One day, she came by to talk with me about the tension she felt between what I was presenting in class and her own views.

Mary's father had abandoned her and her mother, and she and her mother had struggled to live with some degree of happiness in a single-parent home. Her mother was very bitter about what her father had done, and for her entire life Mary had heard her mother fiercely denounce her father and dogmatically condemn men in general. Her mother's bitterness (a common result of such relational dysfunction) had determined Mary's pessimistic view of men and relationships, and she told me that she was not sure she could ever trust and respect a man.

Several semesters later, she brought a young man by for me to meet and told me that they were engaged. I asked her privately how she was coping with the issues she had discussed with me earlier. She told me that she was making progress and that counseling was helping both her and her fiancé. But she also admitted that she was still struggling with the feelings and ideas that had resulted from growing up in unhealthy relationships. Mary will probably have difficulty developing a healthy marriage because poor family relationships had hindered her from developing and maturing as she should. It likely will take many years for her to learn to trust and respect her husband so that they both may experience the fullness of what marriage can be.

During the years in which I have met a number of women like Mary, I have also met at least as many men whose unwholesome attitudes toward women have been shaped by people around them who regularly devalued and demeaned women. The poor role models and the constant exposure to values that are inconsistent with God's order will make it very difficult for these men to respect and appreciate women appropriately and to treat them in ways that illustrate to the world Christ's love for the church. I meet students with very poor opinions of themselves and find that it often goes back to parents, teachers, or friends who constantly criticized and demeaned them. Again, the very relationships that are designed to encourage and nurture children as they develop into adults can also discourage them from developing into mature adults. Relationships play a major role in human development, including spiritual development, and relationships also provide an important context for developing wise and godly character. The glimpses into relationships provided by the Wisdom Literature may be far more relevant to the question of spiritual development than one might initially suppose.

Psychologists agree widely that interpersonal relationships play a crucial role in our development from infants into relatively independent and responsible adults. Most of these experts concur that traumatic experiences, or a serious dysfunction in family relationships, make it very difficult for children to develop normally and likely will hamper their own functioning as responsible adults. In other words, when the basic relationships of life do not function in the way God designed them to work, it is harder for people to become the mature adults that God designed them to be. Many people would add that the immaturity that results affects a person's relationships with both others and God, and personal observation seems to confirm the general accuracy of the theory. Developing healthy interpersonal relationships seems to be an essential element in becoming spiritually mature.

Earlier in this book, we pointed out that the human need for relationships is a fundamental part of God's design. We noted that pride will skew relationships from their God-intended function and can destroy their benefits. But another important benefit comes from human relationships and the way God's order is meant to work: healthy relationships promote spiritual growth. Perhaps for this reason Proverbs gives the attention it does to various human relationships and the way they are designed to function. As is typical of Proverbs, it does not give a comprehensive discussion of interpersonal relationships. Rather, it gives a number of cross sections of truth about relationships, seeds from which we are to cultivate the skills for living among others according to Yahweh's order.

Parents and Children

"Grandchildren are the crown of the aged," teaches Proverbs 17:6, indicating a view of offspring as a blessing, but Proverbs 29:17 instructs, "Discipline your son, and he will give you rest." Many people today would see these two proverbs as implying a contradiction, the first indicating love, the second a harshness that feels to them like a lack of love. But Proverbs 13:24 sets the matter straight: "Whoever spares the rod hates his son, but he who loves him is diligent to discipline him." So the discipline of Proverbs 29:17, even when it includes corporal punishment, is to be motivated by affection. In such cases, the parent who is acquainted with the ways of God will sometimes see his child developing habits contrary to those ways. When reasoning and flat commands both fail to bring the child back to safety, the only alternative that remains is to cause the child to associate wayward behavior with discomfort. This is the only valid purpose and function of discipline, whether it takes the form of withholding expected pleasures or giving the pain of harsher forms of discipline.

Discretion tells us when to correct the child gently with a word or two and when to become more forceful. Discretion says that in punishing a child when our emotions are controlling our actions—whether anger or (yes) enjoyment—we are not punishing because we care for the child's soul but because we ourselves are in the grip of sinfulness. No evidence exists that the book of Proverbs was collected with the expectation that we would follow every individual proverb all of the time; it is evidently designed so that we can learn what is likely to work in certain situations, and it leaves to our wise and humane judgment the decision as to when a particular problem calls for a particular solution. The Bible was not written for automatons but for human beings created in the image of God, that is, people with the ability to reason: to observe a situation, discern its elements, and then either do nothing or intervene with the carefully measured and self-disciplined precision of a brain surgeon. Our growth in wisdom develops the skill to accomplish this in ways that are consistent with Yahweh's order.

Our children, like all other human beings, are of great value to God, and the high value that He places upon them does not diminish when they disobey us or when they irritate us. After all, He did not love us any less when we disobeyed Him; He does not lose His love for us on those occasional days when our faith in His goodness weakens. And what God values, we would do well to value as well, so we must do what is best for our children, whether the thing we do is praise their virtues or correct their faults. And we must do what seems likely to be most beneficial for them in the long run, not what we would like to do for the benefit of our reputations or for our personal pleasure. This is the meaning of *agape,* Christian love.

But the Wisdom Literature also is insistent that children, even adult offspring, imbibe wisdom from their parents. "Listen to your father who gave you life, and do not despise your mother when she is old," says Proverbs 23:22. The New Testament ratifies this command in Mark 7:10, where Jesus quotes the Old Testament approvingly as having said, "Honor your father and your mother" (Exod. 20:12). To listen, to honor, and not to despise might be seen as near synonyms in this regard because, although adult children may pointedly avoid the command to obey all that parents say, each of the three words reinforces the concept that one's parents are at all times to be allowed their dignity. In contrast to this, Colossians 3:20—where Paul instructs the children at Colossae, "Obey your parents in everything, for this pleases the Lord"—seems to address young children still living under their parents' supervision.

Probably no human relationship is more important than that between parent and child. When the relationship works the way God designed it, children develop into responsible adults. They learn essential skills for living, appropriate values, and dangers to avoid in life as these skills, values, and dangers pertain to both their relationship with God and their dealings with others. Children learn to appreciate the value of discipline, even in its more painful forms, as they experience discipline from wise parents, whose loving commitment to their children is obvious to them. Children who learn about discipline in such a context are much more likely to see the goodness of God even when He disciplines them, and they are much more likely to trust God's purposes in such experiences. At the same time, children who have experienced only harsh and abusive discipline, administered in anger and a vindictive spirit, will have great difficulty relating to God's discipline in positive ways. Children who cannot depend on their parents to honor their commitments, or whose love for them is always in doubt, will have great difficulty trusting God's faithfulness to His Word or believing in His unconditional love.

Parenting not only provides an invaluable opportunity for children to learn wisdom, to learn about God's ways, and to develop into responsible adults but also offers parents an important (if sometimes difficult) challenge to practice God's truth and develop the godly character that defines spiritual maturity. For the process to work as God designed it to work, parents must be moving toward spiritual maturity. They must, for example, be developing the patience and steadfast love that will allow them to deal with their children in a wide variety of situations in the way God deals with us. Certain values are characteristic of the wise and the spiritually mature—such values as discretion, self-control, the ability to respond carefully and deliberately rather than rashly, the avoidance of harsh and hurtful words in favor of words that encourage and heal. These values are essential in creating an environment in which children can develop as they should emotionally, intellectually, and spiritually. But few contexts exist where the demonstration of wisdom and values that reflect God's order can pay such high dividends as in the relationship between parents and children, and few settings exist where the failure to do so can produce such disaster.

Marriage

Agape love figures also in the husband-wife relationship, especially when the two hold in common a concept of spiritual excellence. "An excellent wife [i.e., one of noble and upright character] is the crown of her husband, but she who brings shame is like rottenness in his bones," says Proverbs 12:4. To use C. S. Lewis's schematic arrangement of the four types of love (dividing forms of love according to the four Greek terms used for love in the New Testament), this would combine *eros* (romantic love) with *agape* (Christian love) and, because of the couple's unified faith, a strong admixture of *philia* (friendship love). Add to this their mutual familiarity resulting from many years of marriage, and *storge* (familiar love) becomes the final and bonding ingredient in a solid and pleasant marriage. "Rejoice in the wife of your youth" (Prov. 5:18b) is a command to take advantage of this fourth part of marital love, so that the marriage will be as strong and vibrantly healthy as possible, enjoying the inimitable pleasures of a fully developed marriage.

The Wisdom Literature is unfailingly opposed to adultery (Prov. 6:20–35), just as it is opposed to the use of prostitutes (7:1–27). But it is just as insistent on the idea that "it is better to live in a corner of the housetop than in a house shared with a quarrelsome wife" (21:9), where the "corner of the housetop" is presumably parallel in meaning with the "continual dripping" of the similar proverb in 19:13. The effect, then, of a given wife's argumentative habit is to make the husband's life a constant irritation. This would most likely be an element of advice for the young man who is seeking a wife; he would do well to avoid such a prospect for marriage. But it could also suggest to contentious wives that their attempts to change their husbands through nagging are cruel, misguided, and unwise.

Many wives, ranging from the excellent to the woefully inadequate, are mentioned in the Old Testament, but Proverbs 31:10–31 contains the description of the wife *par excellence:* she is trustworthy, industrious, productive, strong, charitable, protective of her family, dignified, wise, kind, and fears the Lord. This song of praise for the ideal wife begins appropriately, "An excellent wife, who can find?" for her virtues are so great, and her faults so pointedly absent, that evidently we are to take her as an ideal; if so, we must attempt always to reach the high standards she sets but should be surprised if anyone were ever actually to do so completely. The passage is certainly not meant to instill guilt in the wife who does not meet her every qualification in real life.

In this same chapter of Proverbs, the young man who is seeking a wife is further advised that "charm is deceitful, and beauty is vain, but a woman who fears the Lord is to be praised" (v. 30). This flies in the face of the usual practice, but, like most biblical standards, it is based on a God-centered worldview rather than on a worldview that either takes pleasure or appearance as the highest good or condones the taking of "trophy wives." In the biblical sense, an ideal wife is not one who would appear on the cover of *Vogue* or in the centerfold of *Playboy* but who approximates the initiative, dedication to family, and devotion to God that the wife in Proverbs 31 displays. Notice, however, that beauty in a wife (or in anyone or anything else) is not condemned as evil; it is only ranked as a lower priority than godliness. "Beauty is vain" simply says that beauty in your wife will be of no real and long-term advantage to you, not that it is necessarily harmful.

As for the husband of the ideal marriage in chapter 31, we see that he trusts his wife (v. 11a), blesses her (v. 11b), and praises her (vv. 28–29). Although it might seem at first glance that he does not contribute to household finances, being found "in the gates [where] he sits among the elders of the land" (Prov. 31:23), the fact is that this was the place for conducting legal arrangements and business transactions, as we can see in Ruth 4:1. (The fact that the "elders of the land" are mentioned makes this even more likely because ten such men were required as witnesses to such arrangements.) The picture we see, then, is of a marriage as a type of partnership, with the wife generally in charge of the on-site labor—which at the time was conducted in the home—and the husband in charge of legalities and transactions conducted in public.

This picture is consistent with the one that we noted earlier from the book of Genesis, where the one-flesh relationship involves the coming together of a man and a woman, both of whom have strengths and weaknesses, with each using his or her strengths to fortify the weaknesses of the other. The entire context of the book of Proverbs implies that the full potential for marriage can be realized only when both partners are wise and when the kind of practical wisdom taught in the Wisdom Literature characterizes their relationship and interactions. Obviously, marriage constitutes a relationship that seems often to be filled with incidents that call for wisdom, and it is also clear that this relationship provides an important context for developing the characteristic traits of spiritual maturity.[1] The New Testament makes clear that husbands are to love their wives in the same way that Christ loved the church and that they are to love their wives as they love themselves (see, e.g., Eph. 5:15–33 or Col. 3:19), with 1 Corinthians 13 defining many of the essential characteristics of this *agape* love. Examples of these characteristics are patience, kindness, humility, selflessness, the absence of anger and arrogance, and a genuine concern for the best interests of the other person.

Whereas the Wisdom Literature identifies many of the practical elements involved in dealing wisely with others, Song of Songs provides a useful example of how marriage can be an admirable matrix for developing those

---

1. This topic is explored at length by Gary Thomas, *Sacred Marriage* (Grand Rapids: Zondervan, 2002). He argues that the primary purpose is not necessarily to make us happy but rather to make us holy (e.g., see his comments on p. 13 and throughout the book).

elements. Although many different opinions exist about how the book should be interpreted, this author (Edward) believes that Song of Songs describes a model relationship between a man and a woman in their courtship and marriage and is possibly intended as a commentary on certain aspects of the one-flesh relationship described in Genesis 2.[2] Certainly the book describes an ideal relationship, and one aspect of that relationship seems especially practical: the man and the woman spend a great deal of time praising one another. Each sees all sorts of things about which the other can be praised, many of which go beyond physical attractiveness. Song of Songs provides numerous examples of this important form of encouragement, with each lover frequently praising the other (e.g., 1:8–9; 2:3–6; 4:1–15). We are likely meant to understand that the mutual praise of the two contributed significantly to the way the partners viewed both themselves and one another. Their mutual praise, we can safely assume, contributed a vital element to the ideal relationship described in the book because as we focus on the qualities in other people that we appreciate and value, we come to appreciate those individuals even more.

At the same time, experience and research make clear that one person's response to another's behavior, whether good or bad, can exert a powerful influence on whether the behavior is repeated. A form of behavior that is praised is more likely to be repeated, perhaps to the point where it actually becomes a habit. Praise has a doubly positive effect in that, for example, as a husband notes praiseworthy things about his wife and commends her for those things, it increases the husband's appreciation for his spouse. At the same time, his praise for his wife often causes the praised aspect of her behavior to become more enjoyable and natural for her. In this way, praise can play a powerful role in deepening relationships among both family members and friends.

Scripture makes clear that believers should actively encourage one another. First Thessalonians 5:11 says, "Therefore encourage one another and build one another up, just as you are doing." Ephesians 4:29 says, "Let no corrupting talk come out of your mouths, but only such as is good for building up, as fits the occasion, that it may give grace to those who hear." Words are one of the most important means by which we can encourage others.

---

2. For a more detailed discussion of this point, see Edward M. Curtis, *Song of Songs,* Bible Study Commentary (Grand Rapids: Zondervan, 1988; reprint, Eugene, Ore.: Wipf & Stock, 2000), 41–48.

The gratifying effect of words is clear from Proverbs 16:24: "Gracious words are like a honeycomb, sweetness to the soul and health to the body." Hebrews 10:24–25 says, "Let us consider how to stir up one another to love and good works, not neglecting to meet together, . . . but encouraging one another." Marriage provides an excellent opportunity to practice and further develop this important virtue. At the same time, praising one's spouse also creates an environment that encourages his or her growth in godliness. A man and a woman who love and respect one another as Scripture indicates they should and who express that love and respect appropriately will grow toward maturity both individually and as a couple. In so doing, they will elevate God's reputation in their marriage.

Discretion Among Friends

Although all relationships provide a context for developing and applying wisdom and the virtues of Christian maturity, Proverbs also recognizes that friendships have the potential for either moving us toward the goal of maturity or hindering our progress toward that goal. "Make no friendship with a man given to anger, nor go with a wrathful man, lest you learn his ways and entangle yourself in a snare" (Prov. 22:24–25). The common saying that "love is blind" will often apply to any of the four loves: the teenage girl who is smitten with the charms of a drug addict and burglar will deny his faults; the fond parent will not easily be persuaded that his daughter is forging checks on his account; the neighbor of the serial murderer will say that he could not be guilty because he was always so polite; and Christians often hesitate to admit that fellow Christians are seriously guilty of anything. But in reality all of us are fallen and therefore subject to sin; as a result, it behooves us to decide carefully how deep and meaningful our relationships will be with the people we meet. If our own weakness is drink, we would be foolish to strike up a friendship with a heavy drinker. If we have a long-established habit of deceiving people, having similarly deceitful friends will only reinforce the sin and make it seem more normal and acceptable than it actually is. Likewise, to use the example cited in the preceding proverb, just being among easily angered people over a long period of time can infect us with the destructive habit of indiscriminately applying anger to all of our problems.

Sometimes we are forced by circumstances to associate with such people, living near them or working with them, so we cannot always avoid completely those who might hinder our spiritual walk. But we can, and should, avoid spending any more time with them than is necessary, and we become close friends with them at our peril. This is not to suggest that we offend them needlessly or denigrate them (even out of their hearing), but it is wise to think of them in terms of the serious threat that they pose to our spiritual growth. We might feel called upon to witness to them or to help them in some other way, but it will not help them to injure ourselves by becoming close friends with them. A Christian acquaintance once told me that she had a friend, a woman who was not only non-Christian but also anti-Christian. She wanted to remain friends with the woman, but someone had advised her that this woman posed a danger to her faith. She asked my opinion, and I told her that her decision to keep or not keep the woman as a friend depended upon her perception of which of the two was more influential on the other. If she asked me today, I would add that she should not become a close friend of the woman but only an acquaintance until the woman began to respect God and accept the Lord Christ. As in all other things, godly wisdom (or *discretion*) is an invaluable aid that is available for our use in interpersonal relationships: "discretion will watch over you . . . , delivering you from the way of evil, from men of perverted speech, who forsake the paths of uprightness . . . , who rejoice in doing evil" (Prov. 2:11–14a).

But one caveat is necessary at this point: when deciding whether someone would make a good companion or friend, it is possible to be either not demanding enough of their beliefs or too demanding. Jesus said, "No one comes to the Father except through me" (John 14:6); He did not say that no one would come to the Father except for those who have been baptized in a certain way or those who believe in a certain doctrine regarding the Lord's Supper. We must not be more demanding than the Lord Jesus lest we call upon ourselves His disfavor. And at the opposite extreme, to consider everyone who is nice, or is merely sincere about his or her beliefs, to be thereby qualified as a good candidate for friendship is not being demanding enough. Once again, no one comes to the Father except through Jesus, and although it might in some cases be arguable as to whether one doctrine or another is scripturally sound, it should be clear enough that people who will not confess to Jesus Christ's lordship are not coming to the Father through Jesus Christ.

Occasionally we meet genuine Christians whose conversation irritates us. They might demand some behavior of us, something that they consider vital to being a true Christian but that we are not comfortable doing and do not believe the Lord wills us to do. They might expect us to accept wholeheartedly and forever some detail of doctrine that they consider nonnegotiable but that we consider optional. We sometimes feel that such people are not of our faith at all but are either hypocrites or heretics. Yet, we must remember that feelings are often unreliable as a test of doctrine. They might very well be as wrong as we feel they are, but they might also be presenting us with a truth that we have never accepted, and this correctional element might make us uncomfortable. It is wise always to remember Proverbs 19:20, "Listen to advice and accept instruction, that you may gain wisdom in the future," and 17:10, "A rebuke goes deeper into a man of understanding than a hundred blows into a fool," along with the many proverbs that begin, "Listen, my son," and then to understand that the voice of wisdom often comes through people who are not our biological or legal fathers. The debate and interaction might also lead to greater understanding and insight, as Proverbs 27:17 suggests: "Iron sharpens iron, and one man sharpens another."

In his book *The Four Loves,* C. S. Lewis distinguishes between companions and friends, a distinction that is vital to any useful discussion of friendship. "Many people," Lewis writes, "when they speak of their 'friends,' mean only their companions."[3] Using the term *companion* to mean the many people with whom we work, live near, and with whom we are perhaps on a first-name basis, he says more fully, "This Companionship is, however, only the matrix of friendship. It is often called Friendship, and many people when they speak of their "friends" mean only their companions. . . . Friendship arises out of mere Companionship when two or more of the companions discover that they have in common some insight . . . which the others do not share." And surely Lewis is right in this distinction because Proverbs 17:17 tells us that "a friend loves at all times," whereas our affection, if we have any, for mere companions will waver from day to day, depending upon circumstances. Proverbs 18:24 distinguishes clearly between the two categories, both by category and by their contrasting results: "A man of many companions may come to ruin, but there is a friend who sticks closer than a brother." And all of this accords well with the finest example of friendship the Old Testament affords us, that between David and Jonathan, whose souls

---

3. C. S. Lewis, *The Four Loves* (New York: Harcourt Brace, 1960), 96.

are said to have been knitted together (1 Sam. 18:1), Jonathan loving David "as his own soul."[4]

Lewis's concept of genuine friendship adheres to this view because when two or more people perceive that their spirits are kindred, they begin to see one another as more or less identical, making it easier to "love one another as we love ourselves." Interest in a sport or in movies or frequency of association might begin the process, but friendship will wilt without something deeper in common, and the deepest of these is a concept of God's sovereignty, power, and Fatherly affection. This clearly was what Saul lacked and what David displayed dramatically before Jonathan's eyes and in his hearing (e.g., 1 Sam. 17:45–47). No wonder Jonathan felt compelled later to protect David when Saul tried to kill him. Given Saul's fears that David would supplant him as king, Jonathan protecting his friend's life, in effect, must have seemed to him like surrendering his own right to assume the throne after Saul's death. This transfer of hereditary right is signified in 18:4, when Jonathan gives to David gifts symbolic of kingship.[5] Unless Jonathan is extremely impulsive (and he gives no such impression elsewhere), the only explanation for this extraordinary donation would seem to be that Jonathan sees David as himself, and his reason for seeing him as such would be the deep and genuine friendship that they share and the abiding faith in God and His purposes that both men possess.

Proverbs makes clear, however, that most human relationships do not function at this deep and selfless level. Some people claim to be our best friends, but they do so only because of the benefits they receive from the relationship. Proverbs 19:4a says, "Wealth brings many new friends," and Proverbs 19:6 adds, "Many seek the favor of a generous man, and everyone is a friend to a man who gives gifts." We get a glimpse of what such pragmatic companionship will do to us when we are no longer of practical use

---

4. We have been conditioned in our day to apply the word *love* to interpersonal relationships only in the case of romantic love, but the Bible does not use the word in such a restricted sense, nor has anyone until our sex-crazed times.

5. Note that Jonathan seems to have been a very capable man, and he displays a number of gifts that would have served him well as Israel's next king. Jonathan's selfless act is a remarkable testimony to both the depth of his friendship with David and his commitment to what he understood to be God's will for his friend. A student once commented about this passage, "I hope that if I am ever in a situation like this where I have the gifts but someone else has the calling, I will be able to respond in the gracious way that Jonathan responded here."

to others: "Wealth brings many new friends, but a poor man is deserted by his friend" (Prov. 19:4). Proverbs 19:7 makes clear that poverty can cause even one's family—and they are generally the ones who are most likely to stick by a person and help in times of difficulty—to abandon him or her: "A poor man is shunned by all his relatives—how much more do his friends avoid him! Though he pursues them with pleading, they are nowhere to be found" (NIV). Proverbs does recognize, however, the existence of faithful friends, like Jonathan or Ruth, who will stick by a person no matter how difficult the circumstances become or how much strain the person's needs place on the friend's resources.

These observations, and similar ones about how people behave, warn us of certain realities about relationships and the potential consequences of failing to understand them. Dependence on the wrong people is unwise and can result in pain and disappointment. Although most of a person's relationships will involve what C. S. Lewis called companionship rather than intimate friendship, the Wisdom Literature does imply that a wise person in his relationships will not be characterized by the kind of self-serving motives that have just been described but rather by integrity, honesty, and faithfulness. In the wide world of general interrelationships, the Wisdom Literature repeatedly prescribes righteous interaction: "Do not plan evil against your neighbor" (Prov. 3:29) and "Do not contend with a man for no reason" (Prov. 3:30). To speak harmfully of one's neighbor is to be "godless" (11:9). Rather than despise our neighbor, we are to be kind, even if our neighbor is powerless to return our kindness (14:21). We are commanded never to alter land boundaries deceitfully (22:28) and are counseled to take disputes to court only after trying honestly to work things out personally (25:8–10). We would be wise to avoid involvement in quarrels that are not our own (26:17); only a fool makes hurtful comments and then tries to claim innocence by saying, "I am only joking" (26:18–19); and we must be careful not to wear out our welcome in our neighbor's home (25:17). We are to be faithful and help our friends in their distress to the limits of our resources. We must be trustworthy and never breech a confidence (11:13; 17:9), and we must be honest with our friends (27:6; 27:9; 28:23).

The Wisdom Literature identifies many other details that are important in relationships, the skillful application of which requires sensitivity to others and a certain amount of insight. Proverbs 25:20 says, "Whoever sings songs to a heavy heart is like one who takes off a garment on a cold day, and like vinegar on soda," and Proverbs 27:14 might make a similar point in saying, "Whoever blesses his neighbor with a loud voice, rising early in the morning, will be counted as cursing." As we noted earlier, Job's "friends" illustrate, with their unhelpful reactions to his troubles, the damage that can be done when limited human wisdom is combined with a lack of insight and sensitivity to another's need. With the best of intentions, but with incomplete wisdom, they diagnose his problem to the best of their ability and are terribly wrong in their conclusions. Their error stems from a pair of faulty assumptions: that *all* disaster and dismay are the direct result of sin and that *all* trouble comes to one in direct proportion to one's sins. "Disaster pursues sinners" (Prov. 13:21) is accurate when taken as a generalization, but Eliphaz and Job's other friends take it as applying invariably to *every* case of adversity. And so, having in their grasp only a part of wisdom, but convinced thereby that they possess wisdom whole, they pontificate. Their folly is even more tragic in that what Job says he needed from his friends in this situation was not answers or theology but rather loving-kindness (Job 6:14).

Which of us has not done so? It is a mistake that is easy for us to make, even at our best, because when we see a friend in pain, we ache to do more than listen. We want to do something, or at least to say something, preferably something godly, certainly something true, so we haul out Proverbs 13:21 or something like it, and we tell the poor soul in agony that he has brought it upon himself. If we are persuasive enough, we can double his pain, just the opposite of what we intended and of what God would approve. Far better that we listen and sympathize. Qohelet says truly, "There are righteous people to whom it happens according to the deeds of the wicked, and there are wicked people to whom it happens according to the deeds of the righteous" (Eccl. 8:14). Better to heed James and be reluctant to assume the role of teacher for fear of a stricter judgment (James 3:1).

All of this might seem to be only common sense, the sort of thing that civilized people do, but two observations are to be made on that score. First, it has come to seem common sense only because its basic principles have been worked out over the millennia to help societies work smoothly, as though wisdom were, in its more practical pronouncements, a lubricant to keep the machinery of society running smoothly. Second, although it is apparently the sort of thing that civilized people do, it is "more honored in the breach than in the observance," as Hamlet says. We know this is the way a godly person behaves, and if asked to assess our lives against these standards, we might casually stamp ourselves as "faultless." But when the city building department has told us that any swimming pool on our property must be tucked into our backyard, and our backyard is just a few feet too narrow for any swimming pool, while our neighbor to the rear is known to be reluctant to part with any of his property, what is our temptation? Might it not be to allow the confusion inherent in construction projects to drift just a little into our neighbor's property? "After all," we reason, "he's not using it, and he'll never miss it." But we will have acted foolishly, to say nothing of sinfully.

And what of Proverbs 3:27? Let's suppose that we are in charge of policy making for a bank. The question arises, How long should deposits be held before they may be withdrawn? All checks, of course, must clear first, both to ascertain their validity and to be available to your bank. But checks issued by the federal government, for example, are hardly to be suspected of invalidity and will normally make funds available, let's say, within two working days. Do you allow such funds to be withdrawn after two days, or do you impose a waiting period of a week, allowing your bank to make an additional profit by investing the money? If your point of view is narrow and secular, you might impose the extra waiting period. But if you acknowledge God's wisdom and the fear the Lord, you must be guided by Proverbs 3:27: "Do not withhold good from those to whom it is due, when it is in your power to do it." And there are many important situations in which to apply this principle (such as mailing our mortgage check or paying our other bills on time), even for those of us who are not in charge of a bank.

If we define spiritual maturity on the basis of lists of the character qualities produced by the indwelling Holy Spirit presented in Galatians 5:22 (love, joy, peace, patience, kindness, goodness, faithfulness, gentleness, and self-control) or the description of the qualities that are consistent with the life that is found in Christ in Ephesians 4:25–32 (truthful speech, control of anger, diligent and honest labor, words that edify, the absence of bitterness and slander, kindness, compassion, and a forgiving spirit) or the similar list in Colossians 3:12–17 (compassion, kindness, humility, gentleness, patience, a forgiving spirit, peace, thankfulness), it becomes apparent that most of the qualities listed are expressed primarily in the context of relationships. In fact, even the primary development of most of these qualities takes place in that same context; patience, honesty, gentleness, kindness, self-control, humility, and the like are normally developed through experiences that, by testing those virtues, further strengthen them. James sees a direct connection between the practice of these virtues and the maturity of our faith, teaching that a religion that pleases God includes visiting widows and orphans in their distress and keeping oneself unstained by the world (James 1:27). The reality of one's faith is demonstrated through living out the truth to which one claims commitment, and this is demonstrated through things such as controlling one's tongue and through good deeds done in the gentleness of wisdom.

The Old Testament Wisdom Literature—with its emphasis on integrity and honesty, common sense and kindness, and faithfulness and a commitment to justice—seems to be the foundation that underlies much of the New Testament teaching. This same Wisdom Literature makes clear that the maturity to which every believer is called is not the result of the instantaneous infusion of these values; rather, with God's help, it results from diligence and daily practice of the skills that characterize maturity. The Wisdom Literature also makes clear what is evident from both Scripture and common sense: all of our relationships, including those within the family, deep friendships, and even casual interactions, play an essential role in the growth of our godliness because by means of those relationships we develop and put into practice the virtues by which maturity is defined.

Another useful caution in interpersonal relationships is to be prepared to admire. Proverbs 3:27 ("Do not withhold good from those to whom it is due, when it is in your power to do it") is often read in conjunction with the verse that follows it ("Do not say to your neighbor, 'Go, and come again, tomorrow I will give it'—when you have it with you"), which would imply that "good" here refers to money or property. But it may well be read as a discrete proverb, in which case "good" can mean good words, or praise. But Proverbs 12:25b carries no such ambiguity: "A good word makes [a man's heart] glad." And Proverbs 21:21 makes a promise: "Whoever pursues righteousness and kindness will find life, righteousness, and honor." And who is to honor such righteous and loyal people if not the people of God?

But many factors work against the human virtue of admiration. One of these is the contemporary feeling among most of us in the Western world that democracy is the only valid system of government; that might be, but the fact that other forms of government have glaring weaknesses does not prove the perfection of democracy. And even if democracy is the best system of human government, one effect of its deeply felt adoption is a secular faith in the equality of every human being. Understood correctly, this faith is helpful in avoiding social prejudices and inappropriate elitism, but understood simplistically, it makes a mockery of individual gifts and individual excellences. Still, this is not the worst of it. Once we have learned by heart that no one is more capable than anyone else, and that therefore no one is worthy of our admiration and respect, we begin to be less able to admire and respect God. Not that we should worship any human being—admiration is not worship. But admiration is the stepping-stone to worship in the same way that learning to walk is a stepping-stone to learning to dance; the first must precede the second, but they are not the same thing. We may call Him "Lord," but our hearts are far from actually considering Him our Lord, our superior, One whose every word and act is unquestionably true, and true not just because He says it is true but because it actually is true. We begin to place God "in the dock" (to use C. S. Lewis's phrase) that is, in the defendant's chair in a court of law, questioning Him and trying Him as though He were merely another human being like us and subject to our human laws, feelings, and opinions. To call this sacrilege is to understate the case; to anyone who has a realistic view of the Father's power, wisdom, holiness, and majesty, it clearly identifies itself as a form of insanity that courts damnation.

Wisdom in relationships, then, is essentially the same as wisdom in other spheres of activity: a reasoning caution that manages emotional impulses. The natural feelings that might otherwise drive us to greed, lust, and self-centeredness are made subject to wisdom, which, far from destroying the impulse entirely, moderates it. As a result, greed is harnessed so as to produce enough wealth to provide for our families and for a judicious generosity, lust is kept within the boundaries of marriage, and self-interest is assigned the task of preserving us from absolute ruin. Similarly, the sinful pride inherent in self-love may be transformed by using this as a standard, loving others as we love ourselves, which means that self-love can be the first step toward holiness. But for the person whose self-love is left in its unregenerate form, the resulting egotism can, and often will, isolate us from both our fellows and our God. When we live in isolation from other people, we remove ourselves from a vital part of our growth in godliness. A refusal to interact with people, or a perverse interaction, can truncate our growth in wisdom, and without wisdom, God will seem very odd to us and very distant.

Questions for Thought and Reflection

1. Many believers who have had a broken or wounded relationship with a parent sense that this has hampered their relationship with God. But some people sense that their unsatisfying relationship with a parent has made them more eager to know the Father in heaven. Does your experience fall into one of these categories, or perhaps both?

2. If you are married, do you and your spouse ever compliment one another? Do you praise one another sincerely and regularly? Do you ever look for things your spouse does that can prompt you to say honestly that you admire him or her? (Caution: don't be put off if your spouse receives compliments awkwardly. Such people eventually learn merely to say, "Thank you.")

   If you are not married, have you ever heard your parents compliment one another? Does the presence or absence of praise seem to have had an effect on their marriage?

3. Ann is a high school teacher who normally takes her lunch break with two colleagues Lynn and Wendy. Ann is currently having problems with her teenage son and sometimes mentions this to her companions. Lynn's reaction is usually that Ann was too lax with her son when he was a child, that children raised with firm discipline never get into trouble. Wendy's comments are different: she says little, but she listens attentively to Ann's woes and then tells her how sorry she is for her. Wendy has had similar problems with her daughter; Lynn, too, has had difficulties with her two children but refuses to admit the fact. Which of the two colleagues is Ann's friend and which is merely her companion? Explain in general terms.

4. Think about your role as a parent, spouse, or friend. During the last month, what opportunities have those relationships afforded you to demonstrate the godly aspects of your character? How did you respond? What opportunities have those same relationships provided you for further developing godly character?

5. Have you ever had a "fair-weather friend," one whose major interest in the relationship seemed to be what he or she got out of you? How did that make you feel? Do you ever do that to other people? What does it mean to be a faithful friend?

Chapter Six

THE FEAR OF
THE LORD AND THE
KNOWLEDGE OF GOD

One of the most striking images from the 1998 winter storms that hit Southern California was a news film of several beautiful hilltop homes crashing down onto a condominium complex in the canyon below. These were large and expensive houses with magnificent views of the ocean and the surrounding hills. They were, I am sure, built with care and fully in compliance with the codes and standards required by all of the appropriate building authorities. But despite the finest materials and excellent workmanship that went into the construction of these houses, they did not survive those storms because they did not have a solid foundation. In this instance, a critical instability existed far below the surface of the ground, and although a few geologists had warned that the hillside was unstable, other experts disagreed. The warnings were ignored, and so the building project went forward.

Although everyone recognizes the need for a solid foundation in a building project, only some people realize that the Old Testament affirms the same principle as applied to the quest for wisdom and knowledge. Proverbs 1:7 and 9:10 are key verses in the book of Proverbs because they state the theme that ties together the entire book: "The fear of the LORD is the beginning of knowledge/wisdom."

These verses make clear that the acquisition of knowledge and wisdom must begin with the fear of the Lord. Although the Hebrew word translated *beginning* can be understood in several different ways, Kidner captures the significance of the word in this verse when he says that *beginning* here signifies "the first and controlling principle, rather than a stage which one leaves behind."[1]

The fear of the Lord constitutes the necessary foundation for the pursuit of wisdom. Any attempt to gain knowledge that proceeds without this foundation is in danger of suffering the same ultimate fate as those houses that slipped into the ravine. People with the finest academic credentials, using their great intellectual abilities, the most sophisticated research techniques, and careful logic can produce some very impressive results in their search for knowledge. From the perspective of Old Testament wisdom, however, any approach that does not begin with the fear of the Lord rests on an unstable and insecure foundation. When it comes to questions of ultimate reality, moral truth, the meaning of life, truth about God, the basic nature of man, or any number of other vital and foundational issues, the flawed nature of the foundation will often become apparent when the structures set on it begin to slip and topple.

The importance of fearing the Lord is affirmed at many other points in the Old Testament. Deuteronomy 10:12–13, for example, indicates that quite beyond its importance in gaining knowledge and wisdom, the fear of the Lord is an essential key to a life that pleases God. The verse says, "And now, Israel, what does the LORD your God require of you, but to fear the LORD your God, to walk in all his ways, to love him, to serve the LORD your God with all your heart and with your soul, and to keep the commandments and statutes of the LORD." Clearly, the fear of the Lord is an idea of central importance in the Old Testament, and this verse from Deuteronomy indicates that it is at the heart of what God desires of His people. But what exactly does it involve, and does the fear of the Lord have any relevance for us today?

A number of different suggestions have been made as to what the fear of the Lord involves, but it seems to this author (Edward) that the fear of the Lord is simply the result of understanding who God is and who we are. Living in the fear of the Lord involves living our lives on the basis of that understanding.

---

1. Derek Kidner, *Proverbs,* vol. 15 of Tyndale Old Testament Commentaries (Downers Grove, Ill.: InterVarsity, 1964), 59.

Learning the Fear of the Lord

Israel's understanding of who God is came to them in a variety of different ways, although always through God's self-disclosure rather than as a result of their own creative thinking about God. Prophets such as Isaiah, Jeremiah, and Ezekiel encountered God through visions and theophanies that profoundly impressed them with God's holiness, majesty, and greatness. Many Israelites learned significant truths about God's power through their experiences at the Exodus; at Mt. Carmel, where Elijah defeated the prophets of Baal; at Jericho; when David defeated Goliath; and in many other instances when God intervened on behalf of His people to deliver or judge them. Through these experiences, Israel learned important lessons about who God is and what He is like. When we look at the number of visions and mighty acts of God that are recorded in Scripture and then consider the approximately one thousand years of Israel's history over which they were distributed, it becomes apparent that the great majority of Israelites never personally witnessed such events. God did send true prophets with genuine messages from Him, but the prophets also denounced as frauds many people who claimed to have a word from the Lord (e.g., Jer. 20:1–6; 23:9–22; 1 Kings 22:8–26).

Yet, neither the dearth of miracles nor the false claims of self-proclaimed prophets relieved Israel of the responsibility of fearing the Lord or prevented the Israelites from achieving that goal. They learned the fear of the Lord through the repeated recollection of the wondrous works of God and the celebration of them in various religious ceremonies. In Deuteronomy 17:18–20, instructions were given for the time when Israel would be ruled by a king. The king was instructed to make a copy of the Law for himself on a scroll. He was to keep that copy and read it regularly to learn to fear the Lord. The result of recurrently reading God's Law was that the king would better understand who God is and would learn more about how God expected him to live and behave. The passage also emphasizes the important role of obedience in learning the fear of the Lord. We seem not only to learn to fear the Lord by studying God's Word, and thus cognitively discovering truth about what God is like, but also reinforce that learning through obedience.

Deuteronomy 14:23 tells us that the fear of the Lord can be learned through worship. In this particular instance, it was the ritual of giving tithes and offerings that contributed to their learning to fear God, but the passage implies that we also can learn to fear God through worship. Certainly the celebration of Passover each year was designed to foster the remembrance of that great event in Israel's history and thus to remind the Israelites about God's great power and His faithfulness to the promise made to Abraham. The regular reflection on these events was meant to reinforce in the minds of the Israelites the reality of God's power and His commitment to His people. As a result of this reinforcement, the people were to commit themselves to a deeper trust in God and a more diligent obedience to His covenant. When the Israelites crossed the Jordan to enter the Promised Land for the first time, Joshua took twelve stones from the river and used them to make a monument at Gilgal. The purpose of the memorial was that when "Your children ask their fathers in times to come, 'What do these stones mean?' then you shall let your children know, 'Israel passed over this Jordan on dry ground'" (Josh. 4:21–22). Such monuments were meant to remind the Israelites of God's power and faithfulness.

A number of psalms are designed to do the same thing. Salvation history psalms such as 78, 105, 106, and 107 and the similar hymn found in Nehemiah 9 reflect on Israel's history to remind the people what God is like so as to motivate them to covenant faithfulness. Clearly, this focus on God's acts of deliverance and His faithfulness to His promises in the past is related to the themes of reflection and meditation that are common in the Psalms and elsewhere. What is taking place here reflects a perspective that characterizes Israel's understanding of the future. A common Hebrew word for the future is *'aharit,* a word that means literally "back or behind." Whereas we normally think of the future as that which is in front of us, the Hebrews thought of the future as that which was behind them, and their perspective makes sense if one thinks about it. We can see that which is in front of us but not what is behind our backs. In the same way, we can see where we have been, our past, but we cannot see the future and all the unknowns it contains. By natural analogy then, the future is "behind" us, for it is unknown and unseen.

Hans W. Wolff has pointed out, "According to this viewpoint man proceeds through time like a rower who moves into the future backwards; he reaches his goal by taking his bearings from what is visibly in front of him."[2] Thus, reflecting on and studying the works of God—both in history (the

---

2. Hans Walter Wolff, *Anthropology of the Old Testament,* trans. Margaret Kohl (Philadelphia, Fortress, 1974), 88.

salvation history psalms) and in the lives of individuals (the thanksgiving psalms)—provides not only concrete examples of what God is like and gives a firm basis for praising Him but also important datum points for orienting the believer while moving into an unseen and unknown future. The parallelism in Psalms 111 and 112 suggests that the person who fears the Lord is the one who studies and takes delight in God's works in the past. This person also delights in and obeys the Lord's commandments.

Obviously, the worship that teaches us to fear the Lord is not primarily performance or entertainment but rather focuses our attention on the Lord such as to bring us to a better understanding of God's nature, character, and activity. Such worship elevates God's reputation. As we reflect on God and what He does, we should come away from worship with a deeper awareness of who God is and what He desires from His people. Participation in such worship encourages obedience and thus teaches us to fear God.

As we noted earlier, an objective basis exists for the knowledge of God that produces the fear of the Lord. Kidner says that "the starting point [of the search] is revelation . . . ; its method is not one of free speculation, but of treasuring and exploring received teachings so as to penetrate to their principles."[3] Our understanding of who God is and what He is like must be based on God's revelation of Himself rather than on our opinions and wishes about Him. We do not have the option of picking and choosing certain parts of that revelation that we like while ignoring other parts that make us feel uncomfortable in our pluralistic and relativistic culture.

Israel's reflection on the mighty works of God began with Creation, and, if Scripture makes anything clear about God, it is that He is the sovereign Creator of all things, including us. Creation speaks volumes about God's great power. When He spoke, all things came into existence; nothing exists that God did not create. Creation also tells us something about God's great wisdom in that God was sufficiently wise to create a highly complex world in which everything works together coherently.

Sometimes I (Edward) try to create things, though never in the same sense that God created them. I have to start with material that is already in existence, and my projects are always on a much smaller scale than God's. Even so, I have major problems getting everything to work together smoothly. My wife and I recently bought a house that needs a lot of work. We have spent a great deal of time thinking about what we want to do, and we often

---

3. Kidner, *Proverbs*, 61.

are stymied by the problem of getting everything to function coherently. We can't put down a floor in one room because we may later move part of a wall, and that will create problems getting the floor to match in both rooms. We can't make a decision about what kind of flooring to put in the kitchen because the floors of two adjoining rooms must coordinate with the kitchen floor. We must get an expert opinion as to whether the hardwood floors in those rooms can be refinished before we can decide how to proceed with those floors. We can't take out the cabinets in the kitchen until we make decisions about replacing windows to avoid problems and extra expense later. From past experience with such projects, I am pretty sure that no matter how long we think about it and no matter what we do, we will later discover some things that we did not take into consideration when we made our plans. God, however, is so wise that He never has such problems, and He is sufficiently powerful always to accomplish whatever He desires to do.

Not only does Scripture make clear that God is the Creator but also that we are creatures. We are significant creatures, to be sure, because we are people made in God's image. God has designed us with significant rational abilities. We can think. We can discover truth about our world as we study it. We can relate to other people. God made us with the ability to perceive and enjoy beauty. God has given people the ability to create beautiful music and art. We are remarkable creatures because God designed us that way, and He gave us dominion over the rest of creation, as both Genesis 1 and Psalm 8 point out. But when all of that has been said, the awareness of our significance and worth in the created order does not change the fact that we are still creatures. I am finite, and I am fallen as well. In addition, and perhaps of even greater significance, is the fact that, as a creature, I am accountable to the Creator. Thus, while my allegiance to God makes sense because He is so much wiser and more powerful than I, it is also required because He is the one who created me, and I am His creature.

The fear of the Lord involves knowledge of who God is and who we are, and significant implications flow from so simple and obvious an idea. Think about what happened in the Garden. God told the man and the woman not to eat the fruit of one particular tree. Then the tempter gave the woman very different advice. He told her to eat the fruit and assured her that very desirable things would result if she did. The woman was confronted with two different sources of information, and as she struggled with what to do, she ended up deciding for herself what to do in this situation. Rather than living in the fear of the Lord and behaving as a creature who acknowledged that the Creator legitimately had authority over her (and that He was all-wise and all-knowing as well), she left the relationship of dependence on God for which she had been designed and chose to be autonomous and independent of God. The consequences were devastating for Adam and Eve and all of their descendants. Had she only functioned as a creature under the authority of the all-powerful and all-wise Creator of the universe, the result would have been far different.

The well-known verses in Proverbs 3 reflect exactly the same idea: "Trust in the LORD with all your heart, and do not lean on your own understanding. In all your ways acknowledge him, and he will make straight your paths. Be not wise in your own eyes; fear the LORD, and turn away from evil" (vv. 5–7). It will be much easier to put this exhortation into practice if we recognize who God is and who we are.

Blocher has said that the fear of the Lord is "the renouncing of autonomy, and trusting acknowledgment of the LORD at every step of one's practical or intellectual progress."[4] Kidner has said that the fear of the Lord is "a worshipping submission to the God of the covenant."[5] If we truly understand who God is and who we are, we cannot do less.

Something is rather perplexing, however, about the idea of the *fear* of the Lord. The term *fear* suggests being afraid and anticipating evil, failure, or other undesirable, disastrous, frightening developments, and we are uncomfortable associating such ominous things with God, even though we also recognize that fear can involve a profound reverence and a deeply respectful awe, and we correctly understand that this is what fearing God primarily involves. It seems clear from Scripture, however, that fearing God does not entirely exclude components of fright and terror. Exodus 20:18–21 describes the Israelites at the foot of Mount Sinai just before God revealed the Law to them. They had been told that God was present on the mountain and that any person or animal who touched the mountain would die. The mountain was covered with fog and smoke, the ground was shaking, fire was coming up from the top of the mountain, there was thunder, and there were sounds that the people associated with the presence of God. Imagine how you would have felt if you had been there. The text tells us that the

---

4. Henri Blocher, "The Fear of the LORD as the 'Principle' of Wisdom," *Tyndale Bulletin* 28 (1977): 18.

5. Kidner, *Proverbs*, 59.

result of this experience was that the people trembled with fear, and rightly so. The people understood something about the power and the holiness of God. They also sensed their own finiteness and their unworthiness in the presence of a holy, righteous God. I cannot imagine anyone being fully aware of those realities and not being afraid. Because the people at Mount Sinai were terrified, they decided that it might be wise to have Moses approach God and then bring God's message back to them. They did not want to risk having God speak to them directly because they were not sure that they would survive the experience. Moses told them not to be afraid, but no doubt that was easier said than done for most of them. Moses went on to tell them that God had revealed Himself to them in this way so they would fear Him and not commit sin.

Exodus 14:31 makes a similar point: "Israel saw the great power that the LORD used against the Egyptians, so the people feared the LORD, and they believed in the LORD and in his servant Moses." Proverbs 24:21 says, "Fear the LORD and the king," and this statement helps us understand how this works. Each year I mail my income tax forms to the IRS. I really do not like to do that, but I am always afraid not to do it. I am careful to observe speed limits, stop signs, and the like in part because I do not want to fall under the power of the law and suffer the consequences that might come from breaking it. According to Woodcock, fearing God and the king "means to respect their authority and to conform to their will."[6]

Certainly the awareness of human sinfulness and the knowledge that God judges wickedness would have contributed to the fear of the Lord in the Old Testament period. I (Edward) became a Christian when I was ten years old, and my decision was in response to a sermon about hell. That sermon scared the daylights out of me. I accepted Christ as my personal Savior to a large degree because I was terrified at the prospect of suffering in hell when I died. Understanding that God's holiness requires that sin be punished and that I was a sinner deserving of condemnation drove me to accept the gracious provision that God had made for my forgiveness through His Son.

Now although I might still be motivated occasionally by that kind of fear in my relationship with God, I would never describe my current relationship with Him primarily in terms of that kind of fear. The Old Testament concept of fearing God involves far more than that. As Deuteronomy

---

6. Eldon Woodcock, *Proverbs*, The Bible Study Commentary (Grand Rapids: Zondervan, 1988), 54.

10:12–13 says, "And now, Israel, what does the Lord your God require of you, but to fear the Lord your God, to walk in all his ways, to love him, to serve the Lord your God with all your heart and with all your soul, and to keep the commandments and statutes of the Lord." This passage makes clear that whatever the fear of God involves, it includes loving God, serving Him with all of our hearts, and keeping His commandments. Perhaps the relationship that comes closest to this is the relationship between a parent and a child. I can remember times when I did what my mother told me to do because of a fear of punishment, but far more often I did what she wanted me to do because I loved and respected her and because I recognized her authority over me.

So it should be in our relationship with God. As we learn about who God is, we recognize that God is more than a powerful and holy being who judges sin and evil. We also understand that He is "merciful and gracious, slow to anger, and abounding in steadfast love and faithfulness . . . forgiving iniquity and transgression and sin" (Exod. 34:6–7). As we realize how deeply and persistently He loves us, and as we experience His gracious provision for us, we come to appreciate His mercy, His faithfulness, and many other things about the God who created us and made us His children even at the cost of His Son. As we grow in the knowledge of God, what the Old Testament calls the fear of the Lord increases, as does our love for God.

The author of Psalm 130 relates the ideas of human sinfulness and forgiveness to the fear of the Lord in a useful way. He says in verse 3, "If you, O Lord, should mark iniquities, O Lord, who could stand?" He then goes on to add in verse 4, "But with you there is forgiveness, that you may be feared." Kidner notes that this verse "confirms the true sense of the 'fear of the Lord' in the Old Testament, dispelling any doubt that it means reverence and implies relationship. Servile fear would have been diminished, not increased, by forgiveness."[7]

The connection between the fear of the Lord and an intimate relationship with God is also apparent in Proverbs 2:5 and 9:10. In both instances, the parallelism in the verses equates the fear of the Lord with the knowledge of God. Proverbs chapter 2 has been emphasizing the need for diligence and persistence in the search for wisdom. As Toombs points out, "It appears that the search for wisdom, demanding as it is, does not lead di-

---

7. Derek Kidner, *Psalms 73–150,* vol. 14b of Tyndale Old Testament Commentaries (Downers Grove, Ill.: InterVarsity, 1975), 446.

rectly to wisdom, but to God. . . . The result of the search for wisdom is that strange admixture of love and awe . . . which the Old Testament knows as the 'fear of the Lord.' The end of the quest is also that intimate personal fellowship with the Eternal which is the 'knowledge of God.'"[8]

The fear of the Lord, which comes out of a clear understanding of who God is and what He is like, together with a clear understanding of who we are as human beings created by God, involves a full-orbed understanding about God that is informed by His revelation of Himself to people. Although attributes of God such as His power, majesty, and holiness are often related to the fear of the Lord, His kindness, compassion, and forgiveness are no less related to the concept.

One Must *Choose* to Fear the Lord

Proverbs 1:20–33 describes Wisdom's public invitation to respond to her and become wise. Whereas some people do accept her invitation, others reject her offer (1:24) and go their own way. At some point, however, they begin to experience the consequences of their folly, and they cry out to Wisdom for help. At that point, she refuses to help them. She tells them that they made their choice and now must accept the consequences. Wisdom explains in verses 29 and 30 that she is refusing to help them "because they hated knowledge and did not choose the fear of the LORD, [they] would have none of my counsel and despised all my reproof."

The decisions involved in choosing to fear the Lord might take many different forms. Certainly we must choose to study God's Word in a world where many different things are vying for our time. Sometimes the necessary choice might require choosing to do God's truth and obey Him in our business affairs even though it appears that such obedience will not contribute to a greater margin of profit. Sometimes the choice might involve rejecting tantalizing opportunities for immoral behavior. It might mean that I will be generous with someone in need even when it seems clear that my generosity will never be repaid by the one who receives it. Choosing the fear of the Lord will sometimes mean doing certain things simply because God says they are right. Certainly choosing to fear the Lord means that I

---

8. Lawrence Toombs, "Old Testament Theology and the Wisdom Literature," *Journal of Bible and Religion* 23 (1955): 194–95.

will be willing to admit that I am sometimes wrong and will accept correction from God and from others who confront me about my folly.

Recently, a former student told me that she had dated a boy in high school and really cared for the young man. He wanted to get married, and although she wanted to marry him, she wanted to finish college and begin to establish herself in her career before she got married. The fellow ended up marrying someone else, much to my student's distress. Several years later, she was still not over the loss, and the young man again appeared in her life. This time he told her the sad story of what a mistake he had made in marrying the other girl. He apologized for treating my former student the way he did and indicated how deeply he regretted breaking up with her. Later, he sent her a letter, essentially asking my friend to take him back (which would, of course, involve his divorcing his wife). My friend still cared for the man and really wanted to be married to him, but she knew that breaking up a marriage was not a thing that would please God. My friend chose to obey God's truth rather than do what she deeply desired to do.

Sometimes, choosing the fear of the Lord means doing what God declares is right despite enormous pressure to do otherwise. My friend's decision not to pursue a relationship with her former boyfriend illustrates the point made by Proverbs 8:13: "The fear of the LORD is hatred of evil." It is this same commitment to do what is right that characterized Job. In Job 1:8, God described Job to Satan as "a blameless and upright man, who fears God and turns away from evil." Choosing to fear God also means choosing to avoid the things that God declares to be evil.

Psalms 111 and 112 make another interesting point about the fear of the Lord. The former, a psalm about God, praises God both for who He is and for what He has done for His people. Psalm 112 is about the person who fears the Lord. The two psalms tell us that the person who fears the Lord obeys God and delights in His commandments. Psalm 111:2 tells us that the works of the Lord are great and that they are studied by all who delight in them. By recalling and reflecting on what God has done in the past—creation, redemption, deliverance of His people, His mercy, and His provision for His people—we come to appreciate more fully who God is, and that contributes to our fear of the Lord.

Psalm 111 describes God and tells us that *God is gracious and compassionate,* demonstrating those characteristics by providing for the needs of His people. It tells us that *God is faithful* to His covenant, and He demonstrated that quality by giving His people the land that He promised Abraham. It tells us that *God's righteousness endures forever.* Psalm 112 describes the person who fears God, and the same words that are used to describe God in Psalm 111 are used to describe the person who fears God in Psalm 112. The person who fears God and greatly delights in His commandments is *gracious and compassionate and righteous.* It also tells us that *His righteousness endures forever.* What we discover is that the person who fears God, who delights in His commandments and keeps them, and who diligently studies the works and words of God will begin to take on certain characteristics of God Himself. That person will become more like God. The two psalms, then, suggest that the fear of the Lord produces God-like character.

The Fear of the Lord and Obedience

The way in which several of the preceding verses connect obedience with the fear of the Lord makes it clear that obedience is both a mechanism by which the fear of the Lord is developed and an essential characteristic of the fear of the Lord. Deuteronomy 17:19 indicates that the king was to read a copy of the Law regularly so that he might learn the fear of the Lord by carefully observing all of the words of that Law. Both reading and obeying seem to contribute to the learning. The idea here is similar to the learning that takes place when a student begins to work math or science problems after hearing an explanation from a professor. In essence, it is the same kind of learning that takes place when a person begins to work in a profession by putting into practice the ideas learned earlier in a classroom.

The connection between obedience and the fear of the Lord is also apparent in Psalms 111 and 112. Psalm 112:1 describes the person who fears the Lord as the person who delights in His commandments. Psalm 111:10 says, "The fear of the LORD is the beginning of wisdom; all those who practice it have a good understanding." The antecedent of the pronoun *it* is not specified, but it most likely refers to the same commandments as were mentioned in Psalm 111:7 (His precepts) and again in 112:1 (His commandments). As Kraus notes on Psalm 111:10, "Fear of the Lord" in this verse "denotes obedience to the divine will."[9] Psalm 119, although not often mentioning the fear of the Lord, presents the same connection between

---

9. Hans-Joachim Kraus, *Psalms 60–150,* trans. Hilton C. Oswald (Minneapolis: Augsburg, 1989), 359.

delighting in the instruction of the Lord and obeying His commandments. Psalm 119:63 does equate those who fear the Lord with those who keep His precepts, while verse 79 equates those who know God's testimonies with those who fear Him.

Perhaps the most remarkable illustration of the connection between obedience and the fear of the Lord is found in the story of Abraham in Genesis 22. God tested Abraham by instructing him to offer his son as a sacrifice at the place that God would disclose to him. Abraham went to the mountain, took his son Isaac to the place where he was to build the altar, bound Isaac, placed him on top of the wood on the altar, and raised the knife, ready to kill his only son. At that point, God intervened in the test, and the angel of the Lord called to Abraham from heaven and said, "Do not lay your hand on the boy or do anything to him, for now I know that you fear God, seeing you have not withheld your son, your only son, from me" (Gen. 22:12). The fear of the Lord is demonstrated through obedience to the Lord. Certainly the omniscient God knew Abraham's heart and mind, but it was through obedience that Abraham demonstrated his fear of the Lord.

The New Testament relates Abraham's obedience to his faith. Hebrews 11:17 says, "By faith Abraham, when he was tested, offered up Isaac, and he who had received the promises was in the act of offering up his only son." When we consider the elements that the Old Testament connects with the fear of the Lord, it becomes apparent that significant parallels exist between what the Old Testament calls fear of the Lord and what the New Testament refers to as faith. Blocher suggests that one reason the fear of the Lord is only rarely mentioned in the New Testament is that "generally speaking, Old Testament fear becomes New Testament faith."[10] Leupold says, "The deep taproot of godly living is the fear of the Lord, which as has been often remarked, is almost the equivalent of faith and trust in God."[11]

As Hoekema points out, the Reformers recognized several aspects of biblical faith. First, it involves knowledge. "We cannot have faith in someone of whom we know nothing or about whom we know the wrong things."[12] Biblical faith, as is the case with the fear of the Lord, is based on knowledge

---

10. Blocher, "The Fear of the LORD as the 'Principle' of Wisdom," 27.
11. H. C. Leupold, *The Exposition of the Book of Psalms* (Grand Rapids: Baker, 1969), 785.
12. Anthony Hoekema, *Saved by Grace* (Grand Rapids: Eerdmans, 1989), 142.

about God and His works as well as on knowledge about ourselves. In both cases, this knowledge results from God's revelation of Himself to us. The Reformers also noted that biblical faith involves an aspect of assent, which, according to Hoekema, means "that activity by which we firmly accept the teachings of God's Word as true."[13] Finally, faith involves trust, and that trust includes obedience, a principle that many passages in Scripture make clear. Hebrews 3:18–19 equates the sin and disobedience of the people who died in the wilderness with their unbelief. The common characteristic of the heroes of faith described in Hebrews 11 is that they obeyed God in situations where it seemed unlikely that they could succeed by doing so. James also insists on the obedient character of faith.

The knowledge with which the fear of God begins comes from God, and when we are confronted with that understanding about God and ourselves, we must acknowledge that it is true. We must then respond to that knowledge in obedience, and as a result of that encounter with the God who created all things, we come to a deeper knowledge of both God and reality. As Calvin states, "The first step in true knowledge is taken, when we reverently embrace the testimony which God has been pleased therein to give of himself. For not only does faith . . . but all correct knowledge of God originate[s] in obedience."[14] To fear the Lord is to commit oneself to Him in faith, and this faith includes the believer's obedience, loyalty, and love. Apart from this commitment, any effort to acquire wisdom rests on an unstable foundation and is doomed to ultimate failure. As the prophet Jeremiah puts it, "Thus says the LORD: 'Let not the wise man boast in his wisdom, let not the mighty man boast in his might, let not the rich man boast in his riches, but let him who boasts boast in this, that he understands and knows me, that I am the LORD who practices steadfast love, justice, and righteousness in the earth. For in these things I delight'" (Jer. 9:23–24). This is a description of the ideal creature, one who fears, knows, and loves the Lord.

---

13. Ibid.
14. John Calvin, *Institutes of the Christian Religion,* trans. Henry Beveridge (Grand Rapids: Eerdmans, 1962). Calvin emphasized in this section the priority of Scripture as the mechanism through which this knowledge comes.

Questions for Thought and Reflection

1. Fear can evoke three different responses: avoidance, defiance, and obedience. When you hear the word *fear,* which of these three responses does your mind automatically attach to it? And which of these three responses do you suppose God desires from you when you fear Him? If the two responses you named are different, how will you respond in a way that pleases God? Have you ever loved and feared the same person? Were you able to do both at the same time?

2. Andy is four years old and lives with his parents in a suburban neighborhood. The people across the street have something in their yard that strongly attracts Andy, so he crosses the street whenever he can. Both of his parents have explained to him clearly and in detail the dangers of traffic, but their efforts have made no difference in his behavior. His father does not like the idea of corporal punishment, but finally, out of desperation, he spanks the child. It takes more than one spanking, but finally Andy stays out of the street most of the time. How is this tale a parable of God's interaction with His people?

3. In preparing to move your family to another city, you search for a job and come up with two offers. One is a well-paying job with a company that takes advantage of the elderly and infirm to make large profits. A second job offer is with a firm that is very helpful to its clients but pays modestly. If you take the first offer, you will be able to buy a house that will make life much easier for your spouse and children. If you take the second one, you will have to rent a modest apartment with no yard. Which job will you take? Explain the reasons for your choice.

Chapter Seven

SCRIPTURE AND SPIRITUAL TRANSFORMATION

For Israel, the time of wandering in the desert between the Exodus from Egypt and their entrance into the Promised Land of Canaan constituted a paradigmatic example of their failure and unbelief. A number of biblical passages (such as Pss. 78; 95; 106; Neh. 9; Heb. 3:7–4:7) make clear that the people of God are, in their journey of faith, to avoid the example of those who left Egypt but failed to enter into Canaan. Although several specific events, such as those at Meribah and Massah, epitomize the failures of the wilderness generation, what happened at Kadesh-barnea was in many ways the defining event in their experience.

When the Israelites reached the springs at Kadesh-barnea, they were just south of their destination in Canaan. From there, Moses sent out spies to gather essential intelligence as they prepared to enter the land that God had promised to Abraham more than four centuries earlier. As the twelve spies brought back their reports, they agreed on one point: Canaan was a very desirable place—truly a land flowing with milk and honey. Nevertheless, they would face some problems in taking the land because of the military superiority of the people who lived there. To make matters worse, some of the Canaanites were giants.

The people knew of the promise of God to their forefathers. The four-hundred-year-old mummy of Joseph that they were carrying with them for burial in Canaan was a reminder of Joseph's confidence in God's promise (see Gen. 50:24–26; Exod. 13:19; Josh. 24:32). Caleb, supported by Moses and Joshua, was confident that God would give them victory over the

Canaanites. He said, "Let us go up at once and occupy it, for we are well able to overcome it" (Num. 13:30). As the rest of the Israelites assessed the situation, however, they rejected Caleb's recommendation and sided with the other spies who said, "We are not able to go up against the people, for they are stronger than we are" (Num. 13:31). Despite the insistence of Moses, Joshua, and Caleb that the majority decision amounted to rebellion against the Lord and an act of unbelief, the people chose not to attempt to take the land at that time. The result was that none of the generation involved in the decision was allowed to enter the land that God had promised to Abraham's descendants.

The Bible's explanation for the radical difference between Caleb's response and that of the other spies is neither precisely theological nor psychological. Unlike the other Israelites who would not be allowed to enter Canaan, Caleb would enter it, and his descendants would possess it because, as Numbers 14:24 puts it, "my servant Caleb, . . . has a different spirit and has followed me fully." Although scholars debate the exact nuance of the Hebrew word translated *spirit,* it here likely refers to that which makes a person a living, dynamic, functioning human being. The point of the passage is that something in Caleb made him the person he was, and that caused him to respond in a way that was different from the way most of the Israelites responded. What that something was is undefined in the biblical text. The Bible simply recognizes that there was an internal difference between Caleb and those who chose not to invade Canaan. As Van Pelt, Kaiser, and Block point out, "To speak of one's *rûaḥ* [spirit] is to discuss his/her character, nature, condition."[1]

They further note that in twenty-one instances the Hebrew word *rûaḥ* is found in parallel with the Hebrew word *leb/lebab,* normally translated "heart," the parallelism indicating that the two words, although not necessarily exact synonyms, can be functional equivalents. Although in most cases the two words refer to entirely different things, the overlap in the semantic range of the two words here seems to result from similar human functions (especially intellectual or volitional ones) being attributed to both spirit and heart. As Van Pelt, Kaiser, and Block suggest, the word *rûaḥ* refers to something that is invisible. It is known, however, primarily from the effect it has on the visible

---

1. Miles V. Van Pelt, Walter C. Kaiser Jr., and Daniel I. Block, *The New International Dictionary of Old Testament Theology and Exegesis,* ed. Willem A. VanGemeren (Grand Rapids: Zondervan, 1997), 3:1074.

world—in this case, the effect it has on human function. Similarly, the heart, the most frequently used anthropological term in the Old Testament, is the core of a person's being. It is what controls virtually all human functions. Again, this core cannot be seen, but its effect on human function is evident. Thus, the two words, although not necessarily precise synonyms, can be used as functional equivalents in the current context.

The term *heart* illustrates the Old Testament perspective well. The heart controls virtually all human functions, but it is especially the source of intellectual activity, and, according to Wolff, this is the most common use of *heart* in the Old Testament. He notes, "Heart in Hebrew describes the seat and function of the reason. It includes everything that we ascribe to the head and the brain—power of perception, reason, understanding, insight, consciousness, memory, knowledge, reflection, judgment, sense of direction, discernment."[2] It is also the seat of such feelings and emotions as mood, fear and courage, desires and longings, and a variety of impulses.[3] The heart is where decisions are made and where the conscience functions (1 Sam. 24:6).

According to some passages, the heart even controls the physical functioning of a person. When Abigail told Nabal what she had done for David and his men, Nabal was very upset, and "his heart died within him, and he became as a stone" (1 Sam. 25:37). But, according to the text, Nabal actually died ten days later, most likely of a stroke that had initially paralyzed him. As Wolfe says, "The ancient narrator therefore thought of the heart here as a central organ which made it possible for the limbs to move."[4]

The heart determines who a person is. It is like a computer that controls a system. It lies deep within a person and is generally hidden to others. God wanted a certain kind of person to replace Saul as king; He wanted someone who would obey Him and lead the people according to His will and covenant. Thus, the choice had to be made not on the basis of the kinds of external criteria that Samuel could discern but on the basis of the kind of heart the man had, and only God has access to those inner depths of an individual (1 Sam. 16:7).

The heart is the focus of the kind of devotion that God desires from His

---

2. Hans Walter Wolff, *Anthropology of the Old Testament,* trans. Margaret Kohl (Philadelphia: Fortress, 1974), 51.
3. For a convenient survey of the evidence, see Ibid., 44–46.
4. Ibid., 41.

people. Deuteronomy 6:5 calls Israel to "love the LORD your God with all your heart." In Deuteronomy 10:12, God says to Israel, "What does the LORD your God require of you, but to fear the LORD your God, to walk in all his ways, to love him, to serve the LORD your God with all your heart and with all your soul." As Wolff points out, what is in view here is devotion to God that involves "the conscious devotion of the will."[5] Solomon's desire for Israel was that their hearts would be completely devoted to the Lord (1 Kings 8:61), and as the context makes clear, the desire was for "complete and unconditional obedience."[6]

Many other Old Testament passages make clear that Yahweh desired neither selective obedience nor an external obedience that came out of obligation. Instead, He wanted an obedience that came from within, that is, from the heart (Pss. 40:6–10;[7] 51:6, 16; Rom. 6:17). Isaiah records the Lord's harsh criticism of those who "draw near with their mouth and honor me with their lips, while their hearts are far from me, and their fear of me is a commandment taught by men" (Isa. 29:13), and Jesus directed these same words against some of the religious leaders of His day (Matt. 15:8).

The idea is expressed interestingly both in the Torah and by Jeremiah. To begin with the Torah, Deuteronomy 10:16 exhorts the people of Israel, "Circumcise therefore the foreskin of your heart, and be no longer stubborn,"[8] and Leviticus 26:41 warns that Israel's stubborn refusal to obey God's covenant (described in terms of their uncircumcised hearts) will result in God's judgment and their banishment from the land. God will, however, return them to the land "if then their uncircumcised heart is humbled." In Deuteronomy's recounting of the covenant blessings and curses, Israel is told that, after they have been banished from the land because of persistent disobedience, and assuming that they then repent, God will gather them and restore them to the land. Deuteronomy 30:6 says that "the LORD your God will circumcise your heart . . . so that you will love the LORD your God with all your heart and with all your soul." Jeremiah indicates that physical

---

5. Ibid., 53.
6. Ibid.
7. Peter Craigie seems to limit the application of this psalm to the king (*Psalms 1–50,* Word Biblical Commentary [Waco: Word, 1983], 314–17). Even if he is correct in this—and I disagree with his conclusion—there are numerous other passages that suggest that it was obedience from the heart that God always desired from His people.
8. See also Jeremiah 4:4.

circumcision without the circumcision of the heart leaves the people of Judah no different than their uncircumcised neighbors. Jeremiah 9:25–26 says that Judah will be punished along with their uncircumcised neighbors. God says, "I will punish all those who are circumcised merely in the flesh . . . all these nations are uncircumcised, and all the house of Israel is uncircumcised in heart." Stephen understood the actions of his fellow Israelites in precisely these terms in Acts 7:51. He says, "You stiff-necked people, uncircumcised in heart and ears, you always resist the Holy Spirit. As your fathers did, so do you."

Both Jeremiah and Ezekiel, speaking in the context of Judah's exile for their failure to keep the covenant, affirm the need for an internal transformation that will change these disobedient people into a people committed to obedience to God's will and God's order. Ezekiel indicates that, even though God has sent them into exile, when they repent of their idolatry, God will restore them. In Ezekiel 36:26–27, God says, "I will give you a new heart, and a new spirit I will put within you. And I will remove the heart of stone from your flesh and give you a heart of flesh. And I will put my Spirit within you, and cause you to walk in my statutes." Jeremiah's treatment of the new covenant promise is similar. God says, "I will put my law within them, and I will write it on their hearts" (Jer. 31:33). Although these passages deal with Israel corporately rather than individually, Psalms 37:31 and 40:8 suggest that some individual Israelites (those who responded to God by faith) were already experiencing some of the blessings that Jeremiah and Ezekiel anticipated for the corporate entity of the people of God.

Clearly, the heart has great relevance for Old Testament anthropology. As Wolff concludes,

> We can see that the spectrum of meaning of this most frequent anthropological term is a particularly broad one. But though it undoubtedly embraces the whole range of the physical, the emotional and the intellectual, as well as the functions of the will, yet we must clearly hold on to the fact that the Bible primarily views the heart as the center of the consciously living man. The essential characteristic that, broadly speaking, dominates the concept is that the heart is called to reason, and especially to hear the word of God.[9]

---

9. Wolff, *Anthropology,* 55.

As he further notes, "The essential activities of the human heart are in the Bible mental and spiritual in kind."[10] The Old Testament clearly attributes a central role to the heart in understanding and responding to God.

In light of the theological purposes of Scripture, perhaps one can expect that the Bible's discussions of the heart would focus on the role of the heart in responding to God's truth, but Scripture also recognizes the broad range of human function embraced by that term. Proverbs 4:23 says that from the heart are "the outgoings" of life, and most commentators understand the metaphor as that of a spring out of which life flows. Thus, the gifts and abilities that God has designed into every human being flow from the heart, and, given the broad range of human function that the term encompasses, this would include the full range of intellectual and artistic abilities as well as attitudinal qualities such as determination, commitment to a task, discipline, or even remarkable interpersonal skills. These qualities are part of God's design of each individual and are what, in an important sense, make people what they are.

Although the Old Testament authors had never developed the idea of human sinfulness in the comprehensive way that Paul was to do in the New Testament, many of the passages cited earlier make clear that they saw human sinfulness and rebellion as residing in the heart. The prophet Jeremiah preached to a group of people who refused to listen to his message and repent, and they rejected his message in spite of the fact that their disobedience to God often resulted in God's judgment.

Jeremiah reflects on Judah's disobedience regularly in the early chapters of his book. In chapter 8, he compares the logic of their behavior to a person who falls down and then just lies there, refusing to get up, or to a person who takes the wrong road, realizes his mistake, and yet continues on that wrong road. As Kidner says, "In matters spiritual and moral we act with perversity which is quite unlike our common sense at other levels. . . . Physically, if we fall we pick ourselves up; if we miss the way we turn back. But spiritually, we can be incorrigible."[11] In chapter 17, Jeremiah distinguishes the person who trusts in the Lord from the person who "trusts in man, who depends on flesh for his strength" (v. 5 NIV). The one flourishes like a deeply rooted tree and is unaffected by drought, whereas the other is like a bush in the desert that barely

---

10. Ibid., 44.
11. Derek Kidner, *The Message of Jeremiah,* The Bible Speaks Today (Downers Grove, Ill.: InterVarsity, 1987), 52.

survives. As the prophet reflects on the stark contrast between the two, he realizes that the problem involves the people's hearts. As Jeremiah phrases it in 17:9, "The heart is deceitful above all things, and desperately sick." Although Bruggemann might be right in his comment that verse 9 "is not carefully formulated theology,"[12] Jeremiah clearly recognized that the problem he observed among people was much more fundamental than simply the rationality of choices based on their outcomes. He recognized that the source of the problem lay at the very core of man's being.[13]

Dallas Willard has described the problem in these terms: "The condition of normal human life is one where the inner resources of the person are weakened or dead and where the factors of human life do not interrelate as they were intended by their nature to do. . . . It is not that we are wrong, but that our inner components are not 'hooked up' correctly any longer. The wires are crossed, as it were. . . . Our thinking, our feeling, our very bodily dispositions are defective and connected wrongly with reference to life as a whole."[14]

Daniel Estes has suggested that wisdom is "skill in living according to Yahweh's order,"[15] but a number of factors work against our success in this. For one thing, we are limited in our ability to understand God's order; as both Job and Ecclesiastes make clear, no matter how hard we try, we understand only the fringes of that order. We live in a fallen world, and our damaged environment discourages us from living according to God's order. Finally, as Jeremiah and many other biblical authors recognized, we have been affected by sin in the very core of our being, with the result being that, in both our understanding and our desires, we incline toward rebellion and folly rather than wisdom, obedience to God, and righteousness. We are unable to organize in a coherent and integrated way the human faculties that are a part of God's design. Wisdom plays a central role in restoring God's order, in both the individual and society.

---

12. Walter Bruggemann, *A Commentary on Jeremiah* (Grand Rapids: Eerdmans, 1998), 160.
13. It hardly seems to be a coincidence that Jeremiah thinks of the solution to the problem in the terms that he does in chapter 31. The solution would involve a new covenant in which God will write His Law within His people; He will write it on their hearts.
14. Dallas Willard, "Spiritual Disciplines, Spiritual Formation, and the Restoration of the Soul," *Journal of Psychology and Theology* 26 (1998): 104–5.
15. Daniel Estes, *Hear, My Son,* New Studies in Biblical Theology (Grand Rapids: Eerdmans, 1997), 26.

The early chapters of Proverbs indicate that wisdom has the power to transform the heart of a person and to enable one to renounce folly and move toward a life that is consistent with Yahweh's order. Proverbs 1:7 and 9:10 make clear that the quest envisioned here begins with faith (i.e., fear of the Lord) and then persists in that same dependence on God (e.g., Prov. 3:5–7). At the same time, the wisdom that moves us toward God's order comes from a variety of sources, including nature ("Go to the ant!" Prov. 6:6–8), parents, the traditional wisdom of the community, life experience, and God's special revelation of Himself to His people in Scripture.[16]

These early chapters of Proverbs view the heart as something very much like a computer that controls a system, and they recognize that the way this computer-like entity is programmed determines how it controls the system. Thus, Proverbs 4:23 warns the disciple to guard the heart carefully, presumably to keep out bad ideas, values, and behaviors such as those suggested by sinners (1:10–19), evil men and women (2:12–22), the adulteress (chapters 5–7), or even self-deception (3:5–7). At the same time, it exhorts the disciple to accept the parent's instruction (1:8–9; 3:1–4; 4:1–27; 7:24–27) and to diligently seek and embrace wisdom (3:13–26; 4:5–9; 8:1–36; 9:1–12). When wisdom enters the disciple's heart, he is delivered from the negative consequences of folly (2:10–22). When the disciple seeks diligently after wisdom, loves it, values it, and keeps it within his heart (4:5–27), he begins to move toward the enjoyment of the pleasant benefits of living according to God's order.

Proverbs 3:13 speaks of the blessedness of the person who finds wisdom and gets understanding. The poem ends in 3:18, using a verb formed from the same Hebrew root as the word translated "blessed" in verse 13. By beginning and ending the poem thus, the author identifies both the desired outcome—blessed/happy/fortunate—and the way the outcome is achieved—by finding wisdom and holding fast to it. Proverbs 3:19–20 then indicate that God by wisdom and understanding created the heavens and earth. As Fritch says, "The purpose of vss. 19–20 is to show that the wisdom which directs human life and brings such bountiful blessings

---

16. David Atkinson says, "The summons to hear Wisdom is really a summons to hear God. The hearers are called to discern God's presence in the world and give attention to it, not only in special times, or when God is, so to speak, 'public,' but at all times, even when God is hidden" (*The Message of Proverbs* [Downers Grove, Ill.: InterVarsity, 1996], 33).

is the same wisdom by which God created the heavens and the earth. He who surrenders himself to the ways of wisdom will therefore find himself in harmony with the world around him."[17] According to Proverbs 8:32–36, the person who lives according to wisdom "finds life and obtains favor from the LORD." Although wisdom includes what human beings can discover about God's order through general revelation, the value of Scripture is not thereby reduced, for it plays a vital and unique role in helping us understand that order. In Scripture, God has revealed truths that people could never discover independently or about which they could never be certain apart from Scripture.

The Benefits of Living According to God's Order

Psalms 1, 19, and 119 are wisdom psalms that focus on the Word of God, presenting different aspects of how that instruction benefits God's people and how those benefits can become a reality for the disciple. Although the blessings noted in these psalms belong primarily in the realm of the spiritual or emotional, there are some indications that the benefits offered go beyond these categories. The metaphor of the tree in Psalm 1 suggests a vitality that extends to every area of life, and the statement made by the psalmist in verse 3, "in all that he does, he prospers," indicates that point as well.

Two of the expressions used in Psalm 19 also allude to blessings that encompass all of life. The effect of God's instruction in 19:7 is that it "restores life." Whereas the expression is often translated "restoring the soul," the use of the idiom elsewhere suggests that this effect involves more than most people understand by the word *soul*. The expression is used in 1 Kings 17:21 of restoring the life of a widow's dead child. It is used in Psalm 35:17 of the relief that comes when one is rescued from those who are attacking relentlessly. The expression is used in Ruth 4:15 of the emotionally energizing effect of a grandson's birth on Naomi, a woman who had been beaten down by the discouraging rigors of life. Similarly, the expression is used in Lamentations 1:16 of the encouraging effect of a comforter on those in despair during a long siege that had left them with no resources or hope. Finally, in Job 33:30, the term is used of the effect of God's discipline in

---

17. Charles Fritsch, "The Book of Proverbs," vol. 4 of *The Interpreter's Bible* (Nashville: Abingdon, 1955), 804.

bringing a wayward person back from the brink of destruction into the fullness of life lived according to wisdom. The expression suggests that God's instruction, welcomed and applied, results in blessings that affect the whole person. Both emotional and physical well-being are nourished by God's instruction.

A second expression in Psalm 19 suggests a similar conclusion. Verse 8 tells us that the commandment of the Lord "enlightens the eyes." The use of this expression elsewhere in the Old Testament suggests that the blessing involves something different than illumination. As Psalm 13:3 makes clear, "enlightening the eyes" means "to give life" or "allow to live." It is the opposite of sleeping in death. The expression is used in Ezra 9:8 to describe the revitalization of people set free from bondage and oppression. An illustration of what is described by the term is provided in 1 Samuel 14:27–29. Jonathan is exhausted from an all-night battle against the Philistines and sees honey in a log. He eats some of it, and "his eyes brightened" (NASB and NIV). The words describe the energizing and invigorating effect of honey on a person who is weary from lack of sleep and great exertion. As Sarna notes, this expression "does not refer to intellectual enlightenment, but rather to revitalization of physical vigor."[18]

The restoration of life is the theme of several verses in Psalm 119, although the psalmist uses an expression different from those noted earlier from Psalm 19. This word means "to cause to live" and is used in several different contexts. Often, it describes the restoration of life and vitality that accompanies deliverance from a threat, such as persecution or illness (e.g., Ps. 119:25, 88, 107, 149, 154, 156, 159). In a few cases (vv. 37, 40, and perhaps 93), it is the "very keeping of God's law that is restorative and life giving,"[19] and this idea is also affirmed elsewhere in the Bible. Proverbs 4:4 says, "Let your heart hold fast my words; keep my commandments, and live." Deuteronomy 30:15–20 also relates life to loving God and keeping His commandments. The Old Testament recognizes that life is more than simply the opposite of physical death. Life in its fullest sense is experienced in a right relationship with God (i.e., in loving God and obeying His commandments). Only through faith and obedience do people experience life as it was meant to be. Certainly a part of what Deuteronomy 30 has in view is

---

18. Nahum Sarna, *On the Book of Psalms* (New York: Shocken, 1993), 86.
19. Derek Kidner, *Psalms 73–150*, vol. 14b of Tyndale Old Testament Commentaries (Downers Grove, Ill.: InterVarsity, 1975), 421.

the enjoyment of the blessings of the covenant in the Promised Land. But by identifying Deuteronomy 6:5 as the Great Commandment, Jesus seems to make clear that loving God and obeying Him result in life, not only under the Mosaic covenant but also today. This is a timeless principle reflecting the order that God has designed into the world. Obeying God's instruction is an essential element in living life as it was meant to be. God's Word, when embraced by faith, is restorative and life-giving in every age.

In addition to these broad descriptions of the blessings that God's revelation is designed to produce, these psalms also identify the blessings in more specific terms. Among the benefits are knowledge, understanding, or insight. Psalm 19:7 says, "The testimony of the LORD . . . [makes] wise the simple." The simple person is a well-known character, with almost all of the occurrences of the word being found in the Wisdom Literature. This is not a person who is lacking intellectual ability; rather, he is naive and uninformed. Sarna says that this is a person "who is wholly inexperienced in the ways of the world, whose moral consciousness is underdeveloped, and who, through . . . ignorance, lacks the critical ability to weigh ethical issues and to make prudent decisions."[20] Fortunately, this person can, by wisdom, be delivered from his naiveté and become wise. As has been noted, fallen human beings are limited in their understanding. But God's revelation in Scripture can instruct those who are naive—whether as a result of finitude, fallenness, or simply lack of experience in the world—and make them wise. As Psalm 119:130 says, "The unfolding of your words gives light; it imparts understanding to the simple."

As Kidner points out, verses like 119:105 ("Your word is a lamp to my feet and a light to my path") make apparent the practical nature of the knowledge. He says that "this is light to walk by, not to bask in."[21] Whereas knowledge is imparted through the revelation, the real goal of the instruction is skills in faith. The idea is similar to that found in Deuteronomy 17, where the king is instructed to make a copy of the Law for himself. He is to read that instruction "that he may learn to fear the LORD his God by keeping all the words of this law" (Deut. 17:19). The knowledge gained from God's truth warns the disciple (Ps. 19:11). It helps him avoid sin and keep his life pure (119:9, 11), and it allows him to identify and reject what is false (119:29, 104, 128). The author of Psalm 19 prays that he may be acquitted of hidden

---

20. Sarna, *On the Book of Psalms*, 85.
21. Kidner, *Psalms 73–150*, 421.

faults (v. 12), and God's instruction is essential in illuminating such faults. As Kidner notes, "A fault may be hidden not because it is too small to see, but because it is too characteristic to register."[22] The knowledge gained from God's revelation in Scripture enables the disciple to remain on the right path despite pressure from others (vv. 21–24, 42), and even in the presence of dissenting opinions from "experts" (vv. 97–100).

Many of the benefits extolled by the psalmist involve the emotional or psychological aspects of life. The psalmist sees God's revelation as a source of strength and comfort in times of affliction and grief (vv. 28, 50, 52, 76), and this is the reason for the psalmist's hope (vv. 49–50, 166). This hope is based on the faithfulness of God (vv. 89–93) and the knowledge that God can be trusted to do what He says. Misplaced trust can leave one embarrassed or disappointed when the person trusted fails to fulfill a promise. The Old Testament commonly describes that situation using a Hebrew word that means literally "to have a red face," a term that the prophets used often to describe the end result of trusting idols or foreign alliances. In contrast to those who trust idols or human resources, those who depend on God will not be left with a red face because God does not fail to do what He promises. As Isaiah 45:16–17 puts it, "They will be put to shame and even humiliated, all of them; the manufacturers of idols will go away together in humiliation. Israel has been saved by the LORD with an everlasting salvation; You will not be put to shame or humiliated to all eternity" (NASB). History attests to God's faithfulness, as is clear in Psalm 25:2–3: "O my God, in you I trust; let me not be put to shame; let not my enemies exult over me. Indeed, none who wait for you shall be put to shame; they shall be ashamed who are wantonly treacherous." This awareness of God's faithfulness in the past, nourished by God's Word, gives the psalmist hope in the midst of difficulty. It is of this promise that the psalmist reminds God throughout Psalm 119 (vv. 31, 46, 116).

God's instruction brings joy and delight to the disciple, as Psalms 19 and 119 make clear. He finds God's words sweeter than honey (19:10; 119:103). They are better to him than gold and silver (19:10; 119:14, 72, 162). Undoubtedly, many reasons exist for the disciple to find delight in God's truth. As we noted earlier, God's instruction is life-giving and energizing to the person who embraces it. It gives comfort and guidance that keeps a person from harm. God's Word, received by faith, nourishes the intimacy with God

---

22. Ibid., 100.

that is the prerequisite for life as it was meant to be (Ps. 25:14 and numerous New Testament passages). The early chapters of Proverbs make clear that the search for wisdom will produce many benefits, and the fruits produced through this search likely will encourage further pursuit because most people will repeat a behavior that brings pleasure. Thus, the delight produced through embracing wisdom motivates the further pursuit of it.

The psalmist sees God's Law in terms that differ greatly from the way most Christians see God's law today. Most people think of words such as *restrictive*, *oppressive*, and *limiting* when they think of law. The psalmist sees God's instruction not as confining or narrow, but rather, as in 119:45, it brings him out into a broad place. As Davidson says, "What is remarkable about this section [of the psalm] are the words used to describe the psalmist's attitude to and response to Torah; 'liberty,' 'freedom' (v. 45), 'delight' or 'joy,' and the repeated 'love' (vv. 47–48). These are not words that you find in the context of a harsh legalism. They are words which the New Testament uses again and again to describe the Christian's relationship with and response to Christ."[23] Kidner writes that what we see in Psalm 119 is "true piety: a love for God not desiccated by study, but refreshed, informed and nourished by it."[24]

Several verses in these psalms indicate that a significant benefit of God's instruction is that it delivers the disciple from sin (119:11) and unrighteousness (119:3). God's Word helps a young man to keep his way pure (119:9), and these verses may provide significant insight into the psalmist's perspective. Most people today see freedom in terms of being able to do whatever they please. The biblical authors seem typically to begin at a different place, a place that more accurately reflects the way God created the world to work. The biblical perspective on freedom begins with the recognition that people are in bondage to sin. True freedom means that we are delivered from our bondage to sin and are given the freedom of living the way God intended His people to live. That way is presented to us in God's Word. Thus, the psalmist sees the Law as liberating, not restrictive. God alone has the power to free us from our bondage, and His instruction in Scripture shows us how life was meant to be lived. The psalmist sees obedience to God's Law as an agent of grace rather than something that stands in opposition to it.

Scripture plays a critical role in transforming the heart because it reveals

---

23. Robert Davidson, *The Vitality of Worship* (Grand Rapids: Eerdmans, 1998), 394.
24. Kidner, *Psalms 73–150*, 419.

to the disciple much about God's order. Transformation is brought about when a person responds, through faith, to God's revelation by applying it to life and then persists in that obedience over the course of one's life. The mechanism for transformation seems similar to that described by Paul in Philippians 2:12–13, where he tells believers to "work out your own salvation with fear and trembling, for it is God who works in you, both to will and to work for his good pleasure." An important outcome of this obedience of faith and the work of God that affects it is an increase in the disciple's desire for God, His truth, and His order. And this is the delight in God's instruction that, according to Psalm 1, is the key to the blessed disciple's success and prosperity.

Although Caleb and Joshua had far less of God's special revelation than we have today, it nonetheless seems that it was their understanding of God and His promises, as received through the special revelation that they did have, that gave them the faith to stand firmly opposed to the majority report at Kadesh-barnea. That same faith in God and the truth of His promises enabled them to lead the successful conquest of Canaan some forty years later. As they were ready to begin that conquest, the Lord said to Joshua, "This Book of the Law shall not depart from your mouth, but you shall meditate on it day and night, so that you may be careful to do according to all that is written in it. For then you will make your way prosperous, and then you will have good success . . . for the LORD your God is with you wherever you go" (Josh. 1:8–9). That this was a new concept to Joshua and Caleb is highly unlikely. Rather, it was a practice that was characteristic of these individuals and a practice that, no doubt, explains the Lord's description of Caleb: "But my servant Caleb, . . . has a different spirit and has followed me fully" (Num. 14:24). It is always the obedience of faith, as informed by God's special revelation, that transforms people and changes them into those in whom God takes delight.

Questions for Thought and Reflection

1. Can you honestly say that, if you had been with the Israelites at Kadesh-barnea and had known only what they knew at that time, you would have supported Caleb? Would you have remained unimpressed by the factual reports of fortified cities, soldiers renowned for their fighting abilities (the Anakim), and warriors of

gigantic size? Given the choice of attacking such a stronghold or to "let sleeping dogs lie," would the Lord's promise of success embolden you enough to do something that has all of the visible signs of your failure and your family's destruction? Or could it be said of you, as the Lord said of Caleb, that you have a different spirit, one that is more pleasing to God? If not, what do you suppose you can do about your predicament?

2. You have read Derek Kidner's comment, "A fault may be hidden not because it is too small to see, but because it is too characteristic to register." What kinds of faults in people are too characteristic of our society to attract notice? Do you have any acquaintances who seem blind to such weaknesses in themselves? Does this characteristic apply to you?

3. Jesus said, "Be wise as serpents and innocent as doves" (Matt. 10:16b). How do you understand this command? In what sense are serpents "wise"? How can one be wise and innocent at the same time? Do you know anyone who fits this description?

Chapter Eight

MEDITATION AS A MECHANISM FOR GROWTH

Despite the fact that I (Edward) have taught Hebrew and Old Testament for many years and would never think of doing a serious study of an Old Testament passage without carefully studying it in the original language, I have never developed real fluency in any language other than English. Although I have mastered the grammar and basic vocabulary of several languages, I could never hold an easy and sustained conversation in any of them. A language learner can apprehend many things about grammar, syntax, and vocabulary, and can even read a lot of literature written in the language, without becoming fully fluent. To move to that next level in terms of proficiency, one normally must spend time totally immersed in that language. Living where all one hears is the language, where one must speak the language if one is to communicate, produces fluency. The Bible suggests that a similar principle operates with respect to spiritual development, and meditation is an essential mechanism by which the "spiritual fluency" that we call maturity is produced.

Psalm 1, a wisdom psalm that presents many of the same ideas found in the early chapters of Proverbs, speaks of the person who rejects the advice and schemes of the wicked and delights instead in the instruction of the Lord as a tree planted[1] by canals of water, which produces its fruit in season,

---

1. The word *shatal* sometimes means "to transplant" (e.g., Ezek. 17:22–23). According to Nahum Sarna, the word here means "well-rooted," not just "planted"

its foliage never withering. That is, the person prospers or succeeds in everything he or she does. The metaphor of the luxuriant, productive tree, deeply rooted in the soil and in constant contact with a source of water, contrasts strongly with chaff that is blown away by the wind. In the parallel passage (Jer. 17:5–8), the firmly established and thriving tree is contrasted with a bush in the desert that struggles just to survive.

The word translated *blessed* (NASB, NIV, NKJV) or *happy* (NRSV) in Psalm 1 is the same Hebrew word used in both Proverbs 3:13 and 8:34. The word is not the normal Hebrew word for *blessed,* although it is used often in the Old Testament Wisdom Literature. According to Sarna, this word reflects "the discriminating judgment of an observer who expresses wonderment and admiration over another's enviable state of being."[2] The psalm's claim is that living according to the principles that it teaches will result in such obvious benefits that others will congratulate us on our enviable state. The other thing noteworthy about the expression with which Psalm 1 begins is that it is the Hebrew counterpart to the term Jesus uses in the Beatitudes—something that must immediately stir our interest. It seems that the psalm is calling believers to a way of living that is not very different from that to which Jesus called disciples in the Sermon on the Mount—and with many of the same results. The idea is that wisdom/instruction has the power to transform its receiver into a person who prospers and enters into the blessings that are a part of Yahweh's order.

Psalm 1 identifies the secret of the person's success: he delights in the instruction of the Lord and meditates on that instruction day and night (Ps. 1:2). Although "instruction of the LORD" here refers to something more specific than the wisdom that is in view in most of Proverbs, it is nevertheless true that the instruction of the Lord is a part of wisdom. The connection between the fear of the Lord and wisdom in Proverbs 1:7 and 9:10 makes that fact clear, as does the fact that wisdom ultimately comes from the Lord (Prov. 2:6). The exhortation to trust God rather than one's own judgment (Prov. 3:5–7) also suggests the connection between wisdom and

---

(*On the Book of Psalms* [New York: Shocken, 1993], 42). As the rabbis pointed out, the normal word for planted was not used here but rather a somewhat rare word, thus emphasizing that something besides "planted" was meant.

2. Ibid., 29.

God's special revelation of Himself in Scripture.[3] Psalm 1 sees delighting in God's instruction and meditating on it day and night as essential keys to the blessedness of the righteous disciple with whom God is pleased, and a number of other passages throughout the Old Testament agree with Psalm 1 about the importance of the practice.

The Hebrew word translated *meditate* in Psalm 1:2 carries a meaning that normally involves a sound of some kind. It is used of a lion growling over its prey or of a dove's cooing. It is used of the deep sighs of a person mourning over a personal loss, and it is also used of normal human speech. Sarna argues that what is in view in this psalm is not meditation and contemplation as is practiced in certain mystical traditions but rather the recitation and memorization of the text.[4] The use of the word elsewhere in the book of Psalms suggests a somewhat broader meaning of the term but clearly one that does not involve mystical practice: in Psalm 77:11–12, the same Hebrew word used in Psalm 1 is used in parallel with Hebrew words meaning "remember" and "muse." In verses 5 and 6 a similar idea is expressed by words that mean "consider," "remember," "muse," and "search out or ponder." The principle in Psalm 1 is similar to that found in Psalm 111:5–6 (another wisdom psalm), where the value of reflecting on and studying the marvelous works of the Lord is affirmed. What is in view is a focused and reflective concentration on both the works and the instruction of the Lord.

The importance of this principle is also recognized in Deuteronomy 6:4–9 and 11:18–20, where, although the word *meditation* is not used, the temptation to embrace the ideas of Israel's pagan neighbors (clearly an act of folly rather than of wisdom) can be counteracted by impressing on the heart the instruction that the Lord revealed to Moses. The commitment to these words is to be assured for coming generations by "teach[ing] them to your children, talking of them when you are sitting in your house, and when you

---

3. Some Jewish tradition equates wisdom and *Torah,* and Sarna argues that because this psalm is "saturated with the vocabulary of Wisdom Literature. . . . It [therefore] indicates that by the time of the author, Hebrew Wisdom . . . had become identified with *torah*" (ibid., 36–37). Although Michael Fox rejects this equation and sees the wisdom in Proverbs as essentially secular and possessing no divine authority, he nonetheless sees the sacred books of Israel as belonging to the wisdom that is in view in Proverbs (*Proverbs,* The Anchor Bible [New York: Doubleday, 2000], 358).

4. Sarna, *On the Book of Psalms,* 38.

are walking by the way, and when you lie down, and when you rise" (Deut. 11:19). The opposing pairs—in your house and walking on the road, lying down and getting up—are examples of a literary device known as merism, which indicates not only the two extremes but also everything between those opposites. The various practices of binding the commandments on the body and inscribing them on the doorposts and on the gates, whether meant figuratively or literally, were designed to produce a constant awareness of God's commandments among the people.

Although the focus of the Deuteronomy passages is the covenant rather than the more general body of wisdom assumed in Proverbs, and probably in Psalm 1 as well, these passages, along with others such as Joshua 1:8–9, make clear that success and prosperity are related to life lived in congruence with God's truth. The passages make clear that meditation is an essential mechanism for bringing about that result. A number of passages point to a dual focus for meditation: God's Law/instruction and God and His works in creation and history.

Meditating on God's Law

Both the Wisdom Literature[5] and passages elsewhere in the Old Testament[6] mention *torah* (law/instruction) as an important focus of meditation, seeing the constant awareness of God's instruction, sustained by means of meditation, as an important antidote to the natural tendency of the disciple toward folly and rebellion. Proverbs 6:20–34 emphasizes the vital role that wisdom and instruction play in delivering the young man from the temptations of the adulteress. By binding the teachings on the heart and tying them around the neck, the young man is constantly reminded of what he should and should not do. When he is confronted by a situation where he is tempted to behave foolishly, this awareness of the right thing to do is one important element in helping him to avoid folly and its destructive consequences. In the broader perspective of Deuteronomy and Joshua 1, it is the constant awareness of God's expectations for His people, as revealed in the covenant, that encourages people to obey the covenant rather than doing either what seems good to them or what wicked people around them

---

5. For example, Psalm 119:15–16, 23, 48, 78, and 148.
6. For example, Deuteronomy 6:4–9; 11:18–20; and Joshua 1:7–8.

propose. Thus, the constant focus on what is true and good plays an essential role in authentic discipleship.

This insistence upon reflecting constantly on what is wise, together with the constant warnings about folly and the need to avoid it, perhaps brings to mind such words as *indoctrination* and *legalism.* Clearly, however, such are not the ultimate goals of meditating on this truth. Although it is important to be aware of the content of wisdom and *Torah,* the goal of the discipline is to internalize the values and principles; it is to write them on the tablets of the heart so that the heart will control the person with wisdom, producing a life that is consistent with Yahweh's order. This goal is entirely different than that of indoctrination and legalism, which leave intact the contrary heart and are content to impose their rule externally.

The way this works is similar to that reflected in the play *My Fair Lady,* in which Dr. Henry Higgins attempts to transform Eliza Doolittle into a woman whose true lower-class origins would not be apparent to people in the highest society circles in London. A major part of his task had to do with her manner of speech. A memorable part of the play deals with his efforts to have Liza correctly say, "The rain in Spain stays mainly in the plain." In the beginning, the task involved intense focus on each syllable; once that was mastered and the entire phrase could be pronounced flawlessly, it then became a matter of getting the phrase so ingrained in her that she could say it correctly without having to think about it. The ultimate goal, of course, was to get her to the point where all of her speech—not just those phrases and sentences that she had slavishly memorized and practiced—was precise and correct.

In much the same way, acquiring wisdom is analogous to learning another dialect or even another language. The initial stages involve learning the mechanics of the language, together with a great deal of repetition, memorization, and practice—things that are neither fun nor exciting. The goal is reached, however, when a person is fluent and is able actually to think in the language. At that point, the language has been written on the tablets of the heart. So it is with wisdom. The goal is neither slavish imitation of certain behaviors nor cognitive awareness of the entire body of Wisdom Literature; even a fool can be taught those things. The goal is to produce wise and godly character. But the emphasis on meditation and persistence in that practice suggests that people must "learn the language of wisdom" if they are ever to reach the goal of wise and godly character. Deliberate and focused attention to the details of wise living—including constant reminders of wisdom's contents, warnings about the consequences of folly, and regular practice applying the precepts—produces the sort of "total immersion" in wisdom that moves a person nearer the goal of spiritual maturity.

In addition, there is more to the Law than just externals involving what to do and what to avoid. As Craigie notes, "An understanding of Torah contributed to long life, peace and prosperity (Prov. 3:1–2) for in its words God has set down the nature of a life which would reach the true fulfillment for which it was created."[7] Meditation on Torah not only helps the disciple internalize these principles but also enables the disciple to discover depths of wisdom in God's revelation that are not always apparent on the surface. Craigie adds, "As instruction, [Torah] contains guidance from the Creator as to the meaning of creation. Life is lived in futility if its fundamental purpose is never discovered. It is the meaning of human existence which is enshrined in the Torah, and it is the discovery of that meaning which flows from meditation upon Torah."[8]

Meditating on God's Works in History and Creation

Many passages throughout the Old Testament affirm the importance of studying and meditating on the works of God in creation and history. Psalm 145 describes both the corporate and the individual dimensions of this focus on the marvelous works of God.[9] The psalmist says in verses 4–6, "One generation shall commend your works to another, and shall declare your mighty acts. On the glorious splendor of your majesty, and on your wondrous works, I will meditate. They shall speak of the might of your awesome deeds, and I will declare your greatness." One of the goals in this proclamation is made clear in verses 10–12: "All your saints shall bless you! They shall speak of the glory of your kingdom and tell of your power, to make known to the children of man your mighty deeds, and the glorious splendor of your kingdom."

---

7. Peter Craigie, *Psalms 1–50,* vol. 19 of Word Biblical Commentary (Waco: Word, 1983), 60.

8. Ibid., 62.

9. The Hebrew word that is often translated "wonderful" regularly refers to those works of God that exceed the bounds of what a person might expect. They are miraculous deeds that only God could accomplish. Man can only stand in wonder and awe in the presence of such deeds.

Psalm 111:2 says, "Great are the works of the LORD, studied by all who delight in them." The Old Testament sees this complex of praising, remembering, studying, and meditating on the works of God as an essential element of discipleship. As Kirkpatrick notes, "All God's works are a revelation of those attributes . . . with which he clothes himself," and he adds, "They are to be studied by all who delight in learning to understand his revelation of himself."[10] The works of God reveal who He is. His power, wisdom, and even goodness are revealed in the marvelous and complex world that He has created.

God's Attributes Revealed in Creation

Throughout the Old Testament, creation is seen as a unique indication of who God is, and for the prophets creation constitutes an irrefutable basis for worshiping and trusting God. The biblical authors seem to have taken it as a given that God created everything that exists, and that fact sets the Lord apart from every other object of trust. Both Isaiah and Jeremiah challenge the people of Judah to abandon their ultimate trust in anything or anyone except the Lord. Isaiah mocks the idols that the people were tempted to worship and declares their utter impotence. He says in Isaiah 44:24, "Thus says the LORD, your Redeemer, who formed you from the womb: I am the LORD, who made all things, who alone stretched out the heavens, who spread out the earth by myself." After pointing out the absurdity of trusting something that a person makes out of wood and metal, Jeremiah says, "Thus shall you say to them: 'The gods who did not make the heavens and the earth shall perish from the earth and from under the heavens'" (Jer. 10:11). In contrast, "It is [the LORD] who made the earth by his power, who established the world by his wisdom, and by his understanding stretched out the heavens" (v. 12). Unlike all of those false gods, says Jeremiah, Yahweh is "the portion of Jacob, for he is the one who formed all things" (v. 16).

The awesome dimensions of God's power, wisdom, and understanding are revealed in the creation when God's glory and majesty are perceived in His handiwork. Isaiah says that one simply has to look at the heavens to understand the incomparability of the Lord. He says, "Lift up your eyes on high and see: who created these? He who brings out their host by number,

---

10. A. F. Kirkpatrick, *Psalms,* The Cambridge Bible for Schools and Colleges (Cambridge: Cambridge University Press, 1906), 672.

calling them all by name, by the greatness of his might, and because he is strong in power not one is missing" (Isa. 40:26). The psalmist's consideration of the heavens, the work of God's fingers, leads him to conclude, "O LORD, our Lord, how majestic is your name in all the earth!" (Ps. 8:1, 9). The author of Psalm 33 says, "Let all the earth fear the LORD; let all the inhabitants of the world stand in awe of him! For he spoke, and it came to be; he commanded, and it stood firm" (vv. 8–9).

It is significant that when Job struggles with the question of God's moral governance of the world because of his personal circumstances, the Lord refers Job to the created world. There Job finds answers that satisfy him and bring him to his knees before the sovereign Lord. God points out to Job example after example from nature, and Job sees enough in those examples to convince him of how limited his own understanding had been while also seeing enough in the created world to convince him of God's goodness. As Andersen says, "To look at any bird or flower—and how many there are!— is a revelation of God in his constant care for the world."[11]

These examples make clear that meditation and reflection on the world can teach us significant things about God and encourage us to trust Him. It is hard to imagine anyone watching the sea pound against a rocky shore, or observing a magnificent mountain such as Mount Rainier or the Matterhorn, without being profoundly struck by the majesty of the physical world. A spectacular sunset always catches our attention, although one wonders how many people, Christians included, regularly connect God with such impressive examples of the natural world.[12]

To gain the full benefit of such meditation on God's creation, we must

---

11. Francis I. Andersen, *Job*, vol 13 of Tyndale Old Testament Commentaries (Downers Grove, Ill: InterVarsity, 1976), 271.

12. Note the comments of Augustine: "I loved beautiful things of a lower order, and I was sinking down to the depths" (*Confessions* 4.13). And C. S. Lewis remarks in *The Weight of Glory and Other Addresses*, "The books or the music in which we thought the beauty was located will betray us if we trust to them; it was not in them, it only came *through* them, and what came through them was longing. These things—the beauty, the memory of our own past—are good images of what we really desire; but if they are mistaken for the thing itself they turn into dumb idols, breaking the hearts of their worshippers. For they are not the thing itself; they are only the scent of a flower we have not found, the echo of a tune we have not heard, news from a country we have not visited" (*The Weight of Glory and Other Addresses* [New York: Macmillan, 1962], 7).

develop a consciousness of our world that notices the remarkable things around us and then sees them as the handiwork of God Himself. We become so accustomed to the world around us that we take it for granted and do not even notice the wonderful things within our view: mountains and butterflies, the ocean and little children, beautiful flowers and magnificent trees, a spectacular sunset or a harvest moon, the fragrance of jasmine or orange blossoms, or the workings of a cell or the strange properties of a water molecule that make possible life as we know it. All of these things are examples of God's handiwork and should teach us about God's greatness, power, wisdom, and understanding.

God's Attributes Revealed Through His Acts in History

God's power and faithfulness are also revealed in the miraculous things that He has done on behalf of His people. The birth of Isaac to Abraham and Sarah, the Exodus, the conquest of Canaan, Elijah's victory over the prophets of Baal on Mount Carmel, and David's victory over Goliath are all demonstrations of various attributes of God, including His commitment to His Word and His people. The celebration of Passover, public praise of God's work in creation, and personal study and reflection on God's works are important because they refresh one's memory about who God is and how He responds to the needs of His people. These works of God demonstrate that His power and wisdom are sufficient for any difficulty that we might face. History also makes clear that God is faithful to His Word and that He can be trusted to do what He promises.

Psalm 78:4, 6–7 describes this rehearsal of God's mighty acts in terms similar to those used in Deuteronomy 6:4, 6–7 and makes clear its intended goal. God's people are to "tell to the coming generation the glorious deeds of the LORD, and his might, and the wonders that he has done . . . that the next generation might know them . . . so that they should set their hope in God and not forget the works of God." The teaching, the public praise of the congregation, and the personal focused reflection on what God has done are essential in encouraging people to trust a God whose reality and presence are apprehended only by faith.

The Old Testament often attributes Israel's disobedience and refusal to trust God to either their failure to understand God's marvelous works or their failure to remember them. The miracles that God did for His people and His ongoing providence demonstrate concretely and visibly who God is and display His power and faithfulness to His Word. The marvelous works of God were supposed to make clear to the people that God can be trusted, that His Word can be believed, and that He is committed to His people.

For example, a central theme of Isaiah's ministry had to do with the focus of the people's trust. He regularly challenged Judah and her leaders to put their trust in God rather than in idols, foreign alliances, wealth, or human wisdom. Yet, Judah refused to trust God despite what Isaiah saw as overwhelming evidence that should have prompted them to put their faith in the Lord. Isaiah argued that they should trust God both because He created all things and is the sovereign Lord of history (Isa. 40:18–26; 10:5–19; 42:5) and because the Lord alone can tell His people what will happen in the future (Isa. 41:21–29). Isaiah found fault with the people because they "rise early in the morning, that they may run after strong drink, [and] tarry late into the evening as wine inflames them!" (Isa. 5:11), a clear parallel, in negative form, of Deuteronomy 6:7: "You . . . shall talk of [these words] when you . . . lie down, and when you rise."

The people of Isaiah's generation, however, focused their attention on "strong drink" and the pleasures of music instead of paying attention "to the deeds of the Lord" and considering "the work of his hands" (Isa. 5:12). The people had the opportunity to understand the Lord; the works of His hands were evident everywhere, but they refused to see them. Their failure to learn from God's works in the past and from the work that God was doing even during Isaiah's time was what the prophet saw as a primary reason for Judah's refusal to trust God and keep His covenant.

The failure of Isaiah's generation was characteristic of Israel throughout her history. God's miracles seldom provoked from the people the desired response of faith and obedience.[13] According to Psalm 106:7, "Our fathers, when they were in Egypt, did not consider your wondrous works; they did not remember the abundance of your steadfast love, but rebelled by the Sea." The failures of the wilderness generation are described in Psalm 106:13–14: "They soon forgot his works . . . and put God to the test in the desert."

---

13. Sometimes, the people did respond as they should, for a time at least. Exodus 14:31 says, "When Israel saw the great power which the Lord had used against the Egyptians, the people feared the Lord, and they believed in the Lord and in His servant Moses" (nasb). The effect, however, seems to have been only temporary, no doubt because they soon forgot those marvelous deeds of the Lord.

In verses 21–22, this psalm goes on to say, "They forgot God, their Savior, who had done great things in Egypt, wondrous works in the land of Ham, and awesome deeds by the Red Sea."

In spite of the miracles they had seen God do in Egypt, when the Israelites were confronted with an insufficient supply of water, they did not trust God to help them; rather, they doubted whether He was even present with them. They "tested the LORD by saying, 'Is the LORD among us or not?'" (Exod. 17:7). Psalm 78:17–20 suggests that even God's miraculous provision of water for the people did nothing to change their unbelief. They put God to the test and said, "Can God spread a table in the wilderness? He struck the rock so that water gushed out. . . . Can he also give bread or provide meat for his people?"

Just as an explanation is given for Caleb's decision to invade the land (a different spirit was in him), so the explanation given for the refusal of the rest of the people to concur in that decision lies in their failure to learn about God from the miraculous deeds that He did for them in Egypt and in the wilderness. Numbers 14:11 describes God's response to Moses after the people had decided not to enter the Promised Land: "The LORD said to Moses, 'How long will this people despise me? And how long will they not believe in me, in spite of all the signs that I have done among them?'" Verse 22 describes the people as those "who have seen my glory and my signs that I did in Egypt and in the wilderness, and yet have put me to the test these ten times and have not obeyed my voice."

Clearly, those who saw and experienced the marvelous deeds that the Lord did for His people were supposed to discern in those acts enough about the nature of God to believe His Word, obey His instruction, and trust Him in times of difficulty. Subsequent generations are expected to learn these same things about God from remembering what He has done and observing His continuing providence. It is focused reflection and meditation, both public and private, that keeps God's people constantly aware of those realities about God. Such meditation nourishes trust and obedience. Failure to learn from such experiences and failure to remember God's works can result in the same sort of lapses in trust that characterized the wilderness generation, as Hebrews 3:7–4:11 makes clear.

In 1 Corinthians 10:11, Paul indicates that "these things happened to them as an example, but they were written down for our instruction." The principle described in these Old Testament passages likely reflects the broader principle that the people of God, both individually and corporately, are supposed to learn about God through the experience of living by faith. They discover in the various experiences of life how God works on behalf of His people. Certainly our experiences are normally much less spectacular than those of the Israelites who escaped from Egypt, just as ours are less dramatic than those of the people who took the land during the conquest. Nor do we have the inspired interpretation of our experiences that Scripture provides for many of the events reported in the Old Testament. Nevertheless, a number of passages suggest that the experiences of life constitute an important mechanism for learning about God and His gracious love.[14]

Psalm 107 describes four different examples of those who have experienced the loyal love of the Lord. In each instance, when people faced serious difficulties, they cried out to the Lord in their trouble, and then He delivered them. The psalm calls on those who have been redeemed by the Lord's loyal love to give thanks publicly for that unremitting concern. After celebrating God's goodness, loyal love, and wonders to the sons of men, the psalm ends by calling on the wise to heed these things and to consider the loyal love of the Lord. The psalmist clearly believed that a certain power resides in reflecting on the examples of those who have experienced God's deliverance and loyal love, the power to teach God's people about Him and to build their capacity for trusting Him. Although meditation on inspired Scripture plays a singular role in teaching us these things, it seems that the experiences of life should also teach us similar things. Keeping a journal, recalling those times when God was clearly at work in our lives, learning to see God's hand and loyal love all around us on a regular basis, and sharing testimonies about God's providence with others are all activities that can teach us about God and help us to grow in our ability to trust Him. Such practices, coupled with meditation on God's marvelous works in creation and history, will stimulate growth in understanding God's order and living in harmony with it.

How Meditation Transforms the Heart

A person's decisions and responses to the circumstances of life are powerfully influenced by a number of factors, including psychological,

---

14. For example, Psalms 32; 34; and 51. The book of Job explores in a different way the question of personal experience and what that teaches a person about God.

emotional, and experiential ones. At the same time, it is true that people's understanding of what is real and true will, in most instances, determine how they live and respond to the various situations that confront them. This was certainly the case with Joshua and Caleb at Kadesh-barnea. And it was also true that, when given the information reported by the spies, those who concluded that the conquest of Canaan was not feasible made their decision based on what they understood to be real and true. But for the biblical authors, God is the fundamental reality on which all others rest, and their claim is that all of life should flow from a correct awareness of God and the order that He designed into the world. These same authors regularly fault the people of God for acting in ways that are not consistent with truth about God and His activity in the world. Often, this discrepancy occurs because people's sense of reality is completely determined by their experience of the concrete world in which they live, ignoring the fact that truth about God and the spiritual realm is known by faith rather than by sight. We are asked to accept the truth that God has revealed to us and then live our lives in ways that are based on that truth. A life that is truly pleasing to God and experiences the fullness of God's blessing is one that is lived by faith. It is difficult, however, to fully comprehend the reality of a spiritual realm that we know about largely by faith because our lives are so dominated by the physical, so we often find it difficult to trust God for deliverance or to respond to circumstances in a way that accords with God's Word. It certainly was so for Ahaz (Isa. 7) and Hezekiah (Isa. 36–39) when attack by a foreign army seemed imminent. Many authors in the Old Testament, when considering the failure of God's people to live in harmony with the reality of God and His providence, attribute the failure to those people's refusal to attend appropriately and consistently to God's revelation in history and Scripture. Meditation is a practice that, over time, has the power to bring balance to our perception of reality by regularly keeping before us truth about God. Such focused reflection on truth about God has the power to transform people psychologically, emotionally, and experientially in ways that move them toward responses and desires that are consistent with reality and God's truth.

The importance of regular meditation, consciously and deliberately focusing one's attention on wisdom and instruction, is clear from many passages in the Old Testament (with the New Testament affirming the basic principle as well). Some of the reasons people need this discipline for spiritual growth are evident. First, these passages recognize that whatever shapes a person's thinking will also shape his life. What a person regularly thinks about strongly influences what he or she does and, in many instances, also determines what the person becomes. As Leland Ryken says,

> People may assent to the proposition that the true end of life is not to make money and accumulate possessions, but if their minds are filled with images of big houses and fancy clothes, their actual behavior will run in the direction of materialism. People may theoretically believe in the ideals of chastity and faithful wedded love, but if their minds are filled with images of exposed bodies and songs of seduction, their sexual behavior will have a large admixture of lust and sexual license in it.[15]

Meditation helps focus the attention on things that are consistent with God's order and thus helps to produce behavior and character that are consistent with God's truth. As Sarna says, "Constant repetition and review, 'day and night,' [function] to incorporate [the] values within the self so that they [become] a part of one's own being, consciously and subconsciously guiding one's actions."[16] This deliberate, reflective concentration on wisdom and instruction[17] changes the heart and brings about closer conformity with Yahweh's order. This focus on wisdom must be the constant preoccupation of the disciple.

Our culture is saturated not only with many ideas that are antithetical to wisdom and Christian truth but also with images the powerful influence of which is difficult to resist. Allen and Borror recognize one important reason these modern images have the power that they do: "An idea (either good or bad) set to a good melody, given rhythmic intensity and harmonic consistency, can really work its way into our minds. . . . Music is a powerful way to get . . . ideas implanted and affect the behavior of mankind. . . . What we sing we remember, because we have combined the power of intellect

---

15. Leland Ryken, "The Creative Arts," as quoted in *The Making of the Christian Mind,* ed. Arthur Holmes (Downers Grove, Ill.: InterVarsity, 1985), 106.
16. Sarna, *On the Book of Psalms,* 39.
17. The same intensity and persistence are regularly called for in the early chapters of Proverbs. The disciple is to "treasure up [the] commandments" (2:1), to "bind them around your neck; write them on the tablet of your heart" (3:3; 6:6; 7:3). He is to love wisdom and not forsake it (4:6).

with emotion."[18] The impression is intensified when the visual images are effectively combined with the power of emotional delivery and the intellect, something that our culture is adept at doing.

When we are regularly exposed to the ideas and images that dominate our culture, we are profoundly influenced in both what we do and what we become. The Old Testament makes clear that constant awareness of God's truth, as reinforced by meditation, is necessary to counteract the negative influences of folly and error on the disciple's heart. The transforming power of meditating on the Law seems to lie in the persistence of meditation, and the form of much of the biblical material seems to make it especially effective in accomplishing this objective. Poetry, music, effective storytelling techniques, and many of the literary genres found in the Wisdom Literature derive their power from the images they leave in people's minds. Such images, when regularly reflected upon, can do much to erase the destructive images that permeate our culture. In addition, the poetic and musical form of many biblical passages makes them easier to remember, stimulating the kind of meditation that leads to internalizing the principles.

The effect of focused concentration on God's truth seems to be similar to that of a good commercial message. The intention of the advertiser is to get a message about the product into a person's system so that he will, often without even thinking about it, whistle the tune or sing the commercial jingle repeatedly to himself. The real goal, of course, is to affect the consumer such that, when he is standing in front of a shelf filled with competing brands, his hand will move inevitably to the advertiser's product. The goal of meditation is similar. Constant reflection and focused repetition get the principle into a person's system such that, when he is faced with a situation requiring a choice, the person will respond instinctively in a way that reflects God's order.

Meditation also helps a person trust God in times of difficulty and distress. Our difficulties never exhaust the reality of God's presence, love, power, sovereignty, and unconditional commitment to us, although pain and frustration often make it difficult for us to see those aspects of reality. It becomes very difficult to trust God in situations where all we see is the problem. But if we have been meditating regularly on the important realities, those about God, we will more easily include them in our view of the

---

18. Ronald Allen and Gordon Borror, *Worship: Rediscovering the Missing Jewel* (Portland: Multnomah, 1982), 162.

situation. Psalm 77 suggests that meditation on God's mighty works confers upon us the endurance to sustain our faith in the face of a personal crisis of such magnitude that it might otherwise persuade us to question God's power and concern. The psalmist is overwhelmed by circumstances that cause him to wonder whether he will ever again experience the Lord's favor (vv. 7–9). In that struggle, he remembers the deeds and miracles that the Lord has done, and he meditates on the works of God. Although the psalm never explicitly states that the psalmist has resolved his doubts as expressed in verses 7–9, the rest of the psalm clearly implies that this resolution has taken place.[19] Remembering, meditating on, God's marvelous works strengthens the psalmist's confidence in God's ability to help and affirms for the psalmist God's commitment to His people (vv. 11–15). Certainly, focusing on God and His works produces a similar transformation in Psalm 63 (see vv. 6–8), Psalm 73 (see v. 17), and Lamentations 3 (vv. 16–24).

Meditation also helps us to focus on those things that will move us toward godliness and closer conformity to the image of Christ. I (Edward) remember when my son began playing baseball at the age of five. One of the major challenges for the players was to stay focused on the game. An airplane flying overhead or an interesting bug often created an irresistible distraction for an outfielder or a base runner. It was not unusual for the outfielder to watch the insect while the ball rolled between his legs, or for the base runner to stop between bases to check out some distracting phenomenon. Similarly, our ability to overcome a sinful habit or develop virtues consistent with God's order is often undermined because distractions in life prevent the sort of sustained focus that enables us to succeed. Meditation keeps the principle before us in a way that contributes to our reaching the desired goal.

Meditation can also help determine what registers with us. Many times, I suspect, we fail to apply God's truth to life because we are not aware of the opportunities before us for applying the principles embedded in that truth.

---

19. Marvin Tate notes that the psalmist does not clearly resolve the tension between his circumstances and the promises of God or answer the question that he raised in verses 7–10, but he says, "The psalm clearly moves in this direction, but . . . the questions are left open. . . . the reader must answer them" (*Psalms 51–100,* vol. 20 of Word Biblical Commentary [Dallas: Word, 1990], 273). He goes on to point out that undoubtedly the psalm is intended to prompt the reader to understand that God has neither changed His nature nor abandoned His people.

When my (Edward's) sons first went to the tide pools to play in the water and on the rocks, we really saw very little there except the rocks and the seaweed. Then one of the boys took a class in which he studied the tide pools and the creatures that could be found there. We were amazed at all that we had missed, in part because we had not known what to look for but also because of the significance of many things to which we had paid little attention.

A student once did a research project for me on what Proverbs teaches about discipline and self-control. When the student turned in the paper, he said to me, "I have never benefited so much from any research paper that I have done. I can't believe how many opportunities the Lord gave me to apply the principles while I was doing the paper." My guess is that no more opportunities to apply the principles occurred than he would have had had he not been doing that project. The difference was that he had become aware of the opportunities for application because he had recently begun to focus on the principles. In my daily experience, I discover many opportunities for application when I am concentrating on a particular virtue or truth, and I think it very likely that I would simply have missed the opportunities had I not been thinking about the principle. Again, meditation helps keep God's truth before us in a way that facilitates application, and that application is an essential tool for internalizing the truth and developing godly character.

Another benefit of meditation is that it often helps to bring God's truth to mind in situations when that truth is needed. We have already noted how this can work in situations of great difficulty and pain because the truths we have invited into our minds through meditation help us to see the bigger picture, including the realities of God. Situations also arise in which we are upset because of what someone has said or done to us, when it is easy to respond rashly and angrily, in ways that are inconsistent with God's order. I can think of times when I was about to respond in anger or when I was mentally preparing to reprimand someone, and a passage on which I had been meditating for some time—a passage such as "A soft answer turns away wrath" (Prov. 15:1) or "The vexation of a fool is known at once, but the prudent ignores an insult" (Prov. 12:16)—came to mind and caused me to back away from a response that would not have been honoring to God. Meditation on God's truth is an essential mechanism by which we avoid conformity to this world and are instead transformed by the renewing of the mind to discern the will of God and discover that it is good, acceptable, and perfect (Rom. 12:2).

Meditation's Potential

I (Edward) often teach classes on Psalms or Proverbs in which I assign my students a meditation project. They are instructed to choose a verse or two from the book we are studying and then write the passage on ten to twelve three-by-five-inch note cards. Then I ask them to put the cards at various places where they will see them throughout the day and night. Each time they see one of the cards, they are to focus briefly on the verse and think about it. One point of the assignment is to show the students that you do not have to block off specific periods of time in which to meditate and reflect on God's truth. It is possible to spread this out into many brief periods of time throughout the day and still find the practice beneficial. At the end of the three- or four-week duration of the assignment, I ask the students to write a brief essay telling me what happened. Following are several examples from a recent class that typify what students discover about the benefits of meditation.[20]

One student chose Psalm 19:14 ("Let the words of my mouth and the meditation of my heart be acceptable in your sight, O LORD") for her medi tation. She wrote, "I have a nasty habit of grumbling and complaining, and as I am planning to get married in a few months, I want to improve my attitude. My boyfriend's roommate really annoys me, and I have trouble not grumbling and complaining about him. Often, just as I was getting ready to say something negative about him, the words of the verse would come into my mind, and I would continue with the verse rather than the complaint that I was about to voice. I was amazed and encouraged to see how much better my attitude was because I was meditating on that verse."

Another student used Psalm 104:33–34 as her verse ("I will sing to the LORD as long as I live. . . . May my meditation be pleasing to him"). In her essay she wrote, "Meditating on the verse caused me regularly to think about singing to the Lord and dwelling on what pleases Him. The project made me more conscious of the music I was singing, and I had to turn a few things off the radio because they focused on things that were not pleasing to God. Seeing the card in the car also changed the way I drive. I am not going to tell everyone to have this verse in the car so they will think about God and drive nicer, but it worked for me. When my roommates saw the

---

20. The essays have been edited, and, in some instances, the details have been modified to obscure the identity of the students.

cards all around the apartment, they laughed, but then at the end of the three weeks, they told me that they were amazed at how the verse made them conscious about the thoughts they were thinking. It made us want to focus more on the Lord."

One student told me that he was struggling with a complex situation that he did not know how to handle. His response included a lot of anger and a generally bad attitude. He said, "When I realized what this was doing to me, I was scared and ashamed, but I really had no idea what to do." The student chose Psalm 119:9 as his verse ("How can a young man keep his way pure? By guarding it according to your word"). He responded, "Despite the simplicity of the message, I have experienced an amazing change. First, as I thought about the verse, simple truths that I know from the Bible began to come to mind—things like 'love one another,' and the reminder helped change my perspective. My situation is still not better, and I do not know how to handle certain aspects of it, but just trying to keep my way according to God's Word has removed so much of my anger. One of the benefits that came to me from meditation is that it helped me focus on something other than me and my problem. I feel as though my spirit is being revived and my heart softened."

The last example that I will include not only notes the benefit of the meditation experiment but also includes a very insightful comment. The student said, "The project was a simple way to think about Scripture throughout the day. I often found myself rehearsing the verse in my mind, even before I realized I was doing it. That was very encouraging; I think the truth was actually getting into my system!" The student went on to say, "As beneficial as the assignment was, I did realize that it takes conscious effort to meditate. The cards [or whatever system one uses to facilitate meditation] can begin to blend in with everything else around them to the point where I do not even notice them. I also see that character is not permanently changed in three weeks. The sort of long-term transformation that I desire, the transformation that brings me into conformity with the image of Christ, will require diligence and discipline in meditation over the entire course of my life. What I have seen through this project is that with God's help and my diligent meditation on His truth the goal can actually be reached."

Questions for Thought and Reflection

1. Think about God's faithfulness toward you in the past. Can you remember times in your life when you knew that God was with you?
   For an entire week, look for examples of God's loving-kindness. List
   these incidents. Try to find at least five such incidents each day. How
   does remembering and reflecting upon God's faithfulness and love
   help you trust God in times of difficulty? Do you see any change in
   your perspective as a result of this exercise?

2. Much of the time, young children take for granted the things their
   parents do for their benefit, thinking that their parents merely looked
   for ways to hinder their fun. Only after they are grown—sometimes
   not until they have their own children—do they reflect on and begin
   to appreciate the loving concern that their mothers and fathers might
   have lavished upon them. At that point, these children's love for their
   parents deepens, and they often become at that time the adults their
   parents had hoped they would become—conscientious, caring, and
   wise. How is this pattern of development similar to that brought
   about in us by meditating on the works of God?

3. Choose a verse from Proverbs and write it on twelve three-by-five-
   inch cards. Place these cards in a number of different places where
   you will see them during the day and night. When you see one of the
   cards, read it and try to apply it to your concern at that moment or
   that day. Read it aloud on separate occasions during the day. Allow
   the exercise to continue for a week or two, and then continue the
   exercise using a different verse. Simply enjoy the experience and note
   what happens. (Remember, this exercise is for *your* benefit; it should
   not be allowed to degenerate into thinly veiled criticisms of family
   members or roommates.)

Chapter Nine

SUFFERING AND SPIRITUAL MATURITY

> Consider it all joy, my brothers, when you meet trials of various kinds, for you know that the testing of your faith produces steadfastness. And let steadfastness have its full effect, that you may be perfect and complete, lacking in nothing. (James 1:2–4)

Although many kinds of uncertainties and difficulties are encountered in a fallen world, one specific difficulty has troubled people since the beginning of recorded history—the problem of suffering, especially suffering that seems to be undeserved. Among the earliest literature that we possess from Mesopotamia are several poems dealing with the question of the righteous sufferer. The issue plagues human beings perennially, as evidenced by the great popularity a few years ago of Harold Kushner's book *When Bad Things Happen to Good People*[1] and by Old Testament Wisdom Literature such as Psalms 37, 73, and the book of Job. These passages not only show us helpful ways to respond to suffering but also identify the important role that suffering plays in moving people toward spiritual maturity.

Few of us find it upsetting when people suffer as a direct result of things they have done. The brutal dictator who is punished for his crimes or who is killed by one of the victims of his evil does not garner much of our sympathy. The same is true of the corrupt CEO who ends up in bankruptcy.

---

1. Harold S. Kushner, *When Bad Things Happen to Good People* (New York: Shocken, 1981).

When wicked people reap the harvest of their own treatment of others, people intuitively feel that they got what they deserved. The problem occurs when good and righteous people suffer. It seems that a just and all-powerful God would reward those who are good with blessings and punish those who are wicked, and generally that seems to be the way things work. For example, Paul, in Galatians 6:7, said, "Whatever one sows, that will he also reap," and many psalms (e.g., Pss. 1; 34; 37) affirm the same principle.

When people who seem to be good and righteous suffer, problems (both theological and experiential) often arise, especially for the person afflicted. The problem is compounded when, at the same time, evil people are prospering. Such situations, to an even greater degree than intellectual issues, generate doubts as people struggle with how God could be who He claims to be given the circumstances in which they find themselves. We know that God is sovereign, but at times the circumstances swirling around us seem so chaotic and confused that it is hard to imagine that God could actually be in control. It is true that difficult experiences and suffering can bring people to deeper faith and understanding, as both Job and Psalm 73 make clear, but they do not routinely bring about that result. We have all heard the saying, "Difficulties make some people better, but they make other people bitter." Some people emerge with even stronger faith from times when life seems to be falling apart, whereas others are never able to pick up the pieces and remain cynical and bitter for the rest of their lives. If these experiences are to move us toward spiritual maturity, it is crucial to understand what makes the difference between the two outcomes. The author of Psalm 73 provides an example of exactly this kind of struggle.

Psalms 73 and 37: Portraits in the Struggle for Faith

Psalm 73 relates an experience involving what one might call the very survival of faith, and the psalmist begins with a statement that presumably expresses a fundamental component of his faith: "Truly God is good to Israel, to those who are pure in heart." The psalmist then goes on to describe an experience that seemed to call his theology into question. Seeing the prosperity of wicked and arrogant people brought him to a place where, as he described it, "My feet had almost stumbled, my steps had nearly slipped" (Ps. 73:2). The Hebrew word translated "prosperity" is the Hebrew word *shalom,* which normally describes wholeness and general well-being. The psalmist was bothered by the fact that these were wicked people, yet everything seemed to be going well for them. They had everything they needed, often in great abundance. They were happy and healthy and were leading what seemed to be ideal lives, despite the fact that they were evil and arrogant and oppressing those around them.

As the psalmist contrasted his own beleaguered situation with the prosperity of these wicked people, he was deeply frustrated and upset, concluding, "All in vain have I kept my heart clean and washed my hands in innocence. For all the day long I have been stricken and rebuked every morning" (Ps. 73:13–14). His experience made him think that his commitment to righteousness was a waste of time and was perhaps even preventing him from prospering.

Many people have become similarly focused on their terrible circumstances and, as a result, have been unable to function in positive ways. But the psalmist understood that such ongoing doubts and struggles could be harmful to both himself and others. In verse 15, he recognized that publicly venting his frustrations and doubts could cause significant harm to others. He says, "If I had said, 'I will speak thus,' I would have betrayed the generation of your children," implying that the psalmist was probably a teacher or public leader of some sort. Certainly, it is important to have people to whom we can complain and bare our souls when we are confused and hurting, but it is also important to do so in appropriate contexts and with people who are stable in their commitment to the Lord, who are faithful friends, and who will hear us with the kind of understanding and gracious love that Job desired when he was in despair (see Job 6:14).

The author of Psalm 73 also recognized the danger that such feelings of despair posed to himself. Constantly thinking about injustice, especially those things that we have no power to change, can raise grave doubts about God and His governance of the world. Struggling with such difficulties can contribute to other problems as well. In verse 2, the psalmist tells us that he was almost tripped up by this situation, and in verses 21 and 22 he says, "When my soul was embittered, when I was pricked in heart, I was brutish and ignorant; I was like a beast toward you." Although some of the implications of this passage remain uncertain, as the psalmist focused constantly on these difficulties, he clearly was unable to function as the person God designed him to be. He was brought down to the level of an animal rather than functioning like a human being made in God's image. A number of studies have indicated that one cause of depression is an ongoing obsession with past wrongs and injustices. Moreover, a failure to forgive and the bitterness that comes from this failure can bring about a variety of physical problems. Clearly, the consequences of such turmoil can go far beyond theological doubts. The consequences can affect all of life and keep us from the *shalom,* or wholeness or well-being, that we all desire. A striking fact is that the wrong kind of concern over the *shalom* of the wicked can radically undermine our own *shalom.*

The psalmist, however, did not allow his anger and frustration over his circumstances to destroy him and his faith, and what he did to turn the situation around illustrates a very important principle for responding to such circumstances. In verses 16 and 17, the psalmist says, "When I thought how to understand this, it seemed to me a wearisome task, until I went into the sanctuary of God; then I discerned their end." As the verses that follow indicate clearly, coming into the sanctuary and worshiping caused the psalmist to remember the fate of the wicked as declared in God's revelation. Such reflection prompted the psalmist to suspend judgment on the basis of his present experience and to wait for God to deal with the wicked as He has promised He will. The rest of the psalm also makes clear that as the psalmist focused on God, he began to realize that his relationship with God constituted something that put into perspective any difficulties he might experience. As he says in verses 25–26, 28, "Whom have I in heaven but you? And there is nothing on earth that I desire besides you. My flesh and my heart may fail, but God is the strength of my heart and my portion forever. . . . But for me it is good to be near God; I have made the Lord God my refuge."

Derek Kidner suggests that the psalmist's entire perspective began to turn around when he turned to God, not as an object of speculation but as the focus of worship.[2] According to Mays, "The reality of God flooded his heart, and became the consciousness by which he understood himself and his experience. The uncertainty of his experience became the certainty of faith,"[3] and this produced a profound change in the psalmist. As he reflected on God in worship, the psalmist began to understand that "the goodness of God is not defined by the *shalom* the wicked enjoy, nor is it denied by the

---

2. Derek Kidner, *Psalms 73–150,* vol. 14b of Tyndale Old Testament Commentaries (Downers Grove, Ill.: InterVarsity, 1975), 261–62.

3. James L. Mays, *Psalms,* Interpretation (Louisville: John Knox, 1994), 243.

affliction suffered by the pure in heart."[4] As a result of focusing on God, the psalmist began to realize that the true good for him was found not in his circumstances but in God Himself and in the psalmist's relationship with Him. The psalmist's circumstances did not change, but his focus shifted from those difficult and frustrating circumstances to a more solid and dependable reality—that of God and His relationship with the psalmist.

The author of Psalm 37 also was disturbed by both injustice and the prosperity of the wicked, and, in telling us how to respond, he says six times in the first eight verses of the psalm, "Don't become angry!" Instead, he says, "Trust God and do good." Few things are more infuriating than injustice and wicked people prospering—especially when they prosper at our expense. The psalmist tells us not to become indignant about such things, but typically we do respond with anger when such things occur, and it is very difficult to avoid that response. The psalmist not only tells us not to become angry but also alerts us to a principle that, if followed, will actually help us avoid the anger that, according to Psalm 37:8, "tends only to evil." As Derek Kidner suggests, "An obsession with enemies cannot simply be switched off, but it can be ousted by a new focus of attention; note the preoccupation with the Lord himself. . . . This includes a deliberate redirection of one's emotions and an entrusting of one's career and reputation to him."[5]

Instead of focusing on the injustice or difficulty, the psalm exhorts the reader to trust God and delight in the Lord (Ps. 37:3–9). An important part of trusting God in such circumstances involves recognizing that the moral governance of the universe is God's job, not ours. We must trust Him to do that job and patiently wait for Him to act.

Another aspect of trusting God includes focusing on attributes of God such as His justice (vv. 9–10, 17, 20, 28, 38) and His goodness to His people (vv. 4, 9, 11, 16–18, 23–24, 28–29, 38–40) even in the midst of the trouble. Seeing the bigger picture, the larger perspective that includes God's wise governance, is essential in avoiding anger and in giving us the patience that allows us to wait for the Lord's deliverance. Psalm 37:3 also tells us to do good and to "cultivate" or "graze on" or "befriend" faithfulness, and the idea is similar to what we see in Job 28:28: Our wisdom consists in faithfully doing God's truth, whether things are going well for us or we are facing

---

4. Ibid., 243.

5. Derek Kidner, *Psalms 1–72,* Tyndale Old Testament Commentaries (Downers Grove, Ill.: InterVarsity, 1973) 149.

sorrow and difficulty. Trusting God and faithfully carrying out our responsibilities will keep the focus away from the circumstances that would otherwise produce anger.

Both of these psalms recognize that reality is never exhausted by our problems or circumstances and that it is important to understand our problems in the light of those broader realities. The broader realities include many things, but two facts that illustrate how the principle works come to mind immediately. First, God is sovereign. The full implications of God's sovereignty are, no doubt, beyond our understanding, but God's sovereignty clearly includes the fact that His purposes, including His purposes for us, are never thwarted. Things such as cancer or some other debilitating illness or a natural disaster do not catch God by surprise, nor are they things that can thwart God's purposes. Knowing that God is sovereign might not always help in trying to figure out why something happened or what to do about it or what the eventual outcome will be, but it can bring a great sense of peace and comfort to know that God is in full control and that, despite this situation, His purposes for us will be accomplished.

Second, we must recognize and reflect on God's unfailing love. Many Old Testament passages describe the reality of that loyal love, and the New Testament shows us even broader dimensions of God's love, such as the affirmation of Romans 8 that nothing can separate us from God's love in Christ Jesus. Knowing the reality of God's sovereignty and His love for us does not eliminate the pain and confusion that is inherent in suffering, but setting the difficulty in the context of such realities provides comfort and stability in the midst of the difficulty. Just as a child with an earache is assured by her mother's confidence in their doctor, even though the pain is still present, so the believer who remembers the Father's sovereignty and love for us will be given confidence in the midst of affliction. Regular meditation on God, reflecting on Him and what He has done for His people, prepares us for the crises and Job-like experiences that are an inevitable part of living in a fallen world, making it easier to experience the assurance described by these psalms.

Job and Righteous Suffering

The book of Job deals with the question of righteous suffering and teaches a number of important lessons about suffering and how to respond to it. Job

1:1 tells us that Job was "blameless and upright, one who feared God and turned away from evil," and God describes Job to Satan using the same words (Job 1:8). The prologue of the book explains to the reader the reason for the experience and for Job's suffering, but Job was unaware of this, so he, like all of us, had to respond to the suffering without knowing its reason. When God pointed out Job to Satan and commended him for his great piety, Satan was not impressed. His response in Job 1:9 was, "Does Job fear God for no reason?" his point being that the only reason Job fears and worships God is that he gets so much in exchange for his piety, that God protects Job and blesses him in every way, and that is the only reason Job—or anyone else—ever serves God. Thus, Satan's claim was that no one sees in God Himself someone worthy of worship and trust, but rather people serve Him only because of what they get out of the exchange. Satan was allowed to attack Job, first by taking his children and his possessions, and then by afflicting him physically. The prologue makes clear that Job suffered because of his piety and that a primary reason for the suffering is to demonstrate to Satan, and then to all who read about Job's life, that there is such a thing as disinterested piety. Job, of course, was unaware of all of this as he tried to understand the suffering and respond to it appropriately without knowing the reason for it or how it fit into the broad scheme of God's purposes.

Job's friends came to comfort him, and because they came from some distance and at some personal expense, it seems clear that their intentions were to help their friend in his distress. Their presence, no doubt, was initially encouraging to Job, but then Job broke the weeklong silence in chapter 3 with an outburst in which he expressed the wish that he had never been born, or at least could have died before experiencing this series of catastrophes. Eliphaz, the first friend to speak, was shocked by Job's words and called them rash, reminding Job that rash words are characteristic of a foolish person, not of a wise and godly man like Job. Eliphaz told Job that he was not following the advice that he had given to others who were experiencing difficulty (4:3–5), and he pointed out that such things happen for a reason (4:7–8). He advised Job to seek God and bring his cause before Him (5:8). If he would only accept God's discipline, he would be restored and perhaps be blessed in even greater ways than before (5:17–26).

Job conceded that his words had been rash, but he argued that the friends had failed to understand the significance of those words—they were simply cries of pain rather than statements of theology that needed to be refuted.

Job insisted that what a person in such unfortunate circumstances needs from a friend is compassion and kindness rather than advice and correction (6:14), and he made clear that the friends were not helping him with their responses. At the same time, Job's response was not what the friends expected, and they, no doubt, felt attacked personally. They quickly became defensive and were increasingly determined to prove their point, though in so doing they only contributed further to his pain. As the emotional level of the debate intensified, the possibility that the friends' efforts might actually help Job or shed light on the issue of suffering began to diminish. In these passages, the book has much to teach us about friendship and ministry to those who are suffering.

Eliphaz's advice to repent and seek God, advice repeated by all of the friends, reveals that the doctrine of retribution (i.e., that a person reaps what he or she sows) was the lens through which they viewed every experience of affliction. This was a doctrine that was well established in wisdom thinking, and even Job began the experience assuming that retribution was the relevant doctrine to explain what had happened to him. The problem with this explanation was that Job could not identify anything he had done that would account for the immense calamity that had befallen him. Job had never claimed that he was sinless, but the disasters that had afflicted him would be appropriate for only immense wickedness, and he was not aware of having done anything that would even come close to that level of guilt. When Job refused to confess to any such hypothetical sin and to seek God's forgiveness, the friends were at first concerned and then insistent that Job must have committed some great sin for such adversity to strike him. His insistence that he was innocent of anything that might account for the suffering made the friends even more certain that he was self-righteous and deserving of even greater punishment. As they saw things, the justice of God required some great sin in Job; an innocent person receiving such treatment would constitute serious injustice and so impugn the character of God. They did not consider that perhaps God works in the world in other ways than the doctrine of retribution. Wisdom tradition affirmed retribution, and as far as they were concerned, it was a comprehensive statement about how God works, one that applied in every individual case. They were not open to Job's claim that he was innocent, because their theology did not allow that possibility.

Job almost certainly began this experience with beliefs much like those of the friends, but his pleas to his friends and to God for help in identifying the decisive sin turned up nothing that convinced him. As the debate continued, he became more and more convinced of his innocence, and because he was a man of integrity, he could not confess an imaginary sin merely to satisfy his friends. At the same time, Job was well aware of the wisdom tradition and its description of the fate of the wicked, and he knew that what was happening to him looked very much like what happens to the wicked according to retribution. Thus, Job was in a situation where he was convinced that he was innocent, yet God seemed to be treating him as if he were an enemy. Job did not have the luxury that the friends had of simply denying his innocence and thereby protecting his theology. The conclusion that God was unjust was as unacceptable for Job as it was for his friends, but he was forced to acknowledge the reality of his innocence as he responded to what was happening to him, and this made it necessary for him to try to find answers that allowed for both his innocence and God's justice.

Although Job's struggle was extreme in its intensity (few of us experience the sort of ideal life that chapters 1 and 29 describe, just as few of us experience the magnitude of tragedy and suffering that Job experienced), his type of experience is paralleled by many people who suffer, especially when they are righteous individuals. Job was in extreme pain, some of which arose from his struggle to harmonize what he knew about God with what was happening to him. Job had no doubts about God's power or wisdom; both Job and his friends clearly recognized those attributes of God. The problem for Job was that his circumstances and his suffering seemed to call into question God's goodness, especially given Job's innocence. The suffering was severe and relentless, and Job did not understand why it was happening. He wanted relief, but perhaps even more significant was Job's confusion because God seemed to be treating him as if he were God's enemy.

So Job struggled to reconcile his circumstances, his understanding about God, and his knowledge about how God works. As the friends insisted that Job could not be innocent, they attempted to bolster their claim by pointing out that these things are simply common knowledge. Everyone knows that retribution is the way God works, and many examples demonstrate that such is the case. Job countered by pointing out that the only way one can support the idea of retribution as the exclusive way God works is to ignore a great deal of data in the world. Numerous and regular examples exist of people who suffer without any apparent reason and, more to the point, wicked people who prosper throughout their lives and die a peaceful death in their old age (21:1–34). The only way a person can support the doctrine of retribution on the basis of the data of human experience is by selecting the examples that support the claim and ignoring the rest.

As frustrating as it must have been for Job to deal with his friends' arguments against him and their lack of personal support for him, the most difficult part of the experience for Job was theological and experiential. Job knew about God from tradition and through his own personal experience, and what was happening to him seemed to be at variance with all of that. Many times in the book, even before the debate with the friends ended, Job's words go past them and are directed to God. Job has little difficulty in concluding that retribution, although generally true, is not a comprehensive statement about how God works. What is much more difficult for him to understand is how all of the pieces relating to God's moral governance of the universe fit together. How can he be innocent, suffer as he is, and God still be just? Is it possible that innocent Job could be vindicated after death?

In chapter 9, Job expresses his desire to argue his case directly before God, presumably either to convince God of his innocence or to have God point out his sin to him. Job dismisses that idea because he recognizes that God is so wise that He could refute all of Job's arguments, and He is so powerful that He could destroy Job even if Job were right. He recognizes in 9:32–35 that, in such a direct encounter, he could not stand alone before God but rather would need a mediator of some kind. Job often cries out to God and expresses his frustration that he finds no relief from his suffering, and he wonders why God persists in attacking him when he is no threat to God (e.g., 7:7–20 and 10:1–22). We see in Job the kind of ambivalence often found in people who are in great pain and emotional distress. They utter bitter cries of pain, confusion, and anger (e.g., 7:1–10; 10:1–7, 18–22; 16:6–17; 17:6–17; 30:16–31). Job demands that God either relent or at least tell him what he has done wrong (10:1–7; 13:20–28). At the same time, we find strong assertions of Job's innocence (16:18–21; 27:1–6; 31:1–40) and statements of confidence that Job will ultimately be vindicated (13:13–19; 17:9; 23:1–7). Although Job does rail at God, he always clings firmly to the conviction that God is his ultimate hope for deliverance and help.

As Job's response continues to evolve, he becomes more fully convinced of his innocence, and he seems to be more emphatic in stating that what has happened to him is unjust. Job 27:2–6 is perhaps the book's strongest statement to that effect. In those verses, Job says,

> As God lives, who has taken away my right, and the Almighty, who has made my soul bitter, as long as my breath is in me, and the spirit of God is in my nostrils, my lips will not speak falsehood, and my tongue will not utter deceit. Far be it from me to say that you [that is, the friends] are right; till I die I will not put away my integrity from me. I hold fast my righteousness and will not let it go; my heart does not reproach me for any of my days.

Certainly, we must understand these statements in the light of Job's pain and emotional state, and in our interpretation of the verses, we must take into account the discussion between God and Satan in the prologue of the book. The book makes clear that Job does not capitulate and do what Satan claims he will do; even in his desolation, he continues to fear and trust God. Yet, at the same time, we must appropriately recognize Job's struggle. Job seems to have come to the point where he is so convinced that he is innocent, and so lacking in any resolution of the tension between God's justice and Job's innocence, that he is more willing to relinquish his faith in God's justice than he is to impugn his own innocence.

We find evidence for this interpretation in the Yahweh speeches and the epilogue of the book. In Job 42:7, God affirms that, unlike the friends, Job has spoken about Him "what is right," so Job clearly did not fail the test; nevertheless, Job's response to God in the Yahweh speeches makes clear that Job has done something for which he needed to repent. After the barrage of questions in chapters 38 and 39, Job says to God in 40:4–5, "Behold, I am of small account; what shall I answer you? I lay my hand on my mouth. I have spoken once, and I will not answer; twice, but I will proceed no further."

In 42:2–6, Job replies to the Lord, "I know that you can do all things, and that no purpose of yours can be thwarted. . . . I have uttered what I did not understand, things too wonderful for me, which I did not know. . . . I will question you, and you make it known to me. I had heard of you by the hearing of the ear, but now my eye sees you; therefore I despise myself, and repent in dust and ashes."

The appearance of the Lord to Job, and the questions that God directed to Job, made clear that Job had jumped to inappropriate conclusions about

the moral governance of God. In a sense, he made the same mistake as the friends in failing to understand the limits of his own knowledge. When confronted with numerous things in nature that God designed and regularly controls through His sovereign providence, Job began to realize that he was in no position to pass judgment on God's justice, and he was forced to confess that he had spoken about that which he did not understand. He was right in insisting on his innocence, but mature piety would have demanded that he be equally vigorous in defending God's justice—even in the presence of circumstances where the two seemed utterly incongruent.

The "answer" for Job did not come in a rational explanation for the suffering; God never told him what we know from the first two chapters. The resolution for Job came from the fact that the Lord's appearance in the theophany made clear to him that his relationship with God was intact and that the suffering did not indicate God's abandonment of or displeasure with him. That fact satisfied Job, and he seems to have been content to allow the mystery of why this happened to remain a mystery. Job 28 has in a sense prepared us for this sort of resolution. The chapter is an interlude that comes after the friends have been silenced in the debate, and many commentators see the chapter as a summary of the "progress" that has been made in the book to this point. The tone of the chapter is very different from that of the debates. It is calm and rational, seeming to step back from the heated discussions that precede it. The chapter begins with a description of what human beings are capable of doing. They are able to find precious gems and metals deep under the earth and bring them out. The human race's extraordinary wisdom is evident in the technology that allows us to accomplish such remarkable things.

At the same time, Job 28:12–22 makes clear that people are incapable of discovering a certain kind of wisdom, and the implication is that the debate between Job and his friends is a display of the inaccessibility of that greater wisdom. Despite twenty-five chapters of debate, no one has come close to the real reason for Job's plight. Job 28:23 makes clear that this kind of wisdom belongs to God, and then Job 28:28 says, "Behold, the fear of the Lord, that is wisdom, and to turn away from evil is understanding." The point of the verse seems to be that many things exist that people will never understand, that God alone knows those things. As human beings, our major responsibility in living wisely does not entail understanding the comprehensive plan of God or figuring out why certain events occur as they do;

rather, our responsibility consists in fearing God and turning away from evil. The point is similar to the one made in Deuteronomy 29:29, which says, "The secret things belong to the LORD our God, but the things that are revealed belong to us and to our children forever, that we may do all the words of this law." Circumstances like those that Job faced, however, can make that task quite difficult.

The Path to Maturity: Living Wisely in the Midst of Suffering

The Old Testament Wisdom Literature teaches many important lessons about suffering, including responses that nourish growth toward spiritual maturity, and recognizes a number of reasons for suffering. Job's arguments against retribution were never meant to deny retribution as one reason why people suffer, and many passages make clear that wicked people regularly suffer the consequences of their evil deeds. From the point made in Psalm 73:17–19 ("I discerned their [that is, the wicked's] end. Truly you set them in slippery places; you make them fall to ruin. How they are destroyed in a moment, swept away utterly by terrors!") to that made in Proverbs 26:27 ("Whoever digs a pit will fall into it, and a stone will come back on him who starts it rolling"), retribution clearly is one principle among several that operate in the world. People do sometimes suffer because of their own wickedness.

Many other passages in the Old Testament recognize that people sometimes suffer as a result of discipline or chastening. Although theologians sometimes make a distinction between the two,[6] the Old Testament generally sees both as a part of *musar* or discipline/instruction. The purpose of *musar* is to correct behavior or attitude, and the method of *musar* is whatever it takes to accomplish that goal. It can involve something as simple as a soft word of correction or something as severe as corporal punishment or suffering of various kinds.

Eliphaz suggests that discipline might explain why calamity has come to Job, and he describes the way this works in Job 5:17–18: "Behold, blessed is the one whom God reproves; therefore despise not the discipline of the

---

6. Discipline occurs when a person has done something wrong and needs to be corrected, whereas chastening is the means by which character is refined.

Almighty. For he wounds, but he binds up; he shatters, but his hands heal." Elihu describes discipline in more detail in Job 33:14–33 as he explains that God subjects people to such things so that "he may turn man aside from his deed and conceal pride from a man" (Job 33:17), and he adds in Job 33:29–30, "God does all these things, twice, three times, with a man, to bring back his soul from the pit, that he may be lighted with the light of life." Their descriptions of discipline are excellent, but unfortunately their attempts to apply this explanation to Job's particular situation were completely off the mark.

The person who wrote Psalm 73 obviously suffered—whether physically or only emotionally is not clear—because of unjust oppression and persecution. Many psalms reveal the same situation, as do instances when people such as David, Jeremiah, or various prophets were persecuted for doing God's will and for standing for what is right rather than surrendering to evil. Job also recognizes that some people suffer because they are oppressed by the wicked. In Job 24, he describes both those who take advantage of the poor and the powerless by depriving them of proper wages and those whose greed and lack of compassion force their victims to live in intolerable conditions (e.g., Job 24:7–12). Proverbs also makes clear that people sometimes suffer because of their own folly. The person whose spending outstrips his or her income, the woman who does not take care of her health, the man who does not control his anger, or the person who takes irresponsible risks will frequently suffer (as will friends and family) as they begin to experience the consequences of those bad choices.

But the story of Job makes clear that God sometimes allows people to suffer for reasons of His own. In this particular instance, God wanted to demonstrate to both Satan and us that some people's faith is not self-serving, and they see in God Himself a Person worthy of their worship and service, even when few overt blessings come to them. Examples such as Job, Jeremiah, and the author of Psalm 44 also show us people whose faith is stretched to the breaking point but who continue to trust God in the midst of their difficulty and suffering. One can imagine that in many instances God allows people to suffer to demonstrate to others the reality of His comfort and faithfulness. God seems sometimes to allow His people to suffer for reasons of His own—but always for reasons that are consistent with His character and for reasons that will bring glory to Himself. One might add that these reasons are always consistent with the affirmation of Romans 8:28 that God works all things together for good for those who love Him and are called according to His purpose.

Robert Gordis has argued that this point is made in Job 39–41, but that, "In accordance with Semitic rhetorical usage [the point] is not spelled out, but [is] left to be inferred by the reader."[7] According to Gordis, these speeches make the point that "the universe was not created exclusively for man's use, and therefore neither it nor its Creator can be judged solely by man's standards and goals."[8] In other words, the purposes of God do not revolve solely around man; thus, humans, like Job, may be called on to suffer as God accomplishes those broader purposes. One has a certain satisfaction in knowing that God uses His children in such ways and that He trusts disciples such as Job in accomplishing those objectives.

Suffering: Responses That Transform

The major contribution of the wisdom books—and the rest of Scripture as well—lies not in the explanations it provides for human suffering but rather in its teaching about responses that transform and lead to spiritual maturity. Both Job and Psalm 73 make clear that the responses to suffering that lead to maturity require neither the knowledge of why the suffering occurred nor an understanding of its significance. In fact, one must endure most suffering with an awareness of neither. The outcome of Job's suffering is expressed in Job 42:5–6, where he says, "I had heard of you by the hearing of the ear, but now my eye sees you; therefore I despise myself, and repent in dust and ashes." As Andersen points out, "He has gained knowledge of God and himself,"[9] and what better indication could one have of significant spiritual growth. The author of Psalm 73 was brought by his experience to exclaim, "Whom have I in heaven but you? And there is nothing on earth that I desire besides you. . . . But for me it is good to be near God; I have made the Lord GOD my refuge" (Ps. 73:25, 28), a response that clearly reflects a significant level of spiritual maturity. But what are the key elements in responses to suffering that make a person better rather than bitter?

---

7. Robert Gordis, *The Book of Job* (New York: Jewish Theological Seminary of America, 1978), 435.
8. Ibid., 235.
9. Francis Andersen, *Job* (Downers Grove, Ill.: InterVarsity, 1976), 292.

Perhaps the most remarkable thing about the response of Job, the author of Psalm 73, or the prophet Jeremiah is their boldness and their honesty with God. They expressed to God their pain, frustration, and confusion. They were at times demanding, and the boldness of their cries to God are sometimes shocking. In Psalm 44, the psalmist expresses his frustration over God's inaction by demanding, "Awake! Why are you sleeping, O Lord?" (Ps. 44:23), and John Goldingay says of this response,

> It is a cry of bewilderment, an astonishing, otherwise unheard of an-thropomorphism, inspired in the poet by his despair. But God allows the saints to plead with him in this babbling manner. The Psalms are a collection of the things that God has been happy for the saints to say to him, prayers and praises that might not every time satisfy the theologian (or the superior kind of believer), but which found acceptance with God because they expressed what was in the heart of his believing people—found such acceptance, in fact, that he welcomed them into his book, and implied the recognition of the activity of his Spirit in inspiring these astonishing prayers and praises.[10]

What is perhaps even more amazing is God's response to Job's bold and sometimes rash words. In chapter 9, Job expressed the desire to argue his case directly with God, and he raises that prospect at other points in the book as well, despite his concern that God's immense wisdom would prevent Job making his point successfully. As he put it in Job 9:3, "If one wished to contend with him, one could not answer him once in a thousand times." He says again in 9:14–15, "How then can I answer him, choosing my words with him? Though I am in the right, I cannot answer him; I must appeal for mercy to my accuser."

When God appears to Job, He does, in fact, ask him question after question that Job cannot answer. The questions are clearly designed to show Job his ignorance, and they do accomplish this objective, but the effect of the questions is very different from what Job had imagined. They do not humiliate Job, despite the rash and challenging words that he has directed toward God. Instead, as Andersen notes, "Their aim is not to crush Job with an awareness of his minuteness contrasted with the limitless power of God,

---

10. John Goldingay, *Songs from a Strange Land* (Downers Grove, Ill.: InterVarsity, 1978; reprint, Toronto: Clements Publishing, 2002), 66–67.

not to mock him when he puts his tiny mind beside God's vast intellect."[11] Instead, they are educative, an example of the point made in James 1:5: "If any of you lacks wisdom, let him ask God, who gives generously to all without reproach, and it will be given him."

God's response involves taking Job into the world that God created and pointing out to him many details of that world that Job did not understand and could not control. This response not only makes Job aware of his limited knowledge, and thus of the absurdity of presuming to pass judgment on God's moral governance of the world, but also causes Job to recognize God's goodness as reflected in His care of His world—the very issue that Job's suffering had caused him to question. At the same time, the very fact that God spoke to Job thus affirmed for Job that his relationship with God was intact. It is essential to note that none of this provided Job with an answer to why he was suffering, but once he was assured that God still cared for him, even though he still did not know the cause of his affliction, he was satisfied.

Although the book of Habakkuk deals with suffering in a very different way than the wisdom passages that we have considered, it nonetheless demonstrates the kind of transforming response that we see in both Job and Psalm 73. The prophet Habakkuk was deeply distressed by Judah's disobedience to God's covenant, and he cried out to God in frustration because God was not punishing Judah for their sin. God assured the prophet that He was, in fact, going to punish them and was going to use Babylon to accomplish that goal. This announcement upset Habakkuk even more because he could not see the justice of using an evil nation such as Babylon to punish a less wicked nation such as Judah. God assured Habakkuk that judgment would finally come on wicked Babylon as well. As the prophet waited for all of this to unfold, he said in Habakkuk 2:1, "I will take my stand at my watchpost and station myself on the tower, and look out to see what he will say to me."

Habakkuk 2:4 describes how people are to respond as they live in the period between the announcement of the judgment and its fulfillment: "The righteous shall live by his faith." What living by faith means in such circumstances is described in a poem in Habakkuk 3, which describes the terror that will accompany the invasion. After describing the disaster that Babylon will inflict on the land, the prophet says, "I hear, and my body trembles; my

---

11. Andersen, *Job*, 271.

lips quiver at the sound; rottenness enters into my bones; my legs tremble beneath me. Yet I will quietly wait for the day of trouble to come upon people who invade us. Though the fig tree should not blossom, nor fruit be on the vines, the produce of the olive fail and the fields yield no food, the flock be cut off from the fold and there be no herd in the stalls, yet I will rejoice in the LORD; I will take joy in the God of my salvation" (Hab. 3:16–18). Living by faith in such times means waiting patiently, despite the turmoil and disaster that prevails around us, for God to do what He has promised.

Whereas the words of Habakkuk are uttered in anticipation of a coming disaster, the words of Job and the author of Psalm 73 come in the midst of the disaster—surely a much more difficult place to be; nonetheless, it is the same response that transforms. Tragedy and suffering may stretch faith to the breaking point and generate cries of pain and confusion, but Job, those like him in Scripture, and others throughout history have continued to trust God and have made Him their refuge, even as the circumstances around them cried out that God must not care. They have found God to be good, providing more than would be adequate for their needs. Through their experiences, they have developed a more intimate knowledge of both God and themselves.

In the mystery of suffering is a transforming power that seems to be almost unique. God's people have, through the crucible of suffering, found a knowledge of God that rarely comes in other ways. A number of years ago, a friend of mine (Edward) injured himself on a hunting trip. When the injury did not heal, he went to a doctor, only to learn that he had leukemia. After several years of treatment, he died of the disease. At his funeral, I was stunned to hear the pastor say that Dick had recently told him that the previous two years had been the best years of his life. He had in those two years, and to a large degree because of his suffering, grown immensely in his relationships with both God and his family. He said that he would not trade for anything the relationships that had developed from his suffering. I have another friend who has been struggling with cancer for a number of years and has recently been told that she has only a short time to live. She has always been a remarkable Christian, but she indicated to me that she has come to know the Lord in a much deeper way through her suffering as she has again and again experienced His care and provision. She also recently told me that the last few years have been the best years of her life.

What my friends have discovered, as they have continued to trust God and cling to Him in their suffering, is what the people of God have always found in such circumstances: God is faithful. He does what He promises, and He is able in such circumstances to provide peace and comfort that goes well beyond what others might imagine possible. Those who trust God in times of immense difficulty truly experience God's all-sufficient grace in their troubles. Moreover, they develop a profound intimacy with God that is, as Job described it, the difference between hearing a rumor about something and experiencing it firsthand. When believers respond faithfully to suffering and continue to seek refuge in God, even though all hope seems to be gone, they find Him faithful and discover the kind of intimacy with God that defines spiritual maturity.

Questions for Thought and Reflection

1. Job's "friends" gave him advice based upon a simplistic reading of Scripture as it existed in their time. That is, they saw Bible passages as applicable in every individual case. One can easily imagine their chagrin when God Himself told them that they were wrong. It is possible even to imagine one of them, Bildad perhaps, saying to the Almighty, "Lord, we only repeated what You said in Your Word. How could we be wrong? Why are You angry with us?" If the Father then left it to you to answer them, what would you say?

2. Your six-year-old daughter Melinda had a pet lizard that escaped into the garden when she put it down to take a drink of lemonade. She has had another lizard now for two months and has been much more careful to keep it in its cage. Nevertheless, the new lizard is missing today. Melinda tells you that she has decided that it makes no difference how careful she is; bad things are going to happen anyway, so she's not going to be careful about anything anymore. What will you say to your child that (a) does not deny the facts of her recent experience but also (b) encourages her to continue taking ordinary precautions in her life?

3. Ask yourself what you expect from God. Everything for which you pray? Eventual life with Him? Encouragement in times of trouble? Making life pleasant for you? A listening ear? Continual excitement in your spiritual walk? Decide which of your expectations are not

valid. Assuming that you trust God's goodness enough to make continual signs of it unnecessary, how does this editing of your expectations change the way you experience disappointment and pain?

Chapter Ten

ECCLESIASTES AND THE MYSTERIES OF LIFE

The book of Proverbs identifies many of the basic principles of God's order, but it does not present anything like a comprehensive philosophy of life or guide to behavior. The principles tend to be general, with some individual proverbs providing specific applications from which the wisdom disciple is expected to generalize. The proper attitude toward money and principles regarding its responsible use, discretion in relationships, and the importance of humility and self-control are standard principles of wisdom that must be learned and applied effectively for a person to succeed in living according to Yahweh's order.

The book of Ecclesiastes, on the other hand, while affirming some of the same principles, goes beyond them to force its readers to acknowledge other realities about life "under the sun," realities that play a very important role in the pursuit of wisdom and maturity. Whereas Proverbs deals largely with the way things normally work, Ecclesiastes focuses on the exceptions, emphasizing not only the struggle that life often involves but also the fact that we do not understand and cannot control many things in life. In such a world, one that includes such realities as Ecclesiastes describes, our lives must be lived and our sanctification must take place. Although the teachings of Ecclesiastes can be difficult to accept, we must acknowledge them as true and integrate them into a scheme for living if we are to grow toward spiritual maturity.

Probably about no other book of the Old Testament has there been so much debate and disagreement over its interpretation and message as about

Ecclesiastes. As Kathleen Farmer points out, "Depending upon whom you read, you might conclude that Ecclesiastes is either 'the quintessence of skepticism' or that it is 'the quintessence of piety.' Interpretive opinions range from the conviction that Qohelet's views run counter to the dominant teachings of the rest of Scripture to the assertion that they faithfully reflect the heart of the tradition and values of Israel."[1]

Although the differences in interpretation of the book often result from the assumptions with which the interpreter approaches the book, such differences are made possible by its apparently conflicting statements. For example, Qohelet points out a number of times in the book (3:16; 5:8; 7:15; 8:14) that injustice is a frustrating reality in the world, and such realities contribute to his conclusion that all is vanity. At the same time, he expresses his confidence that justice will prevail (3:17; 8:12–13). Qohelet affirms the value of wisdom over folly in 2:12–14, but then he realizes that death takes both the wise person and the fool and questions the value of being extremely wise (3:15). Qohelet makes statements that sound very pessimistic and skeptical (e.g., 3:19; 4:2–3; 9:2) while at the same time making other statements that are the epitome of piety and orthodoxy (e.g.,12:13). These tensions in Ecclesiastes are obvious and create confusion for most perceptive readers.

Major debates exist about almost every aspect of the book, and given that reality, it seems somewhat risky to devote an entire chapter to the relevance of Ecclesiastes for spiritual growth, especially when I (Edward) will disagree with many excellent scholars at various points in this brief discussion. I remain convinced, however, that some of the major teachings of the book are of great importance in learning to live according to Yahweh's order in today's world. I am also convinced that some of these truths are not dependent on either a particular interpretive model or specific critical theories about the book and its history; rather, they flow from the final form of the book as it has come down to us in the canon. I do assume that coherence exists in the overall teaching of the Old Testament and that the teaching of Ecclesiastes does not contradict the rest of the Old Testament; therefore, I will sometimes resolve a tension on the basis of ideas that are affirmed elsewhere in the Old Testament.

---

1. Kathleen Farmer, *Proverbs and Ecclesiastes: Who Knows What Is Good?* International Theological Commentary (Grand Rapids: Eerdmans, 1991), 142.

Qohelet the Realist

Without question, Ecclesiastes regularly points out things that many people in the church prefer not to acknowledge, and it is no surprise that the man is often described as a cynic, a skeptic, or a pessimist. But when one looks at many of the things that Qohelet points out to his readers, we must conclude that the man was correct. He is describing accurately the way life often works.

He points out a number of times in the book that life is filled with struggle, toil, and difficulty (see examples of this in Eccl. 1:3; 2:18–19, 21–22; 4:8; 5:18; 9:9), and the Hebrew word translated "toil/labor" often connotes the difficulty and frustration of the labor. Ecclesiastes also emphasizes the injustice that is part of life generally as we know it. In 3:16 he says, "Moreover, I saw under the sun that in the place of justice, even there was wickedness, and in the place of righteousness, even there was wickedness." He says in 4:1, "Again I saw all the oppressions that are done under the sun. And behold, the tears of the oppressed, and they had no one to comfort them! On the side of their oppressors there was power, and there was no one to comfort them." He says again in 5:8, "If you see in a province the oppression of the poor and the violation of justice and righteousness, do not be amazed at the matter, for the high official is watched by a higher, and there are yet higher ones over them."

The reality is that injustice exists, and it often is tolerated and even supported by the political structures. Certainly that is the case in many countries in the world where dictators and oppressive regimes rule, but it is true, though normally to a lesser degree, in democracies as well. Those who are rich often escape punishment because they know the right people or because they can afford the shrewdest lawyers. Often, government laws and agencies created to prevent one sort of injustice end up creating a different kind of injustice, and those injustices are sometimes very difficult to rectify. Often, when injustice is perpetrated by government agencies (e.g., police corruption or IRS errors), the supervising officials "support their own" and will not do anything to correct the wrong that is being done. This reality is not limited to the government; it is found in business when greedy and corrupt corporate executives cover for their colleagues to the great disadvantage of employees or stockholders. It is also found in education, politics, and virtually every other area of life. My mother and grandmother used to say to me (Edward) when I complained that I was being treated unfairly in some activity, "Nobody ever said life was fair," and they were certainly correct.

Ecclesiastes recognizes that such inequities and frustrations do not always result from malicious intent on the part of the people who perpetrate them; sometimes they result from ignorance or incompetence. As Ecclesiastes 9:18–10:1 says, "Wisdom is better than weapons of war, but one sinner [or one person who errs] destroys much good. Dead flies make the perfumer's ointment give off a stench; so a little folly outweighs wisdom and honor." A little folly, we might say, can negate the results of much wise planning and diligent work. One mistake at a crucial time in an athletic contest, a military campaign, or an engineering project can result in disaster.

I (Edward) have a friend who works in what had been a very successful program in a public school in the Midwest. A new administrator was assigned to the program, and he basically destroyed it. Among other things, he required the teachers to spend so much time doing paperwork and filling out forms that they had no time to teach, something that had once been a strength of the program. Even more frustrating was the fact that all of the paperwork went to only this administrator and did nothing more than feed his pathological need for control. No one at either the district or the state level had any interest in it; actually, all of the information was readily available elsewhere. A little folly destroyed a very effective program, and this man's superiors supported him in his folly and refused to do anything to stop it. As 10:5–6 puts it, "There is an evil that I have seen under the sun, as it were an error proceeding from the ruler: folly is set in many high places, and the *rich* sit in a low place."[2] As Longman notes, the verse describes the chaos that results from the ruler putting "the wrong people in the wrong positions."[3] About such abuses in our own time, Qohelet would just shake

---

2. The parallel between "folly set in many high places" and "the rich sit in a low place" does not seem logical to us in a world where we have been conditioned to associate wealth with oppression and injustice. Wisdom, however, is looking at things from a different perspective. Wisdom recognizes that the same qualities that enable a person to become rich are also the ones that are appropriate in leadership in the community. Thus, the situation that is described here is one where the social order has been turned upside down and the wrong people (i.e., the foolish ones) are in control.

3. Tremper Longman III, *The Book of Ecclesiastes,* New International Commentary on the Old Testament (Grand Rapids: Eerdmans, 1998), 242.

his head and say, "See? I told you so." Could anything be more current or true to life than Ecclesiastes?

Qohelet spends a lot of time in the book pointing out that many things in life we can neither understand nor control. He reminds us in chapter 3 that there is a time for all sorts of activities in life. If the activity is timed correctly, the results can be good and positive, and we all understand that poor timing can lead to real disaster. Imagine a doctor who does not get 3:3 right ("[there is] a time to kill, and a time to heal"). Or imagine a contractor who is remodeling your house and gets confused about the second part of that verse ("[there is] a time to break down, and a time to build up"). The problem, of course, is that we do not always know the right time for each necessary activity. Try as we may, we cannot always determine that with accuracy. Qohelet makes clear that this is one of the things that we cannot always understand, and our limited knowledge causes us frustration, sometimes producing an undesirable outcome.

Ecclesiastes points out that many things people do in life are fraught with risks. He says in 10:8–9, "He who digs a pit will fall into it, and a serpent will bite him who breaks through a wall. He who quarries stones is hurt by them, and he who splits logs is endangered by them." Risks are inherent in even the most basic activities of life, and one simply cannot anticipate and avoid every possibility for accidents. Qohelet also makes clear that things are not always what they seem to be. At the end of chapter 6, for example, he states, "Who knows what is good?" and then goes on to cite a number of proverbs describing situations that initially seem bad but might turn out to be good and vice versa. For example, he tells us that it is better to go to a funeral than to go to a party because the funeral forces a person to acknowledge the reality of death, something that rarely comes up at parties. The wise person takes to heart that death is inevitable, and he then lives life differently.

Solomon also forces us to recognize that many things exist over which we have no control but that determine the outcomes of important endeavors in life. For example, he says in 9:11–12, "Again I saw that under the sun the race is not to the swift, nor the battle to the strong, nor bread to the wise, nor riches to the intelligent, nor favor to those with knowledge, but time and chance happen to them all. For man does not know his time. Like fish that are taken in an evil net, and like birds that are caught in a snare, so the children of man are snared at an evil time, when it suddenly falls upon them."

We all have faced situations where important outcomes hinge on things that are out of our control. Sometimes those things work out to our advantage. For example, my wife and I (Edward) once bought a house and discovered in the escrow process that legal issues made it unlikely that we would ever be able to buy the property. The issues had been unresolved for several years, with both sides in the dispute becoming quite determined that they would never agree to the sort of compromise that might resolve the dispute. But, to the amazement of both ourselves and the realtors and lawyers involved in the case, a whole series of things worked out, and we were able to buy the house. On the other hand, there are often situations where, had we applied for a job a day earlier, we would have been hired, or where we called too late to get a badly needed item at a price we could afford. Tragedies overwhelm people (both saved and unsaved) quite suddenly and destroy what seemed to be a future with unlimited potential. And then some people, although their abilities seem to be mediocre, nevertheless enjoy great success because they always seem to be in the right place at the right time. Although Qohelet recognizes that ultimately the sovereignty of God underlies all such events (e.g., 3:9–11; 7:13; 8:16–17; 9:1–3, 11–12), he also makes clear that, on the basis of simply observing life, it is not at all clear that God's sovereign providence provides confidence and comfort— something to which we will return shortly.

Although Qohelet simply describes the reality that he sees and does not normally resort to theological explanations, we immediately understand that many of the things he points out do reflect life in a fallen world: the injustice and unfairness; failure to punish evil promptly, and sometimes not at all; and unjust reversals of fortune. Yet, we must point out once again that in such a fallen world sanctification takes place. The Lord brings us into conformity with the image of Christ in a world that includes precisely the evils and uncertainties that Ecclesiastes describes, and it is doubtful that spiritual development can occur if we do not recognize those realities. As we noted earlier, we are finite creatures with limited ability to understand reality. Although we are able to understand certain segments of life fairly well, the real difficulty in understanding life comes in trying to identify all of the pieces and then discovering their interrelationship in the comprehensive design. Kidner, in his comments on 3:1–15, says of the perpetual change that is an integral part of life,

> The trouble for us is not that life refuses to keep still, but that we see
> only a fraction of its movement and of its subtle, intricate design. . . .
> We catch these brilliant moments, but . . . they leave us unsatisfied for
> lack of any total meaning that we can grasp . . . We are like the desper-
> ately nearsighted, inching their way along some great tapestry or fresco
> in the attempt to take it in. We see enough to recognize something of
> its quality, but the grand design escapes us, for we can never stand back
> far enough to view it as its Creator does, whole and entire, *from the*
> *beginning to the end.*[4]

Growth toward spiritual maturity occurs in a world like that observed by
Qohelet, where we must contend with evil and uncertainty and live without understanding how all of the pieces fit together coherently. Our observation and experience will not provide irrefutable evidence regarding the
meaning of life, or even whether life has any meaning. If we ignore these
handicaps of our fallen world, we will only create further disappointments
and obstacles to our growth, especially when we meet unexpected tragedies
from which we thought Christians were exempt.

Qohelet the Teacher

In the epilogue of the book, Qohelet is commended as an excellent
teacher.[5] He was wise; he taught the people knowledge; and he pondered,
searched out, and arranged many proverbs. He worked diligently to present
his teachings in delightful words, and according to this final section of the
book, he wrote words of truth correctly. We are told that the words of wise
people (presumably including Qohelet) are like goads used to prod animals
(12:11), and the point here seems to be that the words of skilled wisdom
teachers can prod students into thoughts and behaviors consistent with the

---

4. Derek Kidner, *The Message of Ecclesiastes,* The Bible Speaks Today (Downers
   Grove, Ill.: InterVarsity, 1976), 39.
5. For a different understanding of these comments about Qohelet as teacher,
   see Tremper Longman III, *Proverbs,* New International Commentary on the
   Old Testament (Grand Rapids: Eerdmans, 1998), 37–39, 276–81. Longman
   argues that Qohelet is, in fact, a skeptic and that a frame narrator is the voice
   of orthodoxy. He sees these verses describing Qohelet's teaching, but he sees
   them as a description of a kind of teaching of which young people should
   beware.

insights of wisdom. Clearly, these verses depict Qohelet as a skilled craftsman in the art of teaching and persuasion, and I assume that the book of Ecclesiastes provides an example of the kind of teaching for which Qohelet (and no doubt other wise men as well) was famous. Certainly his teaching is different from most of the teaching with which we are familiar, and I suspect that a failure to understand his methods has contributed to the diverse interpretations that scholars offer for the book. Whereas most of our teaching develops logically from premise to conclusion, much of Ecclesiastes (in keeping with many other wisdom passages) is more like a collage in which a number of related passages are arranged around a central theme. Kaplan calls such an organization "an approach by indirection," in which the individual units "turn around the subject and show it from a variety of tangential views, but the subject is never looked at directly."[6]

One of the most obvious techniques that Qohelet used was tensions, or what Loader calls polar opposites,[7] and the tensions do not always seem to work in the same way. Sometimes the tensions produce a better understanding. For example, wisdom and folly are contrasted in 2:12–26 (and throughout much of the book). The initial comparison of the two makes clear that wisdom is superior to folly. At this point, however, the author introduces another tension—the fact that death eliminates any advantage that wisdom generates because wisdom does not deliver the wise person from death. Any advantage that wisdom gains for a person during his lifetime is left behind at death. In this instance, Qohelet uses tension to affirm both the advantage of wisdom over folly and the limits of wisdom. The effect of this technique is to bring the disciple to an awareness of not only the advantages and benefits of wisdom but also its clear limitations. The teacher uses his words as goads to move his students in one direction and then fine-tunes their concept in a slightly different direction as he seeks to bring them to a more accurate understanding.

In some instances, Qohelet uses tension to bring his students to a better balance, as is obvious in 7:15–18, where the author presents the tension

---

6. Robert B. Kaplan, "Cultural Thought Patterns in Inter-Cultural Education," in *Readings on English as a Second Language,* 2d ed., ed. Kenneth Croft (Boston: Little, Brown & Co., 1980), 406.

7. J. A. Loader, *Ecclesiastes: Text and Interpretation* (Grand Rapids: Eerdmans, 1986); see, also, idem, *Polar Structures in the Book of Qohelet* (Hawthorne, N.Y.: De Greyter, 1979).

between the experiences of the righteous and the wicked. He notes that the fate of the two is not always what tradition would lead a person to expect. He then argues that it is not good to be too righteous nor is it good to be too wicked. Although it is not clear exactly what Qohelet means by "too righteous" (perhaps an obsession with keeping the law or with ritual, or "ostentatious showmanship in the act of worship"[8]) or by "too wicked," what is clear is that the person who fears God "comes forth with both of them." Thus even if we remain uncertain as to the exact abuses about which Qohelet is concerned, it is apparent that his goal is to bring a person to a balance that allows one to avoid the problems of either extreme and to draw from the benefits that each pole of the contrast involves. The fear of the Lord provides the key to the balance and makes clear that Qohelet definitely is not saying "sin enough to keep life interesting."

Often, the tension in Ecclesiastes is between the way things are "under the sun" and the way things ought to be.[9] Many of these tensions are not resolved explicitly, and some of them seem to be irresolvable—which is certainly one of the points Qohelet wants his students to understand. Qohelet strongly emphasizes the limits of man's ability to understand and his inability to control various aspects of life, and the tensions set those realities in clear relief. We know that there is a correct time for success in any undertaking, but often we cannot determine what that time is (3:11; 9:1–2; 11:1–6). Beyond that, we cannot understand and determine God's activity and timing. The uneven treatment of the righteous and the wicked creates tension that Qohelet wants us to recognize, and he regularly sets forth the tension between what the religious tradition affirms and the experiences of life that stand in contrast with it. Qohelet also contrasts the activity of God (which people cannot understand or control) with human activity, the outcomes of which often depend on that work of God.

Qohelet does provide some movement toward resolution of these ten-

---

8. Walter Kaiser, *Ecclesiastes*, Everyman's Bible Commentary (Chicago: Moody, 1979), 85.

9. Michael Fox argues that when Qohelet says "all is vanity" he is making a statement "about the logic of the system of worldly events" (*A Time to Tear Down and a Time to Build Up* [Grand Rapids: Eerdmans, 1999], 48–49). His point is that there is no grand causal order on which we can depend under the sun. Fox argues that the "vanity" (Fox would translate the Hebrew word as "absurd") has to do "with the disparity between reasonable expectations and actual consequences."

sions. He points out that sometimes the reason for the anomalies is that things are not always what they seem to be. The whole section of "better than" proverbs in 6:12–7:14 provides examples of this point. Sometimes the reason for the injustice is human depravity (7:29; 8:11). Sometimes Qohelet presents faith as the way to resolve the tension. For example, in 8:12–13, after noting that injustice often prevails in the world, he expresses his confidence that "it will be well with those who fear God. . . . But it will not be well for the wicked," a conclusion that is based on a faith that denies the finality of human experience. Often, however, the tensions are not resolved. Obviously, Qohelet was a teacher who was not afraid of ambiguity and a lack of closure as he taught his students.

Qohelet was also a teacher who challenged his students and was willing to risk allowing them to reach their own conclusions. His teaching often involves indirection and implication rather than explicit and overt propositions, and, of course, this is one reason why so many different opinions exist about what he taught. Qohelet begins the book, for example, with a description of recurring and endless cycles in nature but never states the point of the description explicitly. The intention seems to be to raise for the reader the question of whether man's life has any more meaning and significance than those repetitive cycles of nature,[10] but the student must discover the point of the discourse. The Yahweh speeches in Job 38–41 reflect a similar methodology. Yahweh asks Job one question after another about various aspects of the natural world. As Gordis says, the section shows that "Just as there is order and harmony in the natural world, though imperfectly grasped by man, so there is order and meaning in the moral sphere, though often incomprehensible to man. This, the heart and essence of the God-speeches, is made by implication, but nonetheless effectively."[11]

Qohelet saw questions and tension as important teaching devices. He used his words as goads to direct students, but he left it to them to draw the proper conclusions and to discover the appropriate answers. Not only do we see here Qohelet's confidence in his students' ability to draw the right conclusions (after all, they were, no doubt, his own disciples) but also his methodology suggests that he thought that something important was gained

---

10. Is life only, as Macbeth says, "A tale told by an idiot, full of sound and fury, signifying nothing"?

11. Robert Gordis, *Koheleth: The Man and His World* (New York: Shocken, 1968), 117.

in the process. One of my students said of the book, "Throughout the book the answer that Qohelet is desiring for us to find is the one that remains unwritten until the end of the book. By doing this the book affirms the importance of learning and of individual and corporate thought processes in finding answers." The methodology is similar to that reflected in a rabbinic story told by Perry. Several students asked their teacher a question, and his answer did not correspond to what he had taught them previously. He commended them for their astuteness and then went on to say, "The case was not that he didn't know but rather he wanted to stimulate his students." They then referred to Rabbi Joshuah, who used to say, "Whoever learns but does not labor at it is like a man who sows but does not reap."[12]

Qohelet's methodology likely reflects an awareness that, despite the importance of tradition, the search for wisdom does not involve simply accepting other people's answers to standard questions, and the most important contribution of the book might well lie more in the questions that he raises than in the answers that he provides. The realities of life are far more varied than the paradigm questions might suggest, and only as people forge out answers in the complex experiences of life is genuine wisdom acquired. Wisdom is not mastery of a body of knowledge; it is skill for living in the world. In this fallen world, we are confronted regularly by significant tensions—often even polar opposites—as we seek to integrate our knowledge of God and the world with the diverse circumstances that confront us. Wisdom and spiritual maturity require the skill to develop answers and responses to experiences that are different from the ones that the textbook told us we would encounter. Qohelet not only alerts us to this fact but also, through his methodology, begins to equip his students for these realities and prepare them for living wisely.

Job illustrates the sort of thing for which Ecclesiastes is preparing his students. The difficulty that arose between Job and his friends did so because Job's experience did not correspond to the standard categories. The friends were determined to fit the experience into those categories despite Job's insistence that the categories were not relevant to his case, and so they got it wrong, causing even more pain to an already suffering friend. Job was forced to respond to a situation that did not fit the paradigm, and his struggle brought him to greater spiritual maturity and wisdom. It is for just such

---

12. Tosefta (on Parah 4:1), cited by T. A. Perry, *Dialogues with Qohelet* (University Park, Pa.: Penn State University Press, 1993), 40.

experiences, those for which no clearly defined answers exist, that the methodology of Qohelet prepares us. Both in his description of life in a fallen world and in his method of forcing us to deal with tensions and polarities in our understanding of God and his world, Qohelet provides us with essential grist for the mill that produces spiritual maturity.

One additional point remains to be made about Qohelet and his teaching methods. Perhaps no question has been debated more vigorously than that of whether Qohelet was a man of faith or a skeptic whose work questions the very foundations of Israel's faith. Although most modern commentators see the Preacher as a skeptic, I would argue that, based on the present text of the book, a number of indications exist that the author was, in fact, committed to Israel's faith, although his teaching methodology and his purpose sometimes obscure that fact. He calls his readers to fear the Lord in 3:14; 5:7; 8:12; and 12:13, and his final word is "Fear God and keep his commandments, for this is the whole duty of man" (Eccl. 12:13). At other points in the book, the author's faith in God's providence seems clear (e.g., 8:12–13; 11:9). In fact, Qohelet, in his search for some activity that will generate a profit or advantage that death cannot take from him, seems to be demonstrating what life apart from the fear of God amounts to—it is vanity.[13] As he points out questions and tensions that cannot be answered or resolved on the basis of our experiences under the sun, his point seems to be that there is no way to resolve them apart from God's special revelation and faith. According to Qohelet, life has little meaning and little coherence apart from God and His providence and purposes. Because he recognizes God's sovereign providence behind all of life, the question becomes, "Is God good, and can one take comfort and find hope in His providence?"

I would argue that Qohelet presupposes the fundamentals of Israel's faith

---

13. The Hebrew word translated "vanity" is *hebel,* a word that is difficult to define. The word itself means "breath" or "vapor," and in Ecclesiastes it refers to that which is meaningless or insubstantial, temporal and fleeting, or absurd because it does not produce results that seem appropriate. Sometimes, it refers to that which is untrue (e.g., to idols, which are nothing but lies). Duane A. Garrett summarizes its meaning in Ecclesiastes: "Everything is transitory and therefore of no lasting value. People are caught in the trap of the absurd and pursue empty pleasures. They build their lives on lies" (*Proverbs, Ecclesiastes, Song of Songs,* vol. 14 of New American Commentary [Nashville: Broadman & Holman, 1993], 283).

(e.g., Exod. 34:6–7 or many of the psalms that celebrate God's goodness), and his challenging and provocative questions are set within the framework of Israel's knowledge of God. The words of Kidner about Proverbs 2:1–5 can, in my opinion, be applied equally well to Ecclesiastes: "The search [for wisdom], strenuous as it must be, is not unguided. Its starting point is revelation . . . ; its method is not one of free speculation, but of treasuring and exploring received teachings so as to penetrate to their principles . . . ; and its goal, far from being academic, is spiritual."[14] It is recognizing the broader theological context in which the teaching is set that transforms the message of Ecclesiastes from one of discouragement and hopelessness into one that is "profitable for teaching, for reproof, for correction, and for training in righteousness, that the man of God may be competent, equipped for every good work" (2 Tim. 3:16–17).

Qohelet and Life According to Yahweh's Order

In the light of all that Qohelet says about what we cannot know, about what we cannot control, and about the risks that are inherent in many essential activities in life, one might suppose that he would just give up on life or opt for some of the depressing conclusions of philosophers such as Camus. Qohelet, however, does not see resignation and despair as necessary conclusions from what he has pointed out to us. In 10:11, he says, "If the serpent bites before it is charmed, there is no advantage to the charmer," his point being that knowledge or skill does a person no good unless timely action accompanies it. Something is especially ironic and sad about a financial adviser who has to file for personal bankruptcy because of poor financial management or a marriage counselor who ends up in divorce court because he or she failed to practice the advice given to others. Clearly, this proverb is meant to motivate us to do something with the knowledge we possess.

Ecclesiastes 11:6 points out that we cannot know whether planting seed in the morning will give better results than planting in the evening, so his advice is, "In the morning sow your seed, and at evening withhold not your hand, for you do not know which will prosper, this or that, or whether both alike will be good." Just as the risk involved in digging pits, breaking through

---

14. Derek Kidner, *Proverbs,* vol. 15 of Tyndale Old Testament Commentaries (Downers Grove, Ill.: InterVarsity, 1964), 61.

walls, and splitting logs must not deter us from those activities because the benefits normally outweigh the risks, so the lack of guarantees in life must not paralyze us from activity. We are to engage in our activities diligently, even when we have no way of knowing precisely which approach will give us the best results. We are also to live wisely. That is why so many proverbs are in Ecclesiastes. Given the difficulties that are a real part of living in a fallen world, we need all of the help we can get, and the last thing we need to do is to compound our problems by ignoring the advice of wisdom and thereby making foolish choices.

Qohelet recognizes that ultimately the sovereign providence of God lies behind everything that we experience in life, but human beings are unable to fully comprehend that work of God. He says in 7:13, "Consider the work of God, For who is able to straighten what He has bent?" (NASB), and again in 11:5, "Just as you do not know the path of the wind and how bones are formed in the womb of the pregnant woman, so you do not know the activity of God who makes all things" (NASB). In 9:1, he adds, "For I have taken all this to my heart and explain it that righteous men, wise men, and their deeds are in the hand of God" (NASB).

Qohelet clearly recognizes that the will of God causes things to work out the way they do, but the question is whether the idea is comforting for the Preacher or instead contributes to his frustration and distress. Longman says, "God's sovereignty is affirmed by Qohelet, but this sovereignty actually calls into question God's concern for his people. He has a plan but does not reveal it to his people and those who want to know what it is. . . . Qohelet may well believe in divine providence, but it is no source of comfort to him as he faces the unpredictable chaos of life."[15] As I have already indicated, I see this differently from the way Longman does for three reasons: (1) because of the way I have chosen to understand the teaching methods of the author, (2) because of the way the fear of the Lord idea is interjected at crucial points in the book, and (3) because I see the book as set in the broader context of Israel's faith. Thus, I am convinced that the author's perspective is the perspective of biblical faith.

At the same time, I think that one of the most significant contributions of the book is that it presents this question in such clear relief, a question much more significant than whether Qohelet was a man of faith. The question is also addressed in Proverbs 21:30–31, which says, "There is no

---

15. Longman, *The Book of Ecclesiastes*, 35.

wisdom and no understanding and no counsel against the LORD. The horse is prepared for the day of battle, But victory belongs to the LORD" (NASB). Gerhard von Rad calls this an astonishing sentence. Its point, he says,

> is not to warn man against acquiring and using wisdom or even to prevent him from "making ready" the horse for battle. If one were to remove it from its context one could perceive in it a radical, theological agnosticism. But this would be to misunderstand it completely. Its aim was rather to put a stop to the erroneous concept that a guarantee of success was to be found simply in practicing human wisdom and in making preparations. Man must always keep himself open to the activity of God, an activity which completely escapes all calculation, for between the putting into practice of the most reliable wisdom and that which actually takes place, there always lies a great unknown. Is that a dangerous doctrine? Must not . . . [,] as a result of this great unknown factor, a veil of resignation lie over all human knowledge and action? The question can be answered only by the degree of trust which man is capable of placing in that divine activity which surpasses all planning.[16]

Qohelet is pointing out the importance of the question rather than simply expressing his own opinion on the matter. In the face of experiences in life that seem to be at variance with the idea that God is good, can a person continue to trust God and live by faith? God's providence is often shrouded in mystery and uncertainty, and terrible atrocities occur in a fallen world. Trusting in God's goodness, while waiting patiently for Him to work out His purposes for us, will help us to avoid being overwhelmed with despair in the face of life apparently without meaning and leading nowhere and will enable us to live with confidence and anticipation in the light of God's providence. Qohelet makes clear that we will never understand God's goodness, His faithfulness to His promises, or many of His other attributes if we try to do so on the basis of the evidence presented by life in a fallen world. The data are simply too ambiguous.

In His revelation in Scripture and in His marvelous deeds, both in creation and on behalf of His people, God has given us significant grounds for trusting Him even when we do not understand. We, of course, are in a far

---

16. Gerhard von Rad, *Wisdom in Israel,* trans. James Martin (Nashville: Abingdon, 1972), 101.

better position to answer this question than was any believer in the Old Testament. We have seen God's irrevocable commitment to us demonstrated at the Cross, we have experienced the blessings of God's grace in ways that surpass anything that Qohelet ever could have known, and we have both the Old and New Testaments to tell us about God and His providence.

Once we are assured that God is good and that He is committed to us, the things that we do not understand and the things that we cannot control will seem far less frustrating and ominous. The knowledge that outcomes are determined by the hand of God now becomes a basis for hope, confidence, and even delight. Once we begin to live the way God has instructed us and to trust in Him for the outcomes, we will be better able to apply Qohelet's advice to enjoy and take delight in life. We will begin to live with a growing awareness that the "better than" proverbs have vast dimensions because we will have set the experiences of life in the broader context of God's sovereignty. We will also be more patient about reaching conclusions about the goodness or badness of the things that happen to us. The distress and disappointment of a job possibility that did not work out or a failed relationship might look very different in hindsight, so instead of throwing up our hands in despair, we will wait to see what God might be doing before judging the event.

I suspect that we are often unable to know the true significance and value of the various components that make up our lives. We think that certain things that we do or certain ministries in which we are involved really make an impact, but I think that we would probably be quite surprised if we could see how God views our lives. We would probably be startled at the things He sees as significant and insignificant.

A couple of times in the last several years, graduates have returned and told me about how one of my classes influenced their lives and how it helped them in both life and ministry. In one instance, I (Edward) did not even remember the student until I checked my records and found that he really had been in some of my classes. I was surprised to hear the student's comments; I never would have guessed that God used my ministry in the way he described. I think of Saul when he went out looking for his father's lost donkeys. He was very upset about his failure to find those donkeys, but in reality, in God's providence, the trip was not about the donkeys. It was about leadership in Israel. I also think of friends who met their spouses in circumstances where neither of them had any interest in finding a husband or wife, and in hindsight they discovered that God had different purposes in those situations than they ever imagined.

Diogenes Allen illustrates the point:

> Not long ago, I heard a short story read aloud. Virtually every word of the story seemed to grip the audience, and I wondered why. It was not simply because it was a good story that was read with great artistry; rather, the audience heard it unfold without knowing which part of the story would be important. For someone to come out of a house, get into a car, and slowly drive away is a prosaic event. But when this action is part of a story, it can—as it did in this case—hold our attention because it just might turn out to be significant.
>
> In a well-constructed short story everything makes a contribution to the overall effect, just as every detail in a great painting is important. But we do not experience everything in our actual lives this way; only some of our life is interesting. As our life unfolds, most of it is utterly prosaic. Well-constructed stories appeal to us because all the events make a contribution to the whole. Perhaps we wish that all the events in our lives were as interesting or at least contributed to some overall meaning.[17]

Qohelet raises the possibility that, because of God's providence, each detail—even the seemingly prosaic ones—may prove to be significant and do, in fact, make a contribution to the whole regardless of whether we recognize it. Consequently, I think that we need to view our lives differently. Some events in our life story that we consider insignificant might well turn out, as events unfold, to be much more important than we suppose. Clearly, we must fear God and turn from evil, but we should also attend to all of the details of life—not obsessively, which creates guilt, but in a way that sees every circumstance as a possibility for honoring God and for character development. In whatever situation God puts us, we must respond with diligence and anticipation. Because we almost never know which detail of our own story may prove, in God's providence, to be significant, we should not be so quick to judge the importance of things that come into our lives or the potential outcomes of those things. A certain conversation with a friend

---

17. Diogenes Allen, *Spiritual Theology* (Boston: Cowley Publications, 1997), 7.

might turn out to be more significant than a spotless house or another deal closed. Treating the clerk at the grocery store courteously and kindly might, after many days, make a bigger impact than the Bible study that you lead.

In 11:1–6, Qohelet continues to teach his readers how to live in the light of the realities that he has pointed out. He says,

> Cast your bread upon the waters,
>   for you will find it after many days.
> Give a portion to seven, or even to eight,
>   for you know not what disaster may happen on earth.
> If the clouds are full of rain,
>   they empty themselves on the earth,
> and if a tree falls to the south or to the north,
>   in the place where the tree falls, there it will lie.
> He who observes the wind will not sow,
>   and he who regards the clouds will not reap.
> As you do not know the way the spirit comes to the bones in the womb of a woman with child, so you do not know the work of God who makes everything. In the morning sow your seed, and at evening withhold not your hand, for you do not know which will prosper, this or that, or whether both alike will be good.

In these verses, the author mixes the metaphors of the merchant and the farmer, but his basic point seems clear: the results of our actions will usually reveal themselves—although it might take a long time before those results are clear. But what is always clear is that there is no place for procrastination and indecision. Qohelet is exhorting us to apply the principles of the merchant and the farmer to the way we live our lives.

Francis Glasson, commenting on verses 4–6, points out that something about sowing seed is chancy and unpredictable. Sometimes a gardener may work very hard on a plot of ground and a crop planted there but get little or no results—sometimes because of circumstances that are completely beyond his control. Occasionally, however, a plant or a tree stuck into the ground on a whim may flourish and give unexpectedly good results. Based on these verses, Glasson suggests, "You never know what may happen in unlikely places; you never know what may happen at odd times and even in unfavorable seasons; you never know what may emerge 'after many days;' and you never know what God is doing through your service." He concludes, "We must sow everywhere, even in the unlikeliest places."[18]

It seems absurd to sow among rocks and thistles, but you never know—the most unlikely places can yield a surprising harvest. Now we are not here addressing the question of priorities or time management, although those topics are important aspects of wisdom.[19] What Glasson is saying is that if God has put you in an obscure place, be diligent and sow wherever you can because you never know what may ultimately spring up from some life that you touch. Qohelet reminds us that if you wait for perfect conditions, you will never get anything done.

I am convinced that it is unhealthful for both individual believers and the church to deny the realities that Qohelet points out. We do not know and cannot understand many things, including injustice, oppression, inequity, and the misfortune that is all around us. The outcomes of many situations are determined by factors that are beyond our control and knowledge. Life is filled with times when people's bad choices create problems for both themselves and others around them. In the presence of such realities, Qohelet clearly sees the pervasive work of God, and he recognizes that life does not always provide clear evidence of God's goodness. Believers who naively suppose that bad things do not happen to good people and who live life in denial of the reality that Qohelet describes will never become spiritually mature. The frequent result is that an unexpected and devastating tragedy might do significant damage to their immature faith.

Qohelet raises a truly vital question: Can I trust God and be confident of His goodness in the presence of the troubling realities that Qohelet describes? The answer is that a person's knowledge of God will determine whether he or she will live in this fallen world with hope and anticipation or with fear and frustration. That knowledge must be informed by Scripture and set in the context of an intimate relationship with God. Only as we keep growing in that knowledge of Him will we keep moving toward wisdom and spiritual maturity. Learning to see all of life as being under the sovereignty of

---

18. T. Francis Glasson, "'You Never Know': The Message of Ecclesiastes 11:1–6," *Evangelical Quarterly* 55(1983): 45.

19. I am certain that Qohelet would tell us to practice those skills, although I suspect that he would warn us against becoming a slave to them.

God, and recognizing in our present circumstances (whether abundance or lack, celebration or distress) those gifts that come from God's hand for us to enjoy, will be a powerful aid to our growing in grace and knowledge of God. Learning to trust in God's providence and to wait patiently to see how God will work out His purposes for us gives us a focus that enables us to learn about God and to discover His goodness in all sorts of unexpected places. Learning to live in the fear of the Lord and in the obedience of faith gives us stability and hope when the world seems to be spinning out of control and when we have no idea why things are working as they are and no visible basis for expecting that things will get better anytime soon.

Just as an athlete becomes stronger and perfects his skill through hard work and diligent training, so the struggle to integrate our experience with our faith is part of the process by which God brings us to greater maturity. This enables us to live with hope and excitement, knowing that our times are in God's hands and that we are therefore secure. It will also allow us to enjoy the ride (bumpy though it may sometimes be) as we live in a fallen world and encounter a host of things that we cannot understand or control, knowing that God is working out His purposes. Then we can wait with anticipation as we watch to see which details of our story God may use in surprisingly gracious ways.

Questions for Thought and Reflection

1. Your Bible study group is discussing Ecclesiastes. During the last session on this book of the Old Testament, two people state their opinions on the book as a whole. Person X says, "Ecclesiastes depresses me. I read the Bible to be uplifted, not to be reminded of the problems in real life. I don't know why this book is even in the Bible." Person Y says, "Finally, something in the Bible tells it like it is. I couldn't go on believing a religion that told me that life is all roses when I know it's full of thorns." How can you respond to these two different remarks? (Note that you do not need to agree or disagree entirely with either remark.)

2. Both Ecclesiastes and Job imply strongly that we human beings are unable to understand some things about God's ways with the world. How comfortable are you with that message? Are you at all displeased that God does not explain to us everything that He knows? Has a

young child ever asked you a question that, although you knew the answer, you also knew that the child would not be capable of following your explanation?

3. "In the morning sow your seed, and in the evening withhold not your hand, for you do not know which will prosper," says Qohelet. Compile a list of the opportunities that you regularly have for doing the Lord's work, opportunities that you might have neglected because they seemed unpromising or because you felt that you already were involved in an organized ministry. (This is not advice to overextend yourself; it is meant to encourage you to drop some seeds of the kingdom in places that might look rocky or overgrown with weeds.)

Conclusion

WISDOM, FAITH, AND THE PURSUIT OF GODLINESS

I (Edward) have a friend who can repair almost anything, and I have tried hard to discover his secret because I am frankly envious of his skills. I have come to realize that my friend is blessed with an intuitive ability to understand how things work. But in addition to this intuitive ability, Bill has spent a lot of time carefully observing and studying the things he sees, always trying to figure out what makes them tick. His house is filled with all sorts of amazing gadgets. We have taken a few trips together, and he is always examining things that we see, explaining how they work, and pointing out what could be done to make them work more effectively. He loves to go to museums that display technology, either modern or ancient. He finds genuine delight in understanding how things work, in repairing them, and in making things function better. This combination of innate ability, careful study, and diligent application and practice has made my friend as good as he is at repairing things. I am also certain that the delight he has in doing such things has been developed and intensified by practice, particularly by practice in which he finally experiences the pleasure of success in either fixing something that is broken or making something work more efficiently.

Growth toward spiritual maturity occurs in much the same way. People develop basic skills as they study the way things work and then apply the acquired truths and techniques in a variety of circumstances. Consistent practice enables a person to develop the requisite skills to apply the principles appropriately to more and more complex situations. In this instance as well, delight grows with practice as a person experiences the satisfaction that comes from success in living wisely, from knowing that one has done what is right, or from behaving in a way that honors God.

We have argued throughout this book that the Old Testament Wisdom Literature contains much that is relevant for spiritual growth. The pursuit of wisdom in many ways parallels the growth in "the grace and knowledge of our Lord and Savior" to which Peter calls believers in 2 Peter 3:18. And Proverbs 2:5 makes clear that the goal of both wisdom and Peter's exhortation are one and the same—the knowledge of God. The pursuit of wisdom involves many of the same things as are involved in carrying out Paul's charge to Timothy to "be diligent to present yourself approved to God as a workman who does not need to be ashamed, accurately handling the word of truth" (2 Tim. 2:15 NASB). Paul also says that wisdom, though now more narrowly defined as God's special revelation in Scripture, is "profitable for teaching, for reproof, for correction, for training in righteousness; so that the man of God may be adequate [complete], equipped for every good work" (2 Tim. 3:16–17 NASB). It seems obvious that the process of sanctification will bring a person closer and closer to the goal of living according to Yahweh's order, and wisdom identifies many details of what that order involves.

As we have seen, the Old Testament Wisdom Literature makes clear several things about spiritual growth, one of which is that spiritual growth must be based on wisdom and truth. This means that we must seek that truth through personal study of Scripture, through the world that God created, and through instruction from others. It means that we must be teachable, even when the truth requires that we admit that we were wrong or need help. The Wisdom Literature also makes clear that we must meditate and reflect on the truth that we learn because meditation allows the truth to begin to affect the way we live and writes those truths onto the tablets of our heart. Meditation also allows us to penetrate beneath the surface of the principles and begin to appreciate their depths. Meditation helps us discover broader possibilities for applying the principles to life.

In a documentary about Leonardo da Vinci that I saw recently, I learned that his painting of *The Last Supper* took much longer to complete than was initially thought. Leonardo painted furiously for long hours on several consecutive days and then did not come back to paint for a number of days. The duke who commissioned the painting became very irritated by the delays, but, according to the narrator, Leonardo was walking around Milan thinking about the painting and looking for faces that would allow him to convey in the painting exactly what he wanted to communicate. The time spent reflecting on the painting allowed da Vinci to paint a masterpiece rather than simply draw figures on a canvas. One suspects that a major reason so few masterpieces of godly living exist is the small amount of time Christians spend reflecting on God's truth and values.

The Old Testament also makes clear that we must apply the truth to life if we are to grow in grace. The goal of the process is not knowledge but skills in living, and skill in living does not result from attending intensive six-week seminars on Christian living or memorizing eight essential principles that can be applied mechanistically so as always to ensure success. The skills that constitute wisdom are based upon a knowledge of truth, but the skills are developed only through practice and diligent application of that truth. The process is similar to that of becoming an excellent teacher, which is never achieved by attending a certain number of courses and workshops in education and teaching techniques. If the teacher has innate ability, it will be informed by such academic instruction, but the act of good teaching results from actually working in the classroom and discovering exactly how principles can be applied effectively to lead students to learn. Normally, teachers learn far more from experienced colleagues than they ever learn by taking classes because experienced teachers are the genuine craftsmen of the profession and are thus the most effective mentors. To use a different illustration, a baseball player can learn a lot about hitting a baseball by reading books and watching videos, but apart from diligence in applying the principles, no one ever becomes a good hitter. Ultimately, the number of books one has read or the number of baseball camps a player has attended does not matter. What is important is whether the athlete has developed the skills and can play the game. The same is true for medical doctors, pilots, woodworkers, and almost every other professional in the world.

It is no different when it comes to the ability to think and act in ways that reflect the character of Christ. Ultimately, it is not how much time we spend in personal devotions or how many seminars on spiritual growth that we attend that is important. Rather, the goal is to develop skills for living in ways that reflect God's truth; it is developing character that enables us, in every circumstance, to love God with our whole being and to love others as we love ourselves. The Wisdom Literature makes clear that such a life involves an active application, not merely a general commitment to rather abstract ideas (such as "Love God and love others"). Wise living requires patience and self-control. It means that we must be careful about what we say to others; we must avoid rash and angry responses and speak to others in ways that display God's wisdom and graciousness. We must exercise the same careful self-control in the ways we use our time and manage our finances. We must keep clear before us the goals we wish to achieve, and we must structure our lives so as to create an environment that will move us toward those goals rather than undermine them. It is not sufficient to examine one's life and goals occasionally to see whether progress is being made and then make a few radical changes that will be implemented for a few months or even a few years. These are mere patchwork measures. Rather, the successful acquisition of wisdom requires a consistent, long-term commitment to acquire and practice wisdom.

Skill is needed precisely because life in a fallen world is complicated and unpredictable. The person who must have major surgery does not want a surgeon who is operating for the first time, no matter how brilliant that surgeon might be. This particular medical condition may well turn out to be different from the textbook cases that he studied in medical school, and if an unexpected situation occurs during the surgery, a patient wants a doctor who has had sufficient experience to know how to respond to the complication. If we may call this ability professional maturity, spiritual maturity similarly equips a person to respond to life's challenges and complications in ways that are consistent with God's order.

For example, it is sometimes necessary to confront others because of their inappropriate behavior, and Proverbs makes clear the difficulty that such situations may present. Proverbs 26:4 says, "Answer not a fool according to his folly, lest you be like him yourself," whereas Proverbs 26:5 says, "Answer a fool according to his folly, lest he be wise in his own eyes." Clearly, there is no single correct, response to a fool. In some situations, one approach is correct, whereas in another situation, an entirely different response is more appropriate. The wisdom and maturity that result from diligent practice in dealing with people can generate the necessary skills for determining the effective response in a given circumstance. When David had committed adultery and then tried to cover his sin by murdering Bathsheba's husband, Nathan's rebuke reflects great wisdom because a direct assault probably would have produced a less wholesome response from the king. Such skill comes only as the result of practice.[1]

Paul, too, had to deal with a very difficult situation in the church at Corinth. Power struggles, questions about his ministry and authority, doctrinal aberrations, and issues regarding church discipline required confrontation and rebuke over a period of time. Paul addressed the issues through letters, and he seems to have visited Corinth, where he tried to confront the problems. But at one point in this process, Paul chose not to go to Corinth to spare both of them another very painful visit (2 Cor. 1:23–2:4). Skill and tact sometimes require a living wisdom in one's reaction, not merely a fixed adherence to one prescribed reaction, and the wisdom that results from constant practice equips a person to respond in effective and God-pleasing ways.

The author of Hebrews says in 5:12, "For though by this time you ought to be teachers, you need someone to teach you again the basic principles of the oracles of God. You need milk, not solid food." He then adds in verse 14, "But solid food is for the mature, for those who have their powers of discernment *trained by constant practice* to distinguish good from evil" (italics added). Although a certain amount of debate exists about whether the people addressed in these verses were Christians, the passage nonetheless makes clear that knowledge put into practice is what develops the ability to discern between good and evil and to know how to respond to the diverse and complicated circumstances of life in ways that reflect the character of God. The pattern for growth toward maturity involves both embracing truth and constant practice in applying that truth to life. As we have seen, many other passages make clear that regular meditation and reflection on that truth are also necessary mechanisms in the process in that the practice holds the truth before the disciple. These practices help the disciple to plumb the depths of the teachings and come to a deeper awareness of the broader implications of God's truth as the disciple makes progress in embracing and applying it.

The Importance of Time and Priorities

Buying a first house is for most people a major purchase with a large obstacle to be overcome: saving enough money for the down payment

---

1. Certainly, what is reflected here is Spirit-illuminated wisdom, but that does not normally occur in a vacuum. God uses the skill of the servant to accomplish His purposes.

and closing costs. Lacking large gifts from parents or some major windfall, saving money for a down payment normally requires substantial sacrifice by the first-time home buyers. They will often defer the purchase of things they might otherwise acquire and direct all available resources toward the goal of buying a house. Some people, however, are never able to reach this goal. They are not able to save the money they need because they are continually being diverted from their goal, spending money on such things as clothes, cars, eating out, and other things that drain their resources. Similarly, people are regularly sidetracked from worthy goals by a wide variety of distractions. Evidently, they have not placed their main goal first among their priorities, which almost guarantees that they will not reach their goal.

My wife and I (Edward) know that we need exercise, and we try to walk for at least half an hour every day. We do not always do that, however, because of our busy schedules and a number of responsibilities that sometimes prevent us from doing what we should. I recently spent almost four months teaching at a seminary in the Netherlands, and we had no trouble getting our walk in every day. As I reflected on the difference between our normal lives and our time in Holland, I was struck by the simplicity of life as we experienced it in the Netherlands. I taught only one class rather than the four (or sometimes even five or six) that I normally teach each semester at home. We had only limited access to a car and no daily newspaper, and on many days we did not receive a single telephone call. We walked to the grocery store almost every day to pick up items that we needed. When we needed to purchase items, the small town where we lived had only a few stores where we could shop. The stores closed at six in the evening, did not open until nine the next morning, and were closed on Sunday. We had to make no trips to the doctor or dentist, no trips to the garage to have our car serviced, no phone calls to the insurance company to try to get information, and no trips from store to store to find the exact item that we wanted or to try to find a better price. We did not have to spend time trying to find an appliance repairman and then more time trying to find out why he did not come when he promised. Our life in Holland was very simple, so it was easy to find time to do important things—such as walk for half an hour each day. We also found it much easier just to spend time together and talk about a wide variety of things that would have been difficult to work into our day if not for the simplified schedule in Europe. It was also much easier to think about God and to see His hand in the various details of life because we actually had time to do that.

I realize, of course, that my time in Europe was quite unrealistic; people cannot live their entire lives that way, and if we actually lived in the Netherlands, life would not be as simple as we experienced it during our limited stay. We would need a car and would have to deal with auto mechanics and government bureaucracy, go to doctors and the like, and we might even find those tasks more difficult to negotiate there than in the United States. But the experience provided a concrete reminder of how important time and priorities are for spiritual development. Many people will never become spiritually mature because their schedules simply do not permit it. We all have the same amount of time, but in the modern world a great many things vie for that limited time, and most of those things will not help us grow spiritually. Perhaps as a reaction to this multiplicity of choices, many people allow their major decisions in life to be chosen for them by just letting things happen, but the person who lives thus will never become spiritually mature. Admittedly, we have little control over many of the things that fill our schedules; we must work and eat and sleep, and we all have social responsibilities. At the same time, however, we must work diligently to control our schedules and involvements as much as we can, and it is essential to exercise that control in the light of appropriate priorities, especially the priority of growing to maturity in Christ.

A friend recently shared the following story with me. It makes the point well.

> One day, an expert in time management was speaking to a group of business students. To drive home a point, he used an illustration that those students will never forget.
>
> As he stood in front of the group of high-powered overachievers, he said, "Okay, time for a quiz." He pulled out a one-gallon, wide-mouthed jar and set it on the table in front of him. He also produced about a dozen fist-sized rocks and carefully placed them, one at a time, into the jar. When the jar was filled to the top and no more rocks would fit inside, he asked, "Is the jar full?"
>
> Everyone in the class yelled, "Yes!"
>
> The time management expert replied, "Really?" He reached under the table and pulled out a bucket of gravel. He dumped some gravel in

and shook the jar, causing pieces of the gravel to work themselves down into the spaces between the big rocks. Then he asked the group once more, "Is the jar full?"

By this time, the class was on to him. "Probably not," one of them answered.

"Good," he replied. He reached under the table and brought out a bucket of sand. He dumped the sand in the jar and it went into all of the spaces left between the rocks and the gravel. Once more he asked, "Is the jar full?"

"No!" the class shouted.

Once again, he said, "Good!" Then he grabbed a pitcher of water and began to pour it in until the jar was filled to the brim. Then he looked at the class and asked, "What is the point of this illustration?"

One eager beaver raised his hand and said, "The point is, no matter how full your schedule is, if you try really hard you can always fit some more things in it!"

"No," the speaker replied, "that is not the point. The truth that this illustration teaches us is this: If you don't put the big rocks in first, you'll never get them in at all. What are the 'big rocks' in your life? Time with loved ones? Your faith? Your education? Your dreams? A worthy cause? Teaching or mentoring others? Remember to put those big rocks in first or you'll never get them in at all."[2]

It is hard to imagine a bigger "rock" than spiritual growth and maturity; yet, it is something that we must achieve in a world that is not at all sympathetic with such goals and values. The environment that the world creates is hostile to spiritual growth and regularly attempts to undermine its progress. We must choose such a goal carefully and deliberately, then we must make decisions that will allow time and opportunity to accomplish our objective. Spiritual growth does not take place apart from the instruction of wisdom and Scripture, and we must set aside time for such study.

Another important factor in the process is meditation, so we must develop a mind-set of meditation and reflection on God's Word and His works in nature and history. Although focused periods of time devoted to various

---

2. The story was pointed out to me by my colleague Dan Blied, who got it from the Internet. I have seen the story on a number of web sites but without any indication of the original author.

meditative practices might be helpful, I think that this factor must include the kind of regular return to and reflection upon such truths throughout the day to produce in ourselves a constant awareness of God's loyal love and goodness in all of life. In conjunction with this, we must also recognize that the sanctification that moves us toward Christlikeness involves the development of practical skills for living according to Yahweh's order. Our focused attention on developing those qualities is an essential part of our quest for spiritual development. Unless we deal with our time and lifestyle in a way that ensures that these "big rocks" receive top priority—that is, are among the first things that we put into our schedules—we can give up on the goal of becoming spiritually mature.

The Problem of Motivation

The importance of internal motivation is well described in a nonbiblical proverb of uncertain origin.[3] The proverb says, "Where the heart is willing, it will find a thousand ways. Where it is unwilling, it will find a thousand excuses." This principle can be applied to many areas of life such as relationships, sports, and academics and virtually every other area, certainly including the spiritual realm. We recognize that the sort of deep and intense desire for wisdom and God's ways described in the early chapters of Proverbs or by the author of Psalm 1 does not characterize most of us, and without that motivation it will be very difficult to make progress toward spiritual maturity.

One of the most frustrating things for any teacher (or parent) to deal with is someone who has great potential but little desire to excel. The frustration is multiplied in a church context or a Bible class when, despite a teacher's best efforts, the student remains apathetic about God's truth and shows no interest in applying it to life. Perhaps, like most other things, a person's motivation and drive are products of personality, education, experience, and the like, but given the crucial role of motivation and desire in Christian spirituality, do ways exist to develop and increase one's desire for godliness? How does a person reach the point where he or she can say with the Old Testament authors that the value of wisdom is greater than gold, silver, or valuable jewels or that the taste of God's truth is sweeter than honey?

---

3. I have seen it not only attributed to Arlen Price but also identified as a Dyak proverb.

In Psalm 119:103, the psalmist says, "How sweet are your words to my taste, sweeter than honey to my mouth!" Derek Kidner says of this passage that such tastes are "acquired tastes."[4] Psalm 34 provides some indication of how a person acquires such taste. In the first few verses of the psalm, the psalmist has described how he faced a serious difficulty in which he sought the Lord, and the Lord delivered him from his troubles. The psalmist sees his own experience as a paradigm for others, and in verse 8 he says, "Taste and see that the LORD is good! Blessed is the man who takes refuge in him!" The psalmist's point seems to be that when a person trusts God for help in times of difficulty, he or she will personally experience God's goodness in ways similar to the experience of the psalmist. Such "tastes" of God's goodness develop in the believer a deeper appreciation for God's power and goodness and further define his or her taste for God's truth.

The taste for God's truth seems to be developed in the same way that other tastes are acquired. People sometimes develop a taste for new and different foods simply by continuing to sample the cuisine. Similarly, I (Edward) took a music appreciation class in college and was required to go to a number of classical concerts. I continued to attend classical performances during the rest of my time in college, and by the time I graduated, I had grown to genuinely enjoy classical music; I had acquired a taste for it. At the same time, I found that my taste for other kinds of music that I had enjoyed before college diminished.

I (Edward) know a man whose native language is English but who speaks fluent German. He took several semesters of German in college but was still unsure of himself when speaking the language, so every occasion that called for him to speak was an ordeal for him. Then he married a native speaker of German and traveled to Germany with her, staying there for several months. During that stay, while totally immersed in the language, he stopped the process of first thinking in English, then translating his sentences into German; instead, he began thinking in German. As a result, the words came tumbling out of his mouth. He said that ever since that trip he has actually enjoyed speaking and reading German and has read several books in that language that otherwise would have been closed to him in their original words.

---

4. Derek Kidner, *Psalms 73–150*, vol. 14b of Tyndale Old Testament Commentaries (Downers Grove, Ill.: InterVarsity, 1973), 427.

When we are learning and adopting God's ways, we are learning a language that is, for most purposes, foreign to us. To become fluent in that language, we must not only study but also immerse ourselves in it by all effective means at our disposal: reading it, repeating it to ourselves, and putting it into practice in our everyday lives. At our first birth, we began hearing our parents speak, and our brains organized themselves to handle the structure and nature of that language, whether it was English, Spanish, Chinese, or Navajo. Then, at our second birth, we began hearing the deeper and more real language of justice, faithfulness, honesty, forgiveness, and love. To accommodate these new concepts—the native language of heaven—our entire character must be reorganized. This process of total reorganization is called sanctification, or spiritual growth, and its distant goal is to make it, not a second language for us but our native language, the words that we would use even under stress or if we were awakened from a deep sleep and not allowed to compose our thoughts before speaking.

Although the capacity for delighting in God's truth is made alive through faith in God and His revelation (what the New Testament calls regeneration), that experience rarely produces the sort of full-blown delight in God's truth that the author of Psalm 1 or Psalm 119 exhibits. Such delight must be cultivated and developed, and a person's taste for God's truth is developed by the very same methods that we have seen in the Wisdom Literature. It begins with instruction in God's truth, from both others and Scripture, and it continues to grow as a person savors that truth through reflection and meditation and then applies its principles to life. Then, as we obey the truth and discover the benefit that comes from living according to Yahweh's order, our taste for God's truth and goodness further increases. As the disciple continues to remember and consider the outcomes of that application of truth to life, he or she discovers broader dimensions of the truth, thus developing even more taste for it. Often, when people are put into desperate situations—when they are forced to trust God because they simply have no other available options—they discover what the author of Psalm 34 found; consequently, their taste for God's truth and their appreciation for its value increases greatly. Just as few beginning music students delight in practicing scales and few athletes enjoy the rigorous training that prepares them for competition, so, in the beginning at least, the diligence and rigor that are a part of serious discipleship rarely bring delight to the disciple. Rather, they prepare one for living according to Yahweh's order in a fallen world, and it is putting God's truth into practice, together with a deepened knowledge of God, that produces the delight.

Often, when people face health problems that force them to change seriously their eating habits, they find it hard to break the old habits and form new ones that are more amenable to the goal of good health (or even survival). In such situations, it might be necessary to stop buying candy, chips, ice cream, and other junk foods that undermine health and well-being and to ensure that such items are not in the pantry. Such radical changes might also be necessary for the acquisition of wisdom. It might be necessary to eliminate spiritual junk food such as video games, certain TV programs, the daily newspaper, or any number of other things because they distract us and sabotage our efforts to develop a taste for wisdom and God's truth.

My Help Comes from the Lord

Finally, certain Old Testament authors recognized another very important aspect of spiritual development, but it awaited the New Testament for its fuller explication. The author of Psalm 119 regularly expresses his love for God's Law and his determination to obey it, clearly recognizing that he must have God's help to do so. As Kirkpatrick notes, "If sometimes his professions of obedience seem to savor of self-righteousness, his prayers for grace fully recognize that strength to obey must come from God."[5]

In recognizing that his understanding of God's truth must come from God, the psalmist asks God to teach him (vv. 12, 19, 27, 29, 33, 38, 66, 68), and to show him wonderful things in the Law (v. 18). He understands that his faithful obedience is possible only if God helps him and empowers him. He says in verse 10, "Let me not wander from your commandments!" He says in verses 35–36, "Lead me in the path of your commandments. . . . Incline my heart to your testimonies." He prays in verse 133, "Keep steady my steps according to your promise, and let no iniquity get dominion over me." Clearly, the type of disciple described in the psalm, the disciple who receives the blessings imparted by God's Word, is one who deeply loves God and appreciates the great treasure that God has given in Scripture. He desires intensely to know that truth and seeks diligently to obey it. At the same time, he is clearly aware that, unaided, he will never understand God's truth,

---

5. A. F. Kirkpatrick, *Psalms*, The Cambridge Bible for Schools and Colleges (Cambridge: Cambridge University Press, 1906), 701.

keep God's Law, and persist in faithfulness to God. In this regard, Psalm 119 expresses ideas similar to those found in Psalm 51, where the psalmist not only recognizes his complete dependence on God for forgiveness but also understands that, apart from God's gracious help, there is no reason to expect that his future will be any different from his sinful past. He prays, "Create in me a clean heart, O God, and renew a right spirit within me. . . . [T]ake not your Holy Spirit from me. Restore to me the joy of your salvation, and uphold me with a willing spirit" (Ps. 51:10–12).

God's instruction is life-giving and energizing to the person who embraces it. It gives comfort and guidance that keeps a person from harm. God's Word, received by faith, nourishes the intimacy with God that is the prerequisite for life as it was meant to be, and it is an essential resource in bringing God's people to spiritual maturity. Believers are called to diligence in the pursuit of God and wisdom, but they are assured that such perseverance in their quest will bring them to the knowledge of God (Prov. 2:5). Such pursuit also produces growth in godliness as it changes the heart and produces in the believer the very character of God. The journey will often bring the disciple through times of difficulty and confusion, but God sustains His saints through all of those troubles and is able to work out His purposes even in the midst of the suffering. What both the Old and New Testaments make clear is that the successful outcome of this process is assured precisely because God is working in the process to bring about that result. The consistent picture that emerges from these texts is that the disciple who wants to become spiritually mature must be diligent in the obedience of faith, and such faith and obedience involves careful attention to the attitudes and skills required for living according to Yahweh's order, as described in the Old Testament Wisdom Literature. The picture that is found in these texts also recognizes the need for God's help in the process, a picture that is consistent with Paul's exhortation in Philippians 2:12–13 to "work out your own salvation with fear and trembling, for it is God who works in you, both to will and to work for his good pleasure."

The spiritual development that is described in Scripture is, however, a process. Our knowledge of God and our trust in Him normally develop not in giant leaps but in small increments every day as we learn, meditate, apply God's truth to life, and wait patiently for God to work out His purposes. Such a life will bring us to maturity, it will make us into people whom God will declare "blessed," and it will lead to what is the best prize of all—an intimate knowledge of the King of kings and Lord of lords.

In Luke's gospel, the twelve-year-old Jesus is described twice as "increasing in wisdom" (2:40, 52 NASB). Luke uses the phrase immediately before and immediately after recounting an incident, effectively framing it. Jesus' parents have lost track of His whereabouts and have gone searching for Him in Jerusalem, finding Him at last in the temple discussing God's ways with the teachers there. Mary's comments to the young Jesus, together with His response, are revealing. She says to Him, "Son, why have You treated us this way? Behold, *Your Father* and I have been anxiously looking for You" (italics mine).

Jesus replies, "Why is it that you were looking for Me? Did you not know that I had to be in *My Father's* house?" (again, my italics).

Clearly, Luke is being careful to point out the distinction that Jesus draws between His two fathers—Joseph (whom Mary refers to as His father) and God (in whose house Jesus has been found). The anecdote reveals Jesus' growing wisdom in preferring His heavenly Father over His earthly father, with an added adjustment in verse 51: "He continued in subjection to them." This preference of loves, this recognition of God's fatherly role in His life, together with this continued honoring of His given relationships with others is our model and paradigm for wisdom. We can do no better than this, and wisdom commands us to do no worse.

Questions for Thought and Reflection

Devise a plan for your spiritual development. Allow your answers to the following questions to guide you in developing that plan.

1. How can I simplify my life so that I can devote more of my day to God's concerns?
2. Which of my activities and concerns are necessary, and which are disposable?
3. How can I think and react more as Jesus might have done without trying to fit myself into superficial expectations?
4. How should I change my assumptions about who God is and what I have a right to expect of Him?

5. How can I develop patience with myself as I go through the long process of sanctification while never becoming satisfied with where I am in that process?
6. What device shall I use to help me meditate on God's Word?
7. What can I do to develop a growing awareness of God's presence and providence in my life?
8. What can I do to develop a genuine delight in God's truth?
9. Do I need to practice obedience consciously and deliberately in specific areas?
10. When should I begin? (Answer: Today.)

SCRIPTURE INDEX

SUBJECT INDEX